Loaded Words

Loaded Words

MARJORIE GARBER

FORDHAM UNIVERSITY PRESS

New York 2012

Fordham University Press has no responsibility for the persistence or accuracy of URLs for external or third-party Internet websites referred to in this publication and does not guarantee that any content on such websites is, or will remain, accurate or appropriate.

Fordham University Press also publishes its books in a variety of electronic formats. Some content that appears in print may not be available in electronic books.

Library of Congress Cataloging-in-Publication Data

Garber, Marjorie B.
    Loaded words / Marjorie Garber.
       p.   cm.
    Includes bibliographical references and index.
    ISBN 978-0-8232-4204-7 (cloth : alk. paper)
    ISBN 978-0-8232-4205-4 (pbk. : alk. paper)
       1. English language—Etymology.   I. Title.
PE1574.G26   2012
422-dc23

                                        2012002859

Printed in the United States of America
14 13 12   5 4 3 2 1
First edition

To the Memory of
Barbara L. Packer

Contents

Acknowledgments

Several essays in this collection have been previously published in journals and collections. My gratitude to the following for their permission to reprint: *Critical Inquiry* (for "Loaded Words"), *The Atlantic* (for "Our Genius Problem"), *Profession* (for "Good to Think With" and "Shakespeare in Slow Motion"), *Foreign Policy* (for "Anatomy of a Honey Trap," *PMLA* (for "Dig It: Looking for Fame in All the Wrong Places"), *Raritan* (for "Translating F. O. Matthiessen"), Peter Lang publishers (for "Third-Person Interruption"), Beacon Press (for "The Marvel of Peru") and *Shakespeare Quarterly* (for "A Tale of Three *Hamlets*"). Some of the remaining pieces, published here for the first time, were written initially for audiences at Arizona State University ("After the Humanities"), the University of Buffalo ("Mad Lib"), Wellesley College ("Shakespeare and Character"), and Harvard University ("Radical Education"). I am grateful to those friends and colleagues who invited me to speculate on so broad and intriguing a range of topics, especially John Bender, Joseph Boone, David Hillman, Michael Holquist, Sally Kitch, Yu Jin Ko, Carla Mazzio, Lino Pertile, John Stauffer, and Nancy Vickers. My warm thanks as well to William Germano, whose advice, encouragement, and expert eye and ear have been invaluable; to Helen Tartar and Tom Lay of Fordham University Press; and to Sol Kim Bentley and Alex Raymond, who kindly helped to prepare this manuscript for publication.

Loaded Words

Loaded Questions: An Introduction

Few words are more loaded than *loaded*. From "charged, burdened, laden" (loaded carts, loaded hearts, loaded fruit trees, loaded guns) to "weighted, especially with lead" (loaded dice) to "inserted in a camera" (loaded film) to "equipped with optional extras" (loaded cars) to slang usages from "drunk" to "drugged" to "extremely wealthy," *loaded* tells a story of abundance, excess, danger, and desire. The specific use of *loaded* in connection with words (loaded words, loaded questions) developed in the mid-twentieth century and may be considered, perhaps, as symptomatic of what are now called symptomatic readings—readings that call into question the good faith or the face value of a narrative. Thus the *Oxford English Dictionary*, under *loaded*, provides the following definition and examples:

> d. *fig.* Charged with some hidden implication or underlying suggestion; biased; prejudiced.
>
> 1942 *College Eng.* Oct.16 General Semantics . . . being metaphysical in a particularly partial and dogmatic sense . . . can yield us only a vocabulary of "loaded" general words, calculated to distort rather than to illuminate the writings of any other school.
>
> 1957 *Observer* 29 Dec. 9/2 Is our popular preference for plays of less blatant sexuality a mark of higher civilisation or merely of greater hypocrisy? Is the Dionysiac cult . . . more childish or simply more honest than the religious practices that have succeeded it in the West? These are loaded questions, I admit.
>
> 1958 *Times* 7 July 13/2 You cannot solve the riddle of the universe by giving the answer "Yes" or "No" to a loaded question.

1961 *Listener* 7 Dec. 991/3 He chose to use emotionally loaded words like "scare" and "infection."

1975 D. Bagley *Snow Tiger* xi. 96 It is improper of Mr. Smithers to ask such a loaded question . . . He is usurping the function of this commission.

A close perusal of these quotations will disclose an interesting range of connotations. Loaded words "calculated to distort" resemble loaded dice, constructed to fall with a particular face upward, while "emotionally loaded words" seem designed to elicit heightened or specific reactions. Loaded questions, apparently, can be either coercive or (worse?) damning, putting the respondent in a position that is both pre-scripted and prescriptive.

But what distinguishes these utterances from others? We could say that *all* questions are loaded questions in that they anticipate some kind of reply. "Would you like to take a walk?" may sound like an open question, but try it on (a) your dog, (b) a hothead in a bar, or (c) the person to whom you are about to propose marriage, and see how "loaded" this simple query can become. And loaded words? It's true that words like *scare* and *infection* are often scary and infectious. (I had to check the date of the quotation from *The Listener* twice to correct my assumption that the time was the 1980s and the "scare" the AIDS crisis; 1961 puts it, instead, in the midst of the Cold War.) But which words in the selections above are *not* potentially loaded in this sense? *Partial, distort, blatant, honest, improper*—all of these, which function in context as rational explanations or analyses of the supposedly loaded utterances, are themselves equally susceptible to being called "loaded," biased, and prejudiced. Here that score-settling lexicographer Humpty Dumpty might well be called upon for adjudication.

> "I don't know what you mean by 'glory,' " Alice said.
>
> Humpty Dumpty smiled contemptuously. "Of course you don't—till I tell you. I meant 'there's a nice knock-down argument for you!' "
>
> "But 'glory' doesn't mean 'a nice knock-down argument,' " Alice objected.
>
> "When I use a word," Humpty Dumpty said, in a rather a scornful tone, "it means just what I choose it to mean—neither more nor less."
>
> "The question is," said Alice, "whether you can make words mean so many different things."
>
> "The question is," said Humpty Dumpty, "which is to be master, that's all."[1]

Furthermore, we might want to ask why words and language are described as "loaded" only in a pejorative sense. The following passage, the first stanza of Keats's "Ode to Autumn," invokes a kind of super-charged loading that might well be said to characterize poetic language, Coleridge's "the best words in their best order":

> Season of mists and mellow fruitfulness,
> Close bosom-friend of the maturing sun;
> Conspiring with him how to load and bless
> With fruit the vines that round the thatch-eaves run;
> To bend with apples the moss'd cottage-trees,
> And fill all fruit with ripeness to the core;
> To swell the gourd, and plump the hazel shells
> With a sweet kernel; to set budding more,
> And still more, later flowers for the bees,
> Until they think warm days will never cease;
> For Summer has o'erbrimm'd their clammy cells.
>
> (1–11)

"O'erbrimm'd," like "swell," "plump," "load and bless/With fruit" "and "set budding more,/And still more" all here describe not only the season but also, reflexively, the fecund phrases that bring it imaginatively to life. Keats's poem, too, has questions, maybe even "loaded questions," in that they are what we often call rhetorical questions, questions that each presuppose a certain answer.

> Who hath not seen thee oft amid thy store?
>
> (12)

> Where are the songs of Spring? Ay, where are they?
> Think not of them, thou hast thy music too,—
>
> (23–24)

A reader who responds to the first question, "*I* haven't," and to the second one, "Yeah, what *about* those songs of spring?" might be said to belong to the Humpty Dumpty school of critical reading, or merely to be a spoilsport, but the fact remains that these questions are highly directive and (pleasurably) coercive. They are, that is to say, part of the rhetorical fabric that makes language rich and strange, as well as risky and dangerous.

"Load every rift with ore," Keats advised Shelley, in a letter written a few months before his death. The phrase has been taken to mean something like "enrich your poetic language," as the poet Andrew Motion recently suggested in his praise of Keats: "The language of all his poems, and in particular the great odes and narrative poems of his final (1820) volume, have a delicious velvety weight: They 'load every rift with ore', to use one of his own phrases."[2] But in fact this quotation omits some crucial quotation marks. When Keats wrote his famous letter to Shelley urging him to "'load every rift' of your subject with ore,"[3] he was not entirely coining the phrase. Instead, he was quoting a passage of Spenser's *Faerie Queene* in which Guyon, the Knight of Temperance, visits the cave of Mammon, a place that looks very much like a gold mine, "with rich metal loaded euery rift," the gold hanging so heavy in a space full of dust and "old decay" (2.7.28:5; 2.7.29:2) that the roof of the cave threatens to fall.[4]

A rift is a fissure, a place of splitting or division. To load it with ore is also to load it with *or*, with alternatives, with multiplicities and contradictions—and temptations. If we hear *or* in *ore*, and indeed *riffed* in *rift*, we are following not only the sounds but also the contemporary associations of language. To load a rift is not quite so secure a notion as it may seem at first. It is the contention of this book that *all* words are loaded, and that they are, inescapably, both overbrimming and biased, or weighted. This is indeed why language works, and why it matters. Without such "loadings," language is lightweight.

These essays focus on words that have, in various ways, become "loaded" in recent years—words like *madness, interruption, patriotism, academia, marriage, genius,* and *celebrity. Shakespeare,* the topic of several of these pieces, is perhaps the most culturally loaded name of our time. In the course of these explorations I consider topics as diverse as advertising culture, film and television, Hollywood tourism and IQ tests, education and translation, while also addressing the work of theorists from Kant and Freud to Foucault and Lévi-Strauss. I interrogate both the meanings ascribed to such words and the surprising degree of passion—and occasional animus—that they evoke.

Sometimes the most apparently anodyne words are in practice the most pernicious. The first piece in this collection, "Loaded Words," came about because I was invited to give a keynote lecture at a conference on "Knowledge and Belief." As I told the friend who invited me, I was greatly honored by the invitation, but I had a visceral response to the keywords of the title, or rather to the pieties sometimes uttered in their names. He kindly encouraged me to say what I thought, and this essay was the result. A similar contrariness motivated the second essay, "Good to Think With," initially written for a Presidential Forum at the Modern

Language Association under the general rubric "The Humanities at Work in the World." I suggest that the humanities and the world are coterminous, and that it is not necessary to go "outside" the humanities, or to some "applied" space of culture, science, politics, or the arts, in order to do work—important, indeed essential work—in the world.

Loaded questions, as we've seen, are often regarded as provocations and coercions. But asking pertinent and persistent questions about literature and culture can and should produce a different kind of "loading," making the case for the worth of words and the value of interested inquiry. The essays in this collection argue that saturation of language and saturation of thought are qualities of paramount importance, and that teasing out the myriad and sometimes antithetical implications of the terms we use is part of the necessary, deeply pleasurable work of the mind. Whether they are addressing the history of the concept of "madness" from midsummer rapture to Foucault to *Mad Men*, or the role of "practice" in the humanities and the arts, these essays focus on the specific, the odd, the untypical, the untameable, the suggestive, the thread, the clue. As Raymond Williams has shown, every word has a history that opens up to alternatives, even to opposites, all these embedded senses lying just below the surface, adding patina and burnish to its current use.[5] And as Freud saw, the antithetical sense of primal words often suggests—whether historically, as he thought, or associatively, as I believe—a tension that is both productive and creative.[6] To these insights I would add, as well, the exhilarating assertion of Roland Barthes: "What I claim is to live to the full the contradiction of my time."[7] Barthes wrote this in 1957, but its enduring power for me comes in part from the shifter, "my time."

Writing today, whether it focuses on literature, art, politics, economics, or philosophy, should be fully loaded—highly charged, explosive, weighty, intoxicating, fruitful, o'erbrimming. This is the best way, in fact, to combat narrowness, bias, and prejudice—loaded language in the restricted sense—wherever those attitudes are found, whether in words, in questions, or in intellectual life.

CHAPTER ONE

Loaded Words

What is the other, or opposite, of *knowledge*? Ignorance? Uncertainty? Undecidability? Theory? Belief? What is the other, or opposite, of *belief*? Unbelief? Disbelief? Doubt? Atheism? Agnosticism? Certainty? Knowledge?

How we define the range of signification and connotation here will shape the way we think about these contestatory, overused, and ultimately unsatisfactory terms, terms that are both *empty* and *loaded*. Empty because they can mean so many different things in different disciplines, practices, and semiotic schemes. Loaded because they are stuffed, even overstuffed, with meanings and implications, like a sofa or a fois gras duck or a comic farce. Or a loaded gun.

We are familiar with the theatrical truism about a gun onstage: If it's there, it will be fired sometime before the close of the play. Its very presence implies the necessity of an action. So too with these loaded words. They will go off, somehow, somewhere, within the frame of our expectations. As we are seeing at present with public dialogues on the question of, say, Darwinian evolution versus "intelligent design." Or "faith-based" charities, and politics, and tax exemptions, or Supreme Court nominees. Or the definition of life and death. Or the intentions of the authors of the U.S. constitution.

How can we distinguish between knowledge and belief? You could say that one is "truth" and one is "opinion," but this seems an unreliable gauge. In 2002, President Bush "knew" that there were weapons of mass destruction in Iraq. He had good "intelligence" on this matter. It was for him a matter of firm conviction, of belief. Or so he said.

In 2005, another president, Lawrence Summers of Harvard, incautiously offered some opinions on "diversifying the science and engineering workforce" at a conference of the National Bureau of Economic Research. "It is a fact about our society," he said, that people in their forties who aspire to leadership positions need to offer "near total commitment to their work," and "that is a level of commitment that a much higher fraction of married men have been historically prepared to make than of married women." As for any other differences between men and women, Summers observed that "on many, many different human attributes—height, weight, propensity for criminality, overall IQ, mathematical ability, scientific ability—there is relatively clear evidence that whatever the difference in means . . . there is a difference in the standard deviation, and variability of a male and female population."[1] Summers prefaced his observations with his intention to be provocative, and he certainly was. He based his remarks on "data" which he took as knowledge, and which produced his beliefs, here couched in terms like *provocation* and *hypothesis*. Below the line, underpinning these remarks, was the scholarship (knowledge or belief?) of figures like cognitive psychologist Steven Pinker, whom Summers had actively persuaded to move from MIT to Harvard.

To draw the line here between knowledge and belief is in part to impose a set of frames: professional versus amateur judgments; intuition versus research (although research, as any student of drug-company protocols or think-tank politics can attest, is not itself a neutral category); present versus past. Previous "beliefs" can become obsolete: Does the sun rotate around the earth or the earth around the sun? How many planets are there in "our" solar system? Is Pluto a planet or not? Has it been grandfathered in with major planet status despite the fact that if it had been discovered today, it would not have been called a planet?[2] How many planets are there in our solar system, anyway? Nine? Twelve? Does it matter? Would a "Kuiper belt object"—the proposed new status for the Planet Formerly Known As Pluto—revolve as sweetly? What about the newly nominated tenth planet, nicknamed Xena, though more formally known by the euphonious moniker 2003 UB313?[3] (The name *Xena* comes from a 1990s television show about a Greek warrior princess. Who says popular culture is ephemeral?)

Knowledge and belief are good (or bad) examples of what linguists call shifters: words like *you* and *I*, *here* and *there*, that change their meanings depending upon the location and nature of the speaker. The prototypical child's plaint on a journey, "Are we there yet?" is always going to be answered, strictly speaking, in the negative, since we—whoever *we* might be on any given occasion—are always *here*, and never *there*. This sounds both trivial and casuistic, but it can have devastating effects especially, but not only, when it crosses into matters of "faith." Consider the refrain of Dale Evans's popular folk hymn: "How do I know? The Bible tells me so." Senator Joseph McCarthy claimed that there were fifty-seven "known communists" in the State Department. Or eighty-one. Or two hundred five. You will say perhaps that this is not real knowledge, but rather a dangerous misuse of the term. I would agree. But I think terms like these have encroaching functions both as shifters and as levelers, and that invidious "knowledge" is sometimes even more dangerous than flagrant "belief."

Knowledge and belief. The poet Alexander Pope is often misquoted on this topos—his alliteration made it "a little learning," not "a little knowledge," that is a dangerous thing—and the distinction is significant.[4] The "learning" that Pope urged in the "Essay on Criticism" came from the Pierian Spring, a spring sacred to the Muses (though "Pierian Spring" is today also, inevitably, the name of a software company, a film- and video-production company, a knowledge development consulting firm run by "an acknowledged leader in knowledge management" and a continuing education institute, the Pierian Spring Academy, for retired seniors in Sarasota, Florida). Learning was, in Pope's sense of the word, a product of intellectual, philosophical, and aesthetic encounters with the arts and sciences. It was, that is, an open and continuing question, not, or not only, a content.

Learning had its nine Muses. But Knowledge and Belief have four daughters: Their names are Dogma, Doxa, Dicta, and Data. Dogma and Doxa have gravitated toward the church and toward philosophy and politics. (Doxa's name, so beguilingly like *doxy*, comes from the Greek word for "opinion," that which cannot be proven.) Dicta, quite naturally, given her background in saying and things said, is a favorite among lawyers and politicians. As for Data, whose own name, like that of her sisters, originally connoted some level of doubt or question ("a thing given or granted; something known or assumed as fact"), she has emerged, like all youngest sisters in fairy tales, triumphant. Her name is now synonymous with "facts; especially numerical facts,"[5] and she is herself the mother of a large and growing family from Data Bank and Data Capture to Data Dump, Data Warehouse, Data Mining, and her own eldest and most ambitious child, Information. You will notice that there is a strong family resemblance among all these descendants of Knowledge and Belief; in infancy they may have resembled Belief, but as they grow older they more and more take on the features, and the trappings, of Knowledge. (I will leave to you the interesting question of whether Knowledge and Belief are a gendered couple, and, if so, which is which.)

Relations among these sisters have been further troubled by their dealings with a close cousin, Theoria, whose parentage and prospects were more problematic. Theoria, often called by her modern name of Theory, is sometimes regarded as a *doxy* in the slang sense, a mistress, paramour, or prostitute, and sometimes as a *doxy* in the more sedate sense of "opinion." But the temptation to blur these boundaries has proven irresistible. "Orthodoxy is my doxy, and Heterodoxy is your doxy," quipped John Quincy Adams in his *Diary*.[6]

The idea of Theoria, as many commentators have noted, derives from Latin and Greek terms for viewing, contemplation, speculation, sight, and spectacle and shares a root with *theater*, literally "a place for viewing." But there has been a good deal of argument, in recent years, about whether the word *theory* belongs properly to science or to the humanities and the arts. In the mid-1990s, scientist Richard Dawkins expressed his dismay at the use of the term *theory* in literary studies.

> I noticed, the other day [he told an interviewer], an article by a literary critic called "Theory: What Is It?" Would you believe it? "Theory" turned out to mean "theory in literary criticism." This wasn't in a journal of literary criticism; this was in some general publication, like a Sunday newspaper. The very word "theory" has been hijacked for some extremely narrow parochial literary purpose—as though Einstein didn't have theories; as if Darwin didn't have theories.[7]

Dawkins himself characterized this response as "somewhat paranoid," and—speaking as a literary critic—I would not want to contradict him. Although some of the hysteria about literary theory has subsided (on all sides of the question) in the intervening years, the issue of the proper home for Theory, or Theoria, continues to be debated. Thus for example a flap about the teaching of Darwinian evolution and "intelligent design" led a prize-winning geneticist to write to the *New York Times* urging that it correct the "popular usage" of the term *theory* as "a speculation, not necessarily supported by evidence," with the scientific definition, "a coherent and consistent way to account for a wide array of observations and experimental results," one that "generates testable predictions. When the explanatory and predictive power of a theory becomes overwhelming, it can be regarded as fact." By this precept, Darwinian evolution was "solidly established" as the foundation of modern biology. Nonetheless, the writer wisely noted, "Even the most well-established scientific theory can be disproved by new contradictory evidence."[8] Fact can change. What was once regarded as fact can be disregarded, or discarded.

Consider, for example, the sobering itinerary of phlogiston, the substance or principle of combustion, that which purportedly caused things to catch fire. In the early years of the eighteenth century, phlogiston became the cornerstone of a whole system of chemistry. Scientists and philosophers hotly debated its nature, its properties, and its existence. Learned treatises explained how it was produced, and how it worked. A hundred years later it had been abandoned as a failed theory. Thus one of phlogiston's last proponents, Joseph Priestley, acknowledged in 1785, "Mr. Lavoisier is well known to maintain, that there is no such thing as what has been called phlogiston."[9] If we ever doubt that phlogiston should be regarded as a fit subject for the wandering boundaries of knowledge and belief, we can remember the title of Priestley's famous, and futile, defense at the end of the eighteenth century: *The Doctrine of Phlogiston Established, and That of the Composition of Water, Refuted.* Priestley, one of the key figures in modern chemistry, was also a Unitarian minister; one of his many publications on scripture was called *The Doctrines of Heathen Philosophy Compared with those of Revelation.* Phlogiston, like philosophy, was a doctrine. A published history of the phlogiston theory from the 1930s reads almost like the biography of an idea, beginning with an account of the "Phlogiston Period (ca. 1700–1800)" and ending with a final chapter called "The Last Days of Phlogiston."[10] A more recent postmortem ends with a cautionary citation from Linnaeus: "Whether our ideas are right or wrong, they are such that we may defend them during our life. After our time, children who are now at play will be our judges."[11]

Other examples of what were once facts or knowledge and have now been downgraded (as they say of tropical storms) to the status of discredited belief include the eugenics movement of the late nineteenth century and its effects upon immigration, racial politics, and Nazi policy, and the association of left-handedness with degeneracy, criminal tendencies, and

other "sinister" behaviors (including that mid-twentieth-century favorite, neglect or rejection by the mother). But of course the stock of eugenics is rising again, and indeed has never been higher, with the new
interest in genomics, cloning, and DNA. Well-funded centers and institutes for integrative genomics are popping up on every university campus. There's a Handedness Research Institute, too, at the University of
Indiana, though this one is still seeking major funding. Funding is often
connected, incidentally, to the idea that theories will become facts,
thereby in some sense putting themselves out of business.

When it comes to knowledge and belief, the lady Theory, or Theoria,
has an opposite number, in the concept of empiricism, derived from
the word for "experiment" or "trial." Indeed ancient physicians were
apparently divided into sects according to their relative faith in experience versus philosophical theory: Empiricks, Dogmatics, or Methodists.
"*Empirical* and the related *empiricism* are now in some contexts among
the most difficult words in the language," wrote Raymond Williams in
1976.[12] In the years between that time and this, the stock of the "empirical" has risen dramatically, especially among humanists and what we
tend to call discursive or narrative social scientists. (The stock of *discourse*
and *discursive*, I should note, has plummeted over this same period, since
discourse has been branded as theoretical jargon while *empirical* is, well,
just plain factual common sense.)

Empirical—as, again, Williams was quick to observe—meant something based upon *experience*, a word that in the seventeenth century had
not yet separated itself wholly from *experiment*—as is still true in French.
(The etymology of the word derives both from "experience," in Latin,
and from "trial" and "experiment" in Greek). *Empirical* has not always
been a winner, though, in the status sweepstakes of language. Its early
medical meaning, describing a physician who "bases his methods of practice on the results of observation and experiment, not on scientific theory" quickly modulated into the portrait of a medical quack: one "that
practises physic or surgery without scientific knowledge; that is guilty of
quackery."[13] *Empirical* thus became, by the middle of the eighteenth
century, a word meaning something "guided by mere experience, without scientific knowledge" in matters of art or practice. Because of the
heritage from quackery, *empirical* could mean, then, "ignorantly pre-
sumptuous, resembling, or characteristic of, a charlatan."[14]

In any case, to be *empirical* in English was, whether you used the term
as praise or blame, to be the opposite of *theoretical*. Raymond Williams—

covering all the complicated terrain between empirical science and empirical philosophy in a necessarily short space—calls this definition of empirical as "atheoretical or antitheoretical," a "loose use," and so it is.[15] But in a university context, or the context of a contest of disciplines, the tension between the empirical and the theoretical—whether the empirical is "mere experience" or "real experience"—is one that has come to touch upon, and to impinge upon, our understandings of, and hierarchies of, knowledge and belief.

One set of meanings of *knowledge* is related to "*ac*knowledge," in the sense of recognition, confession, or legal cognizance. But the main sense of the word as we use—or "know"—it today derives from the verbal form *to know* and has migrated, over the years, from the biblical sense ("And Adam knew his wife again" [Gen 4:25], or the film *Carnal Knowledge*) to the possession of information acquired by study or research. The loss in intimacy has been balanced, perhaps overbalanced, by an expansion of what is and can be "known." Information. A branch of learning. Theoretical or practical understanding of an art, science, industry, and so on. (The phrase "the Knowledge" as any anglophile tourist knows, is a slang term for the encyclopedic understanding of London's streets, buildings, and routes required of all aspiring taxi drivers; the verbal phrase for such arcane acquisition is "doing the Knowledge.") The desuetude or over-ripeness of the term *knowledge* can perhaps best be gleaned by a quick rundown of its current use in compound form, of which knowledge worker and knowledge industry are among the more recent, and the least elegant.

Knowledge worker is a term coined in 1959 by management specialist Peter Drucker, the author of nineteen books, including *The Practice of Management, Managing for Results, Managing for the Future, Managing in a Time of Great Change,* and *Managing in the Next Society.* Drucker also published, perhaps inevitably, a book called *Peter Drucker on the Profession of Management* (2003). In a half century, management had been transformed from a practice to a profession. This is the ideology of knowledge-and-belief at work. (As we will see shortly, the term management was also destined to be euphemized, as business schools took upon themselves the more glorious, humanistic, and undefinable task of providing "leadership" instead.)

A knowledge worker works on, and with, "information," which is not at all the same as "learning." As for the knowledge industry, Clark Kerr saw it on the horizon as early as 1963, when he wrote in *The Uses of the*

University that the "growth of the 'knowledge industry'" was "coming to permeate government and business."[16]

If a knowledge worker is someone who deals with networks and technology—an engineer, a research-and-development scientist—what in the world is a "belief worker"? A missionary? A member of the clergy? A medium? A politician? Are "faith-based initiatives," a blatant euphemism (if I may so express myself) for religious charities, schools, and motives, versions of "belief" in action?

The Victorians had Doubt, often spelled with a capital D, to complicate and enrich their lives. The capitalization marked this kind of doubt as religious: Many writers (from Tennyson to H. G. Wells), and not a few fictional characters, confessed to having Doubts about the truth of Christianity or some other religious belief or doctrine, as if Doubt itself—by virtue of its allegorization—was an alternative kind of belief. More than a century later, the theater (the namesake cousin, you will recall, to the concept of theory or *theoria*) has become one of the showplaces for doubt, and for the crossover anxieties between and among religion, science, and art.

The 2000 Tony Award for Best Play went to Michael Frayn's *Copenhagen*, a play about a problematic encounter between the German physicist Werner Heisenberg and his Danish mentor and counterpart, Niels Bohr, in 1941—in the midst of World War II—when science had become, inevitably and self-evidently, political. The play plumbs the depths and heights of the word *uncertainty*, associated with Heisenberg's principle in science but also with the entire concept, which, as Frayn points out in a postscript, would be better rendered in English by the word *indeterminacy* or *indeterminability*. Everything in the play is indeterminable: what was said on various occasions, who said it, what was intended, what was withheld.[17]

The next year saw the Pulitzer Prize awarded to a play called *Proof*, by David Auburn (later made into a film starring Gwyneth Paltrow, cast improbably enough as a brilliant mathematician). The double meaning of the word *proof*—like the double meaning of *uncertainty* in Frayn's play *Copenhagen*—brought theatricality together with science, and, in this case, with gender. The mathematical proof of the title becomes a question of evidence: Was it written by the famous father, whose mental instability had taken him out of the classroom long before his death, or by the daughter who gave up her own career to care for him? Her claim that she didn't find the proof among her father's papers—"I didn't find it. I wrote it"—makes a fabulous curtain line for act 1.[18]

The Pulitzer Prize for Drama in 2005 went to yet another play about doubt and proof, this one called *Doubt: A Parable*, by John Patrick Shanley. The playwright added the phrase *a parable* at the last minute, to indicate that the topic was not so much the specific question of accusations of sexual abuse among the Catholic clergy as it was the general question of certainty versus salutary doubt. (The plot of the play involves a nun's "certainty" about her accusation of a popular priest.) In an essay he wrote for the *Los Angeles Times* that is now published as a preface to his play text, Shanley laments the fact that "we are living in a culture of extreme advocacy, of confrontation, of judgment, and of verdict." Doubt, he thinks, is by contrast a healthy state, the "age-old practice of the wise. . . . Doubt requires more courage than conviction does, and more energy. . . . We've got to learn to live with a full measure of uncertainty. There is no last word."[19]

There are, of course, significant differences among these plays: *Copenhagen* centers on a historical confrontation between scientists dealing with the potential for nuclear destruction; *Proof* singles out questions of intellectual elegance, ownership, and gendered expectations; *Doubt* is about two kinds of belief and many kinds of "fact"—the certainty of the accusing nun, the denials of the priest, the sexuality of an altar boy (or what his mother calls his "nature"), but not about the specific kind of knowledge or belief called science. Still, this cluster of plays—and, more strikingly, the fact that they have won prizes—suggests that they mark a serious issue for our time. It's pleasing to me, and perhaps even significant, that the theater, the staging place for *theoria*, the space for viewing or spectacle, should again become the site of such contestation. I don't think this is an accident. It worked for the Greeks, and for Aristotle, and, indeed, for Shakespeare.

Knowledge and belief. Two dangerous words.

To these problematic terms I would add some other loaded words from our own time, words, like *knowledge* and *belief*, that carry an undeniable whiff of comparable gravitas. Words like *wisdom* and *leadership*, *creativity* and *closure* (not to mention the egregious, and currently ubiquitous, *faith*, *faith-based*, and *person of faith*). *Leadership*, my particular unfavorite in this list of unfavored terms, is now the topic of things called leadership institutes around the nation. These cash cows, or cash bulls, vary from the Institute for Women's Leadership to the right-wing Leadership Institute to the Getty Leadership Institute for museum professionals to the Rotarian Leadership Institute and the Shambhala Institute for Authentic Leadership, and so on. Increasingly, such institutes are also sited within universities. What are these leaders going to lead? It doesn't really matter. *Leadership* has become a free-standing substantive, a skill or attribute desired by "forward-thinking leaders, managers, and change agents of all levels from business, government, education, NGOs, and civil society."[20] Not excluding, of course, those who opt for weekend training in "Personal Leadership, Timeless Wisdom." Some attended such a session in 2005, in fact, at Cortes Island, British Columbia, under the guidance of "some of the world's most accomplished and visionary leadership mentors." Who is this program for? It says right on the website: "For professionals who aspire to lead with authenticity while enacting transformative change."[21]

If you seek loaded words, look about you: *professional, aspiration, authenticity, transformative change* (as contrasted, I wonder, with what other kind of change?). What all these problematic terms have in common is that they seem to be real. And in fact they are placeholders for thinking—even for what might be called, gritting our teeth as we say it, "transformative change."

Loaded words. The problem with loaded words is—as I suggested at the outset—not that they are too full but rather that they are too empty. Knowledge and belief are substantives in our culture, not stages. They represent what Paolo Freire once called the "banking model" of education.

> Education . . . becomes an act of depositing, in which the students are the depositories and the teacher is the depositor. Instead of communicating, the teacher issues communiques and makes deposits which the students patiently receive, memorize, and repeat. This is the "banking" concept of education. . . . In the banking concept of education, knowledge is a gift bestowed by those who consider themselves knowledgeable upon those whom they consider to know nothing.[22]

In the process of becoming nouns, they have forfeited the process of becoming. Instead of knowing and believing, which are active, transitive, and transitory, we have the instantiations of *knowledge* and *belief* as think-tank substantives or research and funding goals. (*Think tank* itself is a good example.) Words like this have become signs and symptoms not of an old, Bourdieu-like cultural capital but rather of a species of *moral capital*, for a society that is running out of real intellectual fuel—the kind of fuel that comes from questions rather than answers. The problem, in other words, is a kind of cultural hypostasis: the desire for knowledge and belief to be entities. Dogma, doxa, dicta, data. If we can get out of the habit of thinking that labeling something is the same as possessing it, or understanding it, or putting it to work—if we can move beyond this kind of intellectual résumé, this c.v. for the achievements of the mind—we can, perhaps, take the first next steps toward reclaiming the processes of knowing and believing. Such a reclamation will depend, crucially, on our willingness to tolerate four other *D* words, four equally legitimate descendants of knowledge and belief: doubt, dissension, disagreement, and debate.

CHAPTER TWO

Mad Lib

COUNTERINTELLIGENCE

> Freud took up madness at the level of *language*, reconstituting one of the essential elements of an experience that positivism had reduced to silence.
>
> Michel Foucault, *History of Madness*

In 1909, Sigmund Freud came upon a pamphlet written by a specialist in ancient languages that seemed to him to have an uncanny resonance with his own recent work on dreams. The pamphlet, like Freud's essay on it, was called "The Antithetical Sense of Primal Words" (or "The Antithetical Meaning of Primal Words"). In it, Karl Abel, a philologist, contended that the vocabulary of ancient Egypt and the "Semitic and Indo-European languages" contained a number of key words whose meanings diverged in apparently opposite directions. To Freud this precisely mirrored—and seemed to validate—a claim he had made in *The Interpretation of Dreams* about how the unconscious mind handles antithetical meanings.

> The way in which dreams treat the category of contraries and contradictories is highly remarkable. It is simply disregarded. "No" seems not to exist so far as dreams are concerned. They show a particular preference for combining contraries into a unity or for representing them as one and the same thing. Dreams feel themselves at liberty, moreover, to represent any element by its wishful contrary; so that there is no way of deciding at first glance whether any element that admits of a contrary is present in the dream-thoughts as a positive or as a negative.[1]

Decades later, Jacques Lacan would assert that the unconscious was structured like a language. In this essay, however, Freud proposed that language was structured like the unconscious: "We psychiatrists cannot escape the suspicion that we should be better at understanding and translating the language of dreams if we knew more about the development of language."[2]

Freud's own characteristic double negative here ("we psychiatrists cannot escape the suspicion that . . .") describes the same mechanism of interior surveillance that he recognized in, or appropriated from, Abel's pamphlet: in essence, the psychiatrist, like the philologist, was on a constant hunt for double agents. In the political realm, double agentry is known, appropriately enough, as *counterintelligence*. And, as we will see, the relationship between intelligence and counterintelligence will have some bearing on this story.

It might be worth noting that Lacan's essay on language in this connection is titled (in English) "The Agency of the Letter in the Unconscious, or Reason since Freud." Language, for Lacan, is clearly a double agent. Here is his apostrophe to madness in that essay:

> Madness, you are no longer the object of the ambiguous praise with which the sage decorated the impregnable burrow of his fear; and if after all he finds himself tolerably at home there, it is only because the supreme agent forever at work digging its tunnels is none other than reason.[3]

The radical nature of Freud's insights in the *Interpretation of Dreams* was not fully appreciated immediately, Lacan says, because that book was written "before the formalization of linguistics for which . . . it paved the way."[4] But this "radical revolution" produced by "the procedures of exegesis" is now felt in every aspect of life. And here he gives a list: "the destiny of man, politics, metaphysics, literature, the arts, advertising, propaganda."[5] The direction of this list is indicative: it is the move from the Renaissance to the twentieth century.

We might note, too, that Derrida's Freudian reading of Foucault's idea of madness is directly cognate to this discussion of language as a double agent. The passionate and impassioned debate between Foucault and Derrida turned, to a certain extent, on which was the "outside" of the other. Was madness to be subsumed under the category of history, or of philosophy? For Derrida, dreams and doubt were key philosophical positions. Foucault retorted scathingly, "How could a philosophy which places itself under the sign of origin and repetition think the singularity of the event?"[6] This was before the 24/7 news cycle and the global media conflated origin, repetition, and event in an endless loop. But it was not before the notion of the antithetical *within*: By that logic, by that reasoning, to think *singularity* was itself already double-think.

To explain the concept of "antithetical meanings" Freud provided, in his essays, some Latin and modern German examples (Latin *sacer*, "sacred" and "accursed"; German *Boden*, "garret" or "ground," the highest and the lowest place in the house; English *cleave*, "to split" and "to cling," etc.). But one example that Freud did *not* offer in his list of antithetical words—although it is intrinsic to his argument about dreams and dream logic—was the word that, conspicuous by its absence in his writings, nonetheless demarcates the very concept with which his work was, for a long lifetime, engaged. Or—what is for Freud the same thing— engaged in resisting.

If you seek out the word *madness* in the General Subject Index of the *Standard Edition* of Freud's works, you will find only two brief subheadings: "and poetry," one page; and "fear of," a few pages, almost all in the very first volume of this chronological edition of his life's work. (So, from the first, the term is bifurcated here, too, between the exalted and the dejected.) Needless to say, Freud did not make his own index, and the English language index attempted to synthesize the various local indices for each of the twenty-four volumes. But nonetheless these sparse listings are suggestive. For if you look at the citations under "fear of madness," you will find that these are the words of a patient, not of Freud himself: Having been told by a maidservant that "a woman living in the same house had gone mad," the patient was thenceforth "never free of an obsession . . . that she was going to go mad too."[7]

Freud's collective term for what an earlier era called *madness* was *psychosis*, a term to which the indexers refer the reader, and here we do find a wide range of specific terms, from *collective, confusional, hallucinatory, hypnotic,* and *hysterical* psychosis to *narcissism, neurosis, religion,* and the more clinically described—and named—psychoses, including *paranoia* and *schizophrenia*. These terms were current and specific when Freud wrote about them; it is not his fault that many of them have become, like *madness*, broad cultural and journalistic terms rather than precise diagnoses of individual conditions.

I will return later to the question of the popular dissemination of clinical terms and their emptying out of diagnostic specificity—as I will also return, and at the same time, to the matter of counterintelligence.

But first let me say something about the antithetical history of *madness* in English.

From its beginnings the English word *mad* was already forked: pointing at once toward insanity and toward infatuation. *Mad* meaning "unwise," "imprudent," "wildly foolish," segued into *mad* meaning "carried away with enthusiasm or desire." Mad with longing. Mad about a woman (or, in the Noel Coward version, "Mad about the Boy"). "He was mad for her,"[8] Shakespeare writes in *All's Well That Ends Well*. But one could, and can, be mad about things, and ideas, as well as about persons of either, or any, gender. Dryden reports that "the world is running mad after farce, the extremity of bad poetry."[9] In a Jane Austen novel one fashion-conscious woman describes another as as being "mad for such a house,"[10] D. H. Lawrence declares in *Sons and Lovers* that "everybody was mad with excitement,"[11] and a food review from the 1960s avers that though the diner "wasn't mad about the parsley sauce," the snails were great.[12] In short, although it would be tempting to guess that *mad* meaning "infatuated" was a corruption, over time, of the "purer" or "original" definition of *mad* meaning "insane," both meanings are recorded as early as the fourteenth century and can readily be found in the same canon of major authors. Furthermore, this can also be said of a third meaning which almost always, these days, is regarded as colloquial: "I'm *mad* at you." *Mad* as "angry, irate, cross" is found as early as the beginning of the fifteenth century. As alternative terms—*wod* or *wood* for "insane," *wroth* for "angry"—began to lose currency, *mad* triumphed, and emerged as the common word covering the entire spectrum of the primal passions from hate to love. *I'm mad at you. I'm mad about you. You've driven me mad.*

The bifurcation (or trifurcation) was already clear by the time Shakespeare wrote *A Midsummer Night's Dream* (a play in which one baffled lover exclaims in frustration that he is "wood [i.e., mad] within the wood"), for toward the end of that play he gives its most conventional thinker, the well-meaning but profoundly unoriginal Duke Theseus, lines that are both hauntingly beautiful and flatly bromidic.

> Lovers and madmen have such seething brains,
> Such shaping fantasies, that apprehend
> More than cool reason ever comprehends.
> The lunatic, the lover, and the poet
> Are of imagination all compact:
> One sees more devils than vast hell can hold;

That is the madman: the lover, all as frantic,
Sees Helen's beauty in a brow of Egypt:
The poet's eye, in a fine frenzy rolling,
Doth glance from heaven to earth, from earth to heaven;
And as imagination bodies forth
The forms of things unknown, the poet's pen
Turns them to shapes, and gives to airy nothing
A local habitation and a name.

    (5.1.4–17)

Despite the popularity of this speech in the Romantic period, it is far from an unalloyed praise of the power of the imagination. "Cool reason" and "comprehension" are clearly Theseus's preferred categories. But my main point for the present purpose is to underscore the equivalence of madness, love, and poetic inspiration. The antithetical sense of primal passions.

We might note in passing that *lunatic*, like *mad* and *madman*, has now moved into popular discourse as a term of affectionate praise as well as political condemnation: Thus actor Alan Arkin can describe his role in the film *Get Smart* as "10% raving lunatic," while praising—in the same interview—"insane, stupid comedy" in general and Second City founder Paul Sills in particular: "he was a maniac, he was impossible, but he was the heart and soul of the place."[13] Concurrently, on the political front, Arianna Huffington published a book with the not-so-succinct title *Right Is Wrong: How the Lunatic Fringe Hijacked America, Shredded the Constitution, and Made Us All Less Safe (and What You Need to Know to End the Madness).* *Lunatic fringe* has been around since at least the time of Teddy Roosevelt, who declared in 1913 that "there is apt to be a lunatic fringe among the votaries of any forward movement."[14] Meanwhile, it is perhaps needless to say, the word *lunatic*, once used to designate the kind of insanity generated by the phases of the moon—and technically still in use through the nineteenth century in the names of lunatic hospitals and "lunatic asylums"– has disappeared from medical vocabularies. The phrase "he's a lunatic" may denote popular success or political denunciation, but whatever it means today, it is not a clinical diagnosis.

*

Foucault famously began his *History of Madness* by suggesting that the medicalization of madness was a displacement—"madmen" and "madwomen" filling the place of social ostracism that had been previously occupied by lepers. In what follows I argue that words like *mad, insane,* and *crazy,* always already antithetical to themselves, emerged in the late twentieth and early twenty-first centuries as post-medical vocabulary for rescripting the vatic role of the seer (the modern "pundit") and the clown (the modern "stand-up comic"). This talk could thus be described as an exploration of the deinstitutionalization of *mad-*ness through the deinstitutionalization of the word *mad.*

Borrowing from the title of Foucault's text, I propose here not a *History of Madness* but a history of "*mad-*ness," a history of the word *mad* as it has been redesignated, rebranded, and redeployed in the twentieth and twenty-first centuries. For the one thing that this flexible term no longer seems to designate is clinical mental illness—at least, not among humans.

Unsurprisingly, *mad* as a clinical term does not appear in the *Diagnostic and Statistical Manual of Mental Disorders* (*DSM*) published by the American Psychiatric Association.[15] Even so-called Axis II disorders, including paranoid personality disorder, schizoid personality disorder, borderline personality disorder, antisocial personality disorder, narcissistic personality disorder, histrionic personality disorder, dependent personality disorder, and obsessive-compulsive personality disorder, are exempt from such labeling. The madwoman in the attic is a book title and a fictional type, not a clinical persona. To the medical community, and indeed, I presume, to the legal community, the term of art is not *madness* but *mental disorder.*

When *mad* is used in a semidiagnostic way, it is usually in the press (describing, for example, the "Mad Bomber" of the fifties, George Metesky; Charles Manson; or the Unabomber, Ted Kaczynski).[16] Mass murderers, torturers, and megalomaniacs are still called "mad" in the media and in written accounts. When law professor Noah Feldman reviewed Osama bin Laden's collected speeches, interviews, web postings and other public statements, he wrote that what made these "different from, say, 'Helter Skelter,' is that bin Laden is not clinically mad. He gives reasons for his actions that, while morally outrageous and religiously irresponsible, could be accepted by otherwise logical people who shared his premises." In Feldman's view this made bin Laden "more, not less, dangerous than the Charles Mansons among us."[17]

But as a term, *mad* is no longer a clinical diagnosis, nor yet an exclusionary epithet. Instead it is an iconic example of the emptying out of keywords over time in the direction of the allusive and the preposterous inversion. *Bad* is good, *wicked* is great, whether these words are wielded by a Michael Jackson or a George Orwell. *Mad*, in other words (but which other words?), has made its move back into popular discourse.

FREE ASSOCIATION

What is said in such a language is of little importance, as are the meanings that are delivered there. It is this obscure and central liberation of speech at the heart of itself, its uncontrollable flight to a region that is always dark, which no culture can accept immediately. Such speech is transgressive, not in its meaning, not in its verbal matter, but in its *play*.

Foucault, *History of Madness*

Decades before the word *lib* appeared as an abbreviation and a combining form for various kinds of liberation, from women's lib to gay lib to children's lib, the phrase *mad libs*, itself a play on the Latin-derived *ad lib* (*ad libitum*, "at one's pleasure"; something spontaneous, unrehearsed, improvised) had made its way into American popular culture.

Mad Libs was invented in 1953 by the television writer Leonard Stern (*Get Smart, The Honeymooners, The Phil Silvers Show*) and the humorist Roger Price, who also invented the Droodle. As Stern tells the story, he was seeking an adjective to describe Ralph Kramden's nose for an episode of *The Honeymooners*, and he asked Price for some adjectives: "I said, 'I need an adjective that—' and before I could further define my need, Roger said, 'Clumsy and naked.' I laughed out loud. Roger asked, 'What's so funny?' I told him, thanks to his suggestions, Ralph Kramden now had a boss with a clumsy nose—or, if you will, a naked nose. Roger seldom laughed, but he did at that time, confirming we were onto something—but what it was, we didn't know." They spent the rest of the day writing stories with key words left out, and took them to a party that night, where they were a great success. The title for the concept was said to have come from an overheard conversation at Sardi's, the show-business hangout. An actor was arguing with his agent about wanting to ad-lib an interview; the agent thought the idea was "mad."[18]

The Mad Libs concept got a big boost from *The Steve Allen Show*, for which Stern was head writer and comedy director. He persuaded Allen to use the Mad Libs approach to introduce guest stars: The audience was asked to fill in the blanks. Allen held up a copy of the first Mad Libs book as Bob Hope came onto the stage. Hope's theme song, "Thanks for the Memories," was subjected to the Mad Libs treatment ("Thanks for the _____ [plural noun]") and emerged as "Thanks for the Communists."[19] The year was 1958. A few days later the first edition (14,000 copies) had completely sold out.

That the word *Communists* could be genially suggested as a random noun gives some sense of the relatively safe space occupied by Bob Hope (and NBC), for in 1958 the Hollywood blacklist, or entertainment industry blacklist, was still very much in force. If Steve Allen's guest had been Paul Robeson, or Lee J. Cobb, or Judy Holliday, or Zero Mostel, or Burl Ives (the list goes on and on), presumably this "mad" suggestion would not have been made—or would not have been taken as humor.

Mad Libs were a kind of pop-psychological free association: you said what popped into your mind (Ralph Kramden had a "clumsy nose" or a "naked nose"), and after a while you tried for the offbeat, the hilarious non-fit that fit. But it did not take a Freud (or a Hollywood blacklist, for that matter) to indicate that no "association" was really "free."

In the same years that Mad Libs was developing from a party game to a well-selling series of books (published by the authors under the imprint Price Stern Sloan), a countercultural comic book became an enormously successful magazine called *Mad*. Originating in the supposedly conformist Cold War '50s, *Mad*, once derided by *Time* as a "short-lived satirical pulp," became the chief vehicle for political satire for young people and adults. "The summer of *Mad*'s first appearance in 1952," wrote the authors of a twenty-five-year retrospective, in 1977,

> was the summer Dick Nixon was attacking Adlai Stevenson as soft on Communism, corruption and costs. The big names-in-the-news in *Mad*'s first years, as it struggled out of the red, were John Foster (Brinkmanship) Dulles, Tailgunner Joe McCarthy, and Engine Charlie (What's Good for General Motors is Good for the Country) Wilson—men for whom the world was grim, dangerous and humorless. Into the middle of that world and loudly giving it a Bronx cheer skidded *Mad*, a (in its own terms) tiny, trashy, disgusting, demented and probably anti-American publication that just happened to speak to some of the deepest fears and perceptions of a nation's puzzled kids.[20]

Those "kids," the article went on to point out, became us. "The skeptical generation of kids it shaped in the 1950s is the same generation that in the 1960s opposed a war and didn't feel bad when the United States lost for the first time and in the 1970s helped turn out an Administration and didn't feel bad about that either." The fascination of *Mad* to the "air-raid-shelter generation," and indeed to those in the generations that would follow, was that the magazine seemed to tell the truth about lying: "*Mad* told us that everything was askew—that there were lies in advertising, that other comic books lied, that television and movies lied, and that adults, in general, when faced with the unknown, lied." Which was *mad* here—the magazine, or the world?

Although the magazine's headquarters were for many years on Madison Avenue (always printed as "MADison" Avenue on the masthead), from 1957 through 2001 *Mad* eschewed advertising. Bill Gaines, for forty years *Mad's* publisher, told *60 Minutes* that they couldn't take money from Pepsi and make fun of Coke. From its "What, Me Worry?" mascot, Alfred E. Neuman, through features like "Spy vs. Spy," in which the Black Spy and the White Spy, identical in every way except the color of their outfits, conspired to outwit one another (and were always themselves outwitted), *Mad* created indelible signs of the changing times. The "Spy vs. Spy" cartoon, indeed, brought to vivid, visible, and risible life a doctrine of military strategy that became a key Cold War tactic aimed at avoiding full-scale war between the United States and the Soviet Union. Sometimes known as nuclear deterrence, this scenario was also given another name: mutually assured destruction, or MAD.[21] The idea was that nuclear nations with second-strike capability could retaliate against a first strike in so quick and devastating a way as to result in the destruction of both sides.

Mad magazine epitomized one aspect of the fifties: the paranoia of the Cold War, and the distrust of elders which were to become the hallmark of a generation. It thus came into interesting conjunction with an organization known as SANE.

SANE was an antinuclear NGO founded by Coretta Scott King, Albert Schweitzer, Dr. Benjamin Spock, and others. Despite its striking name, always spelled out in capital letters, SANE, unlike MAD (Mutually Assured Destruction), or indeed NGO (nongovernmental organization) was not an acronym. The name was a reference to the title of a 1955 book by Erich Fromm, *The Sane Society*. SANE's initial goal, as set forth in a full-page ad in the *New York Times*, was to make the American public aware of the threat posed by nuclear weapons. (In the realm of coincidence, we might note that Steve Allen, who had introduced Mad Libs on his television show, also hosted the first meeting of the Hollywood branch of SANE.)

SANE, like *Mad* (the magazine) still exists today. Originally founded in 1957—that same fifties decade—it is now called Peace Action, an organization formed by the merger of the Committee for a SANE Nuclear

Policy and the Nuclear Weapons Freeze Campaign.[22] SANE/FREEZE supported candidates pledged to work for peace in Vietnam, endorsed Eugene McCarthy for president in 1968, opposed the U.S. military buildup in the Persian Gulf that became the first Gulf War, and changed its name to Peace Action in 1993. After 9/11 it made calls for justice rather than war, and supported the national coalition called Win Without War. But the other MAD, the theory of Mutually Assured Destruction, also remains, although these days one can also find articles reflecting upon—or calling for—"The End of MAD?" (and the "rise of U.S. nuclear primacy").[23]

Which of these manifestations from the fifties is sane, and which is mad? What seems clear is that the word *mad* itself became a cultural marker, much as—perhaps—the Fool in the Renaissance was a cultural marker, an "allowed fool" or "licensed fool" whose antics, doubletalk, and insubordination gave pleasure, provoked thought, and spoke truth to power.

MAD IN CRAFT

> The marvelous logic of the mad seems to mock that of the logicians, as it shadows so closely, or rather because it is exactly the same, and at the heart of madness, at the basis of so many errors, absurdities, aimless words and gestures, what is sometimes to be found is the deeply buried perfection of a discourse.
>
> Foucault, *History of Madness*

Polonius had a phrase for it: "Though this be madness, yet there is method in't." And Hamlet, whose madness had so puzzled Polonius, will later caution his mother not to tell her husband, King Claudius, the secret, "that I essentially am not in madness,/But mad in craft."[24]

What is the craft of madness? In the Romantic period, we might have said that it was poetry, from Christopher Smart to Yeats's Crazy Jane. By the middle of the twentieth century (as a recent television hit has reminded us), the craft of madness was advertising: "Mad Men," advertising executives, were the lords and heroes of Madison Avenue.

Sometime in the 1940s, Alfred Hitchcock announced that he was going to make a film of *Hamlet*, with Cary Grant in the title role. The project never came to fruition,[25] but in 1959 Hitchcock made another film starring Grant as a Madison Avenue advertising executive caught in a web of mistaken identities, spy stories, and assassination plots: The film was called *North by Northwest*. The allusion to *Hamlet* is unmistakable, whether or not it was intended (accounts on this question vary, as one might expect of anything to do with Hitchcock). The phrase occurs at a crucial moment in Shakespeare's play, the moment when Hamlet, already undercover as a mad man, offers his own version of double-agent-speak to the perfidious Rosencrantz and Guildenstern: "I am but mad north-north-west."[26]

Early in the film, Grant tells his secretary, "In the world of advertising there is no such thing as a lie," only "the expedient exaggeration." Later he is assailed by his archfoe, the head of a Cold War enterprise bent on stealing U.S. government secrets: "Has anyone ever told you that you overplay your various roles . . . ? First you're the outraged Madison Avenue man who claims he has been mistaken for someone else. Then you play a fugitive from justice, supposedly trying to clear his name of a crime he knows he didn't commit. And now you play the peevish lover, stung by jealousy and betrayal." We do not need to remind ourselves of Hamlet's advice to the players ("Nor do not saw the air with your hand, thus, but use all gently . . . O it offends me to the soul to hear a robustious periwig-pated fellow tear a passion to tatters, to very rags, to split the ears of the groundlings")[27] to see that this "Madison Avenue man" accused of overplaying his roles is the missing hero of the missing film: Cary Grant as Hamlet. The aptly named Jon Hamm, the actor who stars in the AMC hit show *Mad Men*, set in an advertising agency in the early 1960s, is Grant's equally elegant and soigné successor. (Commenting on love, that most commonly accepted form of madness, Hamm's character, Don Draper, tells a woman that it doesn't exist: "What you call love was invented by guys like me to sell nylons.")

An imaginative reading of *North by Northwest* could tease out more Hamlet themes. The "ghost" figure of Old Hamlet in this reading is arguably split between the larger-than-life head of Abraham Lincoln on Mount Rushmore and the character called "The Professor" (played by Leo G. Carroll), an American spymaster who is trying to keep the villain from smuggling microfilmed secrets out of the country. The Grant character's closeness to his mother—marked at the beginning of the film by his date to go to the theater with her and his need to be in touch with her as he sets out on his adventures—falls away as he becomes more involved with the spy plot, and with the adventuress Eve.

And I can't help thinking, too, that the fact that the fictitious government agent Grant chases and then impersonates has a Jewish name (George Kaplan) is also a marker of the times. There is no Jew in this

1959 film of espionage—but in order to extricate himself from the tangled trap that began when he was mistakenly identified as Kaplan, the hero has to *become* the Jew, to take on the identity of "George Kaplan" and abandon his Waspy identity as Roger O. Thornhill (the initial O, he explains in response to a question, "stands for nothing"). Here too is a ghost, a ghost of the past and the present. The ad man takes on the name of a Jew. Matthew Weiner's *Mad Men* is set in the early 1960s and has emphasized the anti-Semitism of the white-shoe firms of the period. The Internet and the print media alike were abuzz at one point with speculations that Don Draper's secret was that he was Jewish, and working for a firm that hires no Jews except in the mail room.[28]

The choice of the "man in the gray flannel suit," the advertising executive, as the main character in this thriller about mistaken identity, counterintelligence, and cultural disorientation is, as we will see, significant. Although Ernest Lehman's script describes Roger Thornhill as "far too original to be wearing the grey-flannel uniform of his kind,"[29] Hitchcock's film has Grant impeccably dressed in gray. By combining these two conflicting modes of belief and truth (madness and advertising) with the crisis of belief which is the slippery slope of espionage (Claudius's "lawful espials"; Polonius's "bait of falsehood" to take a "carp of truth")[30], Hitchcock deftly touched upon themes that would be central to mid-century culture, providing a narrative for the Cold War and its discontents.[31]

NONE DARE CALL IT REASON

> One [madman] who suffered from persecution mania could produce an infinitely extended induction: "A, B, and C are my enemies. They are all men. Therefore all men are my enemies."
>
> Foucault, *History of Madness*

The word *paranoid* is now common in headlines and in articles on social and cultural trends, as well as on domestic disputes: Check your LexisNexis (or your daily paper) and you'll immediately see what I mean. Dozens of books, from novels to histories to self-help, use *paranoid* in their titles, and a recent release called *Paranoia: The 21st Century Fear*, featured the results of a "Paranoid Thoughts Questionnaire" which the authors had circulated to 1,200 respondents. A *Boston Globe* book critic suggested to a colleague that paranoia was an interesting new theme in the books sent her for review; I'm sure she wasn't being paranoid. But in fact the term has been in play at least since the early sixties, when historian Richard Hofstadter spoke at Oxford on the topic of "The Paranoid Style in American Politics"—a phrase that became the title of his well-received book.

Hofstadter noted a long-term trend in "right-wing thought," including the contention that "top government officialdom has been so infiltrated by Communists that American policy, at least since the days of Pearl Harbor, has been dominated by sinister men who were shrewdly and consistently selling out American national interests," and that "the country is infused with a network of Communist agents . . . so that the whole apparatus of education, religion, the press and the mass media are engaged in a common effort to paralyze the resistance of loyal Americans."[32] As Daniel Patrick Moynihan observed many years later, Hofstadter "was at the time primarily concerned with the conspiratorial fantasies of the right—Ike as a tool of the Reds, etc.—and certain of their characteristics, such as the redemptive role of ex-communists in exposing the conspiracies. . . . But he knew well enough the paranoid style of the left."[33] "I call it the paranoid style," Hofstadter explained,

> simply because no other word adequately evokes the qualities of heated exaggeration, suspiciousness, and conspiratorial fantasy that I have in mind. In using the expression "paranoid style," I am not speaking in a clinical sense, but borrowing a clinical term for other purposes. I have neither the competence nor the desire to classify any figures of the past or present as certifiable lunatics. In fact, the idea of the paranoid style would have little contemporary relevance or historical value if it were applied only to people with profoundly disturbed minds. It is the use of paranoid modes of expression by more or less normal people that makes the phenomenon significant.[34]

So here, too, the fact that the word has migrated from the diagnostic to the metaphorical makes all the difference: If the paranoia or lunacy were merely literal, it might have dark consequences but it would not be a *style*, "a way of seeing the world and seeing oneself."

> There is a vital difference between the paranoid spokesman in politics and the clinical paranoiac: although they both tend to be overheated, oversuspicious, overaggressive, grandiose, and apocalyptic in expression, the clinical paranoid sees the hostile and conspiratorial world in which he feels himself to be living as directed specifically *against him*; whereas the spokesman of the paranoid style finds it directed against a nation, a culture, a way of life whose fate affects not himself alone but millions of others. . . . His sense that his political passions are

unselfish and patriotic, in fact, goes far to intensify his feeling of righteousness and his moral indignation.[35]

The conspiracy theory of the time was supported by writers like Phyllis Schlafly, who contended in *A Choice Not an Echo* that "a small group of secret kingmakers, using hidden persuaders and psychological warfare techniques, manipulated the Republican National Convention to nominate candidates who would sidestep or suppress the key issues."[36] This was in 1964, a whole Republican revolution ago. But what I want to underscore here is the connection between fears of Communist infiltration and the rhetoric of the "hidden persuaders"—the title of Vance Packard's 1957 book on the advertising industry, motivational research, and the manipulation of the populace both by product marketers and by political operatives.[37] By the early and mid-fifties a merchandising approach to American politics had taken off within both major parties. Leonard Hall, the Republican National Committee chairman, announced in 1956 that the party "has a great product to sell . . . You sell your candidates and your programs the way a business sells its products."[38]

By contrast, as we saw, *Mad* magazine banned advertising from its pages from 1957 until 2001, since the editors regarded it as unethical to take money from firms that might become targets of satire. (Will the real counterculture please stand up?) Comic send-up "ads" for products from Likely Strife cigarettes to Blech Shampoo to the Bilked Telephone System ornamented its pages, as did a reverse ad from the NRA (Nature's Revenge Association) in which a deer in an orange jacket and carrying a rifle urged hunters to "keep your guns in the cities where they belong."[39]

In both the 1952 and the 1956 national campaigns, the Republicans were identified with the New York advertising agency Batten, Barton, Durstine and Osborn (BBDO)—just as the fictional Sterling Cooper firm, on television's *Mad Men*, was retained to sell the candidacy of Richard Nixon. Political essayist Richard H. Rovere wrote at the time that Nixon was "a politician with an advertising man's approach to his work," able to switch from intervention in Indochina to anti-intervention "with the same ease and lack of anguish with which a copy writer might transfer his loyalties from Camels to Chesterfields."[40] But despite the fact that in the fifties both major parties proudly made use of advertising as a new mode of political persuasion, the idea of insidious and subliminal manipulation by dangerously "hidden" persuaders matched all too well—as

Schafly's screed suggests—with the concomitant paranoia about Communists hidden everywhere in American life. Not for the first time, the illogic of combining capitalism (the advertising industry) and Communism came together to give additional force to the "logic" of the claim. "A small group of secret kingmakers, using hidden persuaders and psychological warfare techniques," were manipulating the populace.

A similar set of accusations forms the centerpiece of John A. Stormer's diatribe on "the communist-socialist conspiracy to enslave America," *None Dare Call It Treason* (1964). Stormer's book quoted J. Edgar Hoover on the back cover—"They have infiltrated every conceivable sphere of activity: youth groups, radio, television and motion picture industries; church, school, educational and cultural groups; the press; national minority groups and civil and political units"—and exhorted readers on the front cover: "1964 is a year of crisis and decision. Will America continue to aid the communist enemy. . . . The decision is yours!" Madness was a subtext here, too, from chapter 1, "Have We Gone Crazy?" to chapter 9, "Mental Health," which excoriated health professionals for wobbly permissiveness.

> Do you hold rigidly to "outmoded" concepts of right and wrong? Do you reject socialism? Do you oppose foreign aid waste? Do you object to letting African cannibals vote on how we should live under a world government? If so, you are by "definition" well along the road toward mental illness and in need of "treatment."[41]

Stormer's chief target is G. Brock Chisholm, a Canadian who was the first director-general of the World Health Organization (WHO) and who is quoted as having written, in 1946, that psychiatrists "should be trained as salesmen and be taught all the techniques of breaking down sales resistance."[42] So here too the worlds of advertising and mental health would seem to collide, at least rhetorically. The title of Stormer's book comes from a well-known couplet by Sir John Harington, the witty and mischievous godson of Queen Elizabeth I.

> Treason doth never prosper, what's the reason?
> For if it prosper, none dare call it treason.[43]

Harington himself was well aware of the dangers, having been caught in the middle during the Essex Rebellion (Essex was his champion, Elizabeth his relation) and stood surety for a cousin who was implicated in the treasonous Main and Bye plots against King James. But perhaps in this case the rhyme of *reason* and *treason* can be said to do double duty, for the title of the book—written at a time when Robert W. Welch Jr., the founder of the John Birch Society, was labeling President Eisenhower "a dedicated, conscious agent of the Communist conspiracy"[44]—could benefit from the elided *t*: None dare call it reason.

Is Harington's terse epigram an advertising jingle avant la lettre? What is the relationship between Mad Men and madmen?

DOUBLE EXPOSURE

> Since Freud, Western madness has become a non-language because it has become a double language (a language which only exists in this speech, a speech that says nothing but its language).
>
> Foucault, *History of Madness*

In July 2008, the *New York Times* reported that the U.S. military had patterned its interrogation methods at Guantánamo Bay on "Chinese Communist techniques used during the Korean War to obtain confessions, many of them false, from American prisoners." A chart outlining such "coercive management techniques" as sleep deprivation, prolonged constraint, and exposure, drawn up in an Air Force study from 1957, appears to have been used, without disclosing its source, in an interrogation class in December 2002.[45] The chart was copied from an article entitled "Communist Attempts to Elicit Confessions from Air Force Prisoners of War."[46] The Chinese interrogators had filmed some of the prisoners confessing to a wide range of atrocities, and the resulting outcry led to assertions that the Americans had been "brainwashed." Fans of *The Manchurian Candidate* were quick to spot the connection—as was columnist Maureen Dowd in that day's *Times*.[47]

The Manchurian Candidate, which became an iconic Cold War film (1962), was first published as a novel in 1957. Perhaps at this point it will not come as a surprise to learn that its author, Richard Condon, began his career in advertising in the 1930s and then became a publicist for the American film industry for twenty-one years before writing his first book.

The perfect paranoid thriller, *The Manchurian Candidate* tells the story of an American platoon captured during the Korean War and brainwashed into believing their sergeant saved their lives in combat. The Communists want to use Sergeant Shaw as a sleeper agent, using a deck of playing cards as subliminal triggers: The queen of diamonds, representing his powerful mother, is the key, and (in true fifties "Momism" style) it is his mother, a pillar of American conservatism, who turns out to be the paradigmatic double agent, in league with the Communists to overthrow the U.S. government.

Paranoia is only regarded an illness if it runs counter to majority expectations; in this case, the fear of a vast conspiracy turns out to be (simply) true. *Brainwashing*, a coinage of the early fifties, is defined as "the systematic and often forcible elimination from a person's mind of all established ideas, especially political ones, so that another set of ideas may take their place."[48] If this is madness, there is method in it: And the method is that of subliminal advertising.

That term, it will again not surprise you to learn, was coined in 1957 by a market researcher, James Vicary, who claimed that flashing messages on a movie screen for a fraction of a second would subliminally persuade audiences to "Drink Coca-Cola" or "Eat Popcorn." The device he used, the tachistoscope, was used in World War II to detect enemy airplanes. Vicary's claims were given wide publicity in Vance Packard's *The Hidden Persuaders* and triggered warning responses by the CIA and the FCC, even though Vicary himself later conceded that the device was a gimmick rather than a provable experiment. In other words, the story about the story about subliminal advertising was good advertising.[49]

Double agents, brainwashing, subliminal advertising, hidden persuaders—all were thought to be useful in "liberating" secret thoughts, or tendencies, or predispositions. As the CIA paper cautioned, "If the subliminal cue is to work by tripping off an existing motive to action, one must know what motives are positive and operant at the moment. . . . The percentage of instances will be high where the opposite motive to that desired will be tripped off."[50] So indeed it proves in *The Manchurian Candidate*, when Raymond Shaw, turned into an assassin, assassinates his mother. (The CIA author calls this "a 'flashback,' . . . inadvertently producing just the opposite effect to that desired.")

By the end of the twentieth century, *brainwash* had made its way into popular culture and style. "Fashion may not seduce everyone, but it has an amazing ability to brainwash its own," writes a style reporter for the *New York Times*, noting that the "return to glamour" in women's wear had spurred a similar movement among designers for men.[51] We might compare this emptying-out of affect to what has happened to the word *madness* in a phrase like *March Madness*, used as an instantly recognizable shorthand for a spring basketball tournament. (Or, for another example of this trend, the smiley-face version of *hysterical*: "I was laughing hysterically through most of the interview," reported a television entertainment journalist who spoke, on camera, with Barack Obama, his wife, and their daughters. "They're such a charming, beautiful family.")[52] But the emptying-out of these terms, their conversion into what used to be called dead metaphors, endowed them with new demotic life. They had become commodified: They were now names—not for conditions, but for desires.

*

We began this inquiry with the idea of madness as linguistic counterintelligence, and, concurrently, with the observation that (in English at least) madness itself was a double agent, seeming to signify both the most exalted and the most abjected states of human fantasy: both infatuation and insanity. The equivalent cultural markers we have been observing at work are espionage (or treason) and advertising. And as we have seen, these "double languages"[53] (to quote again Foucault on madness after Freud) are often—we may think uncannily—either derived from the same sources or linked by association, advertent or inadvertent (Schlafly's and Packard's "hidden persuaders"; Allen and Hope's "Thanks for the Communists"). Following the signifier where it led, we saw that *Mad* magazine, for example, contained a popular spy cartoon feature that mimicked, though never explicitly mentioned, the tactics of the nuclear policy called MAD, Mutually Assured Destruction. The protagonist of 1959's *North by Northwest* is an advertising executive caught by mistake in a spy plot; the protagonist of 1959's *The Manchurian Candidate* is a "brainwashed" ex-military man who is manipulated by methods concurrently being explored by American advertising (in a novel written by an author who was once a Mad Man himself). Are you getting the subliminal message here?

It may be useful to remind ourselves of a few key dates.

1952: the founding of *Mad* magazine

1953: the invention of Mad Libs
        Richard Hofstadter speaks at Oxford on "The Paranoid Style in
        American Politics"

1957: the founding of SANE (the Committee for a Sane Nuclear Policy)
        the publication of Vance Packard's *The Hidden Persuaders*

1959: the publication of Richard Condon's *The Manchurian Candidate* the release of Alfred Hitchcock's *North by Northwest*

1961: the publication, in French, of Michel Foucault's *History of Madness* (*Folie et déraison: Histoire de la folie à l'âge classique*)

1962: the release of the film version of *The Manchurian Candidate*, directed by John Frankenheimer

1964: the publication of both Phyllis Schlafly's *A Choice Not an Echo* and John A. Stormer's *None Dare Call It Treason*

And off our chart, but definitely on our path,

1968: the publication of *The Selling of the President*, by Joe McGinniss

Politics, popular culture, and play thus come to restage the debate about madness between Derrida and Foucault. Instead of being located within something called "history" or something called "philosophy," the itinerary of Mad Libs, *Mad* magazine, and Mad Men (or of Hitchcock, Condon–Frankenheimer, and Weiner) pitches madness as a living script for Abu Ghraib and Guantánamo Bay.[54] A war of necessity, or a war of choice?

> President [George W.] Bush: You can't rely upon a madman, and [Saddam Hussein] was a madman. You can't rely upon him making rational decisions when it comes to war and peace, and it's too late, in my judgment, when a madman who has got terrorist connections is able to act.
>
> Tim Russert: In light of not finding the weapons of mass destruction, do you believe the war in Iraq is a war of choice or a war of necessity?
>
> President Bush: (after a long pause) I think that's an interesting question. Please elaborate on that a little bit. A war of choice or a war of necessity? It's a war of necessity. We—in my judgment, we had no choice when we look at the intelligence I looked at that says the man was a threat. And you know, we'll find out about the weapons of mass destruction that we all thought were there.[55]

The "singularity" of the event was then *all about* repetition and origins. Military intelligence and counterintelligence were texts waiting to be performed. By this reckoning, Foucault's *History of Madness* appeared on the scene just at the point at which a new such history might have begun.

CHAPTER THREE

A Tale of Three *Hamlets*

or, Repetition and Revenge

For Heaven's sake don't get a wrong impression. Men don't shoot one another because of literary disagreements, however bitter they may have been in print.

   —J. C. Masterman, *An Oxford Tragedy* (1933)

Quite early we had become alive to the possible use of so-called secret weapons by the Germans, and we learned in fact a great deal about their probable nature and the extent of the menace through the traffic of the agents. . . . It was subsequently agreed that we should use ARTIST to the full for this purpose and not attempt to use HAMLET, who had also been suggested as a possible source of information.

   —J. C. Masterman, *The Double-Cross System in the War of 1939 to 1945* (1972)

HAMLET: A LOVE STORY

Over the course of my career I have written about many kinds of love, including house love, art love, Shakespeare love, and dog love. All of these have been essential and continuing in my life, as resonant as equally precious human relations: different, but also the same. After a lifetime of experiences, I thought I had taken cognizance of my passions. But—isn't it always the way of these things?—I was unprepared for, and surprised by, and overwhelmed by another new love, one to which I thought I was actually pretty immune: the love of a rare book.

I am a literary scholar; I've spent my professional life in libraries, including rare book libraries. My work as a Shakespearean has brought me into contact with Shakespeare folios and quartos and with play texts by Shakespeare's contemporaries. I began as a modernist and experienced the pleasure of seeing firsthand, and cautiously handling, first editions and even manuscripts. When I was in college, a friend of mine worked at the Rosenbach Foundation Museum in Philadelphia, where the manuscript of James Joyce's *Ulysses* is housed. The Rosenbach was then open to the public only a few hours a week, though scholars, curators and art lovers could apply for private periods of study and contemplation. During some of those off-hours I had the amazing privilege of holding the *Ulysses* manuscript in my hands, reading Joyce's distinctive handwriting on those pages and pages of graph paper. I've never forgotten it.

Still, I have always imagined myself to be immune—and, indeed, I thought happily immune—from the bibliographic passion for old books. Indeed, I half-congratulated myself on the fact that *this*, at least, was not one of my extravagances. And then I was asked to give a talk in honor of one particular book, "*The Tragedie of Hamlet Prince of Denmarke*, edited by J. Dover Wilson, Litt.D. From the text of the Second Quarto printed in 1604–5, 'According to the True and Perfect Coppie,' with which are also printed the Hamlet Stories from Saxo Grammaticus and Belleforest and English Translations Therefrom. Illustrated by Edward Gordon Craig and Printed by Count Harry Kessler. Weimar: Cranach Press, 1930."[1]

I have to say that I'd never heard of it. I knew who Edward Gordon Craig was—I work on modern theater and performance, as well as on Renaissance drama, and I have had a passion for woodcuts and engravings ever since, as an undergraduate at Swarthmore College, I studied them at the Lessing J. Rosenwald Collection in Jenkintown, Pennsylvania. There I did get that "boing-boing" feeling of passionate encounter with artwork and text—one that has stayed with me my whole life. But I never associated it with bound books, "rare books," or book collecting. As for *Hamlet*—well, I'm a Shakespearean. I have taught *Hamlet* regularly (one might even say, incessantly) over the years. I've seen innumerable *Hamlet* productions. I own *Hamlet* T-shirts in a variety of fetching styles. I've published many essays and chapters about *Hamlet*, including a long piece called "*Hamlet*: Giving Up the Ghost."[2] A few years ago I taught a graduate course called "The *Hamlet* Complex," and I venture to say that not only scholars but also students and audiences have a version of a *Hamlet* complex, if we understand a "complex" to be a fixed mental tendency or obsession.[3] I have never shared the view of D. H.

Lawrence that Hamlet is "boring."[4] But I did think that very little, perhaps nothing, connected to *Hamlet* could surprise me any longer—or
obsess me. I'd seen it all, I thought, until I saw the Cranach *Hamlet*. And
could not get it out of my mind.

Many of the grand love stories of history and fiction occur, as it were,
by accident: a chance encounter, a glance across a crowded room (for
Dante and Beatrice, the church; for Romeo and Juliet, the Capulet ball).
And so it was with me and the Cranach *Hamlet*. I'd been told that I
could speak about anything I wanted on this occasion, even though the
event was configured around the acquisition of a rare book. But I was
interested, and curious. I didn't, and don't, consider myself a specialist
in old books, or rare printed books—or even, in the collector sense of
the term, a bibliophile. So I took myself over to the Houghton Library
to do what I initially regarded as "due diligence": I thought I should at
least have a quick look at the book about which all this fuss was being
made.

Quick look, indeed. When I saw the book, I was enraptured. There is
perhaps no other word for it. I turned the pages, slowly, and read
through the text. I stared—covetously, it must be said—at the illustrations, sublime and witty woodcuts by Craig, some droll, some pointed,
all of them compelling "readings" of Shakespeare's play at the same time
that they were stand-alone images of clean lines and surpassing beauty. I
touched the handmade paper. I looked at the type and the typeface. I
read through Dover Wilson's textual notes at the end of the play. I was
hooked. I couldn't, in fact, bear to leave it—I lingered in the reading
room, revisiting what had already become favorite images, favorite pages,
reading the marginal text from Belleforest and Saxo Grammaticus. What
was I going to do about this unexpected crush? It was like falling for a
movie star, or a rock star. But it was a book.

As it happens, the Gordon Craig papers are held at Harvard, and so,
it turned out, were proofs, sketches, and handwritten notes connected
with the illustrations for the Cranach *Hamlet*. So I had other materials—
manuscript notes in pencil in Craig's hand, proofs on a variety of surfaces
including paper and silk, and, most interesting to me, some block prints
that had not been used in the book.[5] But it was the book itself—the
bound, finished book, with its red morocco cover and its remarkable
rhythms of play text, image, marginal source texts, the complete consort
dancing together—that seemed to me so compellingly beautiful. I
couldn't get over it. It may therefore seem surprising that my topic is

revenge, when I have begun with *love*. But it doesn't take a Freudian to find a connection between the two. And in the case of *Hamlet*—Shakespeare's *Hamlet*—the two themes are very much interconnected. Hamlet's love for his father leads him to want to revenge his father's murder. Hamlet's love for his mother leads him to want to revenge himself against her new husband. Hamlet's love for Ophelia, thwarted by circumstance, leads him to lash out at her with instinctive cruelty. Which is the more powerful emotion? Can the one masquerade as the other? Can the one be the other? Revenge tragedies are love tragedies, tragedies of love thwarted, love denied, love opposed by politics and the social world, the love dyad become a triangle with the entry of the third actor, Death.

In what follows I will tell three parallel stories about Hamlet, each of which could fit under the general rubric of "Hamlet, Repetition, and Revenge." I begin with Edward Gordon Craig and his complicated relation to the play, and then move on to a story about the scholar John Dover Wilson (the textual editor of the Cranach *Hamlet*), and finally to another story involving a literary scholar, J. I. M. Stewart, who, moonlighting as detective novelist "Michael Innes," was the author of a terrific mystery called *Hamlet, Revenge!* Each of these inset narratives turns on a book: a book that incarnates the idea of *Hamlet*—the play—as repetition and revenge.

I will claim that there are times when revenge takes the form of homage, and homage takes the form of revenge. And I will also suggest that there is something about *Hamlet*—let's call it the *Hamlet* effect—that not only generates this cycle, but also, ultimately, casts the play itself in the position of the revenger.

PLAYERS AND PAINTED STAGE

Let me set the stage with a pair of passages, one from the Renaissance and one from the twentieth century. Both speak to the tension between scenery (or, more properly, the *mise en scène*) and language or acting—a tension that was crucial to Edward Gordon Craig.

The first is a famous couplet from Ben Jonson's "Expostulation with Inigo Jones" (1631), a poem that describes the rivalry and stress that had developed between Jonson, a poet, playwright, and author of court masques, and Jones, his collaborator, a scene designer and architect. Jonson's tone is, needless to say, deeply ironic: "O, to make Boards to speak!

There is a task!/Painting and carpentry are the soul of masque!"[6] My second quotation, which might be said to espouse something of the same content, has a very different tone, although it is also written by a poet and playwright—in this case, Edward Gordon Craig's friend and admirer, William Butler Yeats in his poem "The Circus Animals' Desertion":

> and yet when all is said
> It was the dream itself enchanted me:
> Character isolated by a deed
> To engross the present and dominate memory.
> Players and painted stage took all my love,
> And not those things that they were emblems of.[7]

This description of the theater as a dreamscape could have come directly from Craig, and especially from Craig's own designs for the Moscow Art Theatre production of *Hamlet* on which he collaborated with Konstantin Stanislavski. But although he was initially buoyed (" 'Hamlet' was a success—I can't say anything else," he wrote to a friend before leaving Moscow),[8] Craig later decided that the production had been a failure, and he ultimately turned away from the theater—and toward the book.

I am, though, getting slightly ahead of my story—or my stories. Let me start with Craig's initial encounter with *Hamlet*—which was, appropriately enough, a family affair. Edward Gordon Craig was a brilliant scene designer, an admired and imaginative theater director, a book illustrator of remarkable ability, and a visionary puppet theorist. He was also, briefly, an actor.

His mother, the celebrated Victorian actress Ellen Terry, was married to someone else when she met his father, architect Edward William Godwin. Terry and Godwin never married; they had two children, Edward and Edith, and they separated in 1875, three years after Edward's birth. (His sister Edith chose the surname Craig, and it became Edward's as well.) Ellen Terry would marry twice more and had a number of other romantic relationships. It is perhaps not entirely a surprise that her son became fascinated with the play of *Hamlet* and imagined himself in the title role. Terry was famous for her portrayals of Shakespearean women. Playing opposite Henry Irving as his leading lady at the Lyceum Theatre for twenty years, she gained celebrity as Portia in *The Merchant of Venice*, Beatrice in *Much Ado about Nothing*, Cordelia in *King Lear*. But her first part, and the one that made her reputation, was as Ophelia to Irving's

Hamlet. And it was as Ophelia, Hamlet's beloved—not as Gertrude, Hamlet's mother—that her son remembered her.

Terry's biographer Nina Auerbach describes Henry Irving as in effect the actress's other "husband," and dates the time when she became his "wife" to December 30, 1878, the night of her Lyceum debut and her first performance as Ophelia.[9] Terry had conceived the idea that instead of wearing the traditional white dress, the sign of virginity and female madness onstage, her Ophelia would wear black—"a transparent, black dress." Henry Irving, without batting an eye, referred the question to his production advisor, Walter Lacy.

> The next day [Terry reported in her *Memoirs*] Lacy came up to me:
>
> "You didn't really mean that you are going to wear black in the mad scene?"
>
> "Yes, I did. Why not?"
>
> "*Why not!* My God! Madam, there must be only one black figure in this play, and that's Hamlet!"[10]

From this experience, Terry learned her role: she would take second place in the theatrical company to the famous actor-manager. In many stock companies of the time, the lead part for a woman in *Hamlet* was Gertrude, the queen. Nonetheless, Terry, then aged thirty, was cast as Ophelia. Whether or not Henry Irving became her offstage lover (on this, accounts and biographers differ), her onstage role was clear.

Nina Auerbach sees the complicated relationship between mother and son as in part a Hamlet-like Oedipal struggle, with Craig as Hamlet, Henry Irving as Claudius, and Terry vacillating between the role of Ophelia, in which she was cast, and the role of Gertrude, which "should" have been hers. But Craig's own account suggests that Irving, in both his personal relations with Terry and his deliberately artificial and stylized acting style, was as much an Old Hamlet—admired, emulated, proudly tied to the past and the future rather than the present—as he was an interloping Claudius. Indeed, one critic notes that Craig "idealized" Irving: just the right word for Hamlet's relationship to his father.[11]

In 1894, Edward Gordon Craig founded his own touring company. He had been a juvenile lead in Irving's company; he was, of course, Prince Hamlet in his own. But even this move, we may think, was haunted by repetition. A playbill for "Mr. Gordon Craig's Company" announced, "The costumes for all the Plays have been kindly lent by

Mr. Henry Irving."[12] ("*My father, in his habit as he liv'd!*" [3.4.137].)[13] One of Craig's last onstage performances was as Hamlet at the Olympic Theater in 1897, where he wore Henry Irving's own costume for the role.

When later on Craig articulated his famous—and often misunderstood—theory of the actor as a marionette, it was in part Henry Irving's deliberate eschewing of mere naturalism that he had in mind. "Irving was the nearest thing ever known to what I have called the Ubermarionette," he wrote.[14] Stylized, avoiding a "debased stage-realism," the marionette transcended the accidents of humanity, the entire false goal of impersonation.[15] "For, while impersonation is in the Theatre, the Theatre can never become free."[16] The overly personal, the merely emotional, is "bad art."[17] Thus, Craig contends with pleasurable bravado that "the actor must go, and in his place comes the inanimate figure—the übermarionette we may call him, until he has won for himself a better name."[18]

Hamlet haunts the marionette essay as he, or it—the character or the play—haunted Craig throughout his career. Craig quotes the Romantic critic Hazlitt in support of his argument: "Hamlet himself seems hardly capable of being acted."[19] When he describes the modern actor as being at the mercy of his emotions, Craig invokes Hamlet's advice to the players: "Hamlet's calm directions (the dreamer's, not the logician's, directions, by the way) are thrown to the winds."[20] And when he comes to the "flamboyant or drooping artists whose works and names catch the eye of to-day," he complains that they "do not so much speak like men as bawl like animals, or lisp like women," echoing Hamlet's misogynistic outburst to Ophelia: "I have heard of your paintings well enough. God hath given you one face and you make yourselves another. You jig and amble, and you lisp" (3.1.144–46).[21]

Even before the essay on the marionette, Craig was turning against the stage as a vehicle for the performance of plays, again using *Hamlet* as his example, authority, and guide. In his "Art of the Theatre: The First Dialogue," a Stage-Director (Craig himself) and a Playgoer hold an extended conversation, part of which centers on *Hamlet*.

> STAGE-DIRECTOR *Hamlet* has not the nature of a stage representation. *Hamlet* and the other plays of Shakespeare have so vast and so complete a form when read, that they can but lose heavily when presented to us after having undergone stage treatment. That they were acted in Shakespeare's day proves nothing . . . no one will say that they find *Hamlet* dull or incomplete when they read it, yet

there are many who will feel sorry after witnessing a performance of the play, saying, "No, that is not Shakespeare's *Hamlet*." When no further addition can be made so as to better a work of art, it can be spoken of as "finished"—it is complete. *Hamlet* was finished—was complete—when Shakespeare wrote the last word of his blank verse, and for us to add to it by gesture, scene, costume, or dance, is to hint that it is incomplete and needs these additions.

PLAYGOER Then do you mean to say *Hamlet* should never be performed?

STAGE-DIRECTOR To what purpose would it be if I replied "Yes"? *Hamlet* will go on being performed for some time yet, and the duty of the interpreters is to put their best work at its service. But . . . the theatre must not forever rely upon having a play to perform, but must in time perform pieces of its own art.[22]

"No, that is not Shakespeare's *Hamlet*." This imagined response to an imagined production anticipates the "no" of T. S. Eliot's Prufrock— "No, I am not Prince Hamlet"—just as the idea that the play should not be performed chimes with Eliot's (rather different) reasons for thinking the play itself to be an artistic failure.[23] Eliot's Prufrock poem was published in 1917, his essay on *Hamlet* in 1919; Craig's provocative observations on the play and the theater, so "modern" in feel and tone, date from more than a decade earlier, 1905.

A few years later, Craig revisited these questions, confirming what he had said in the "First Dialogue."

I still remain of the same opinion—that Shakespeare's plays are not for representation, more especially because I am myself now working on several Shakespearean representations, and therefore have occasion for passing in review the many different "editions," as they are called, of Shakespeare, especially the stage editions, and I am struck by one fact, and it is this: that the people who hold that Shakespeare was a master of theatrical art cut away from these plays lines, passages—nay, whole scenes: these words, passages and scenes which, they say, were written for the stage. To say a thing is perfect and then to mutilate it, is most peculiar.[24]

He goes on to discuss some specific scenes from *Hamlet* that are often cut in production and criticizes the ceremonial way in which the lines are often delivered: "It is this slow delivery of Shakespeare's lines which have made Shakespeare a bore to so many people." But even if well-acted, the project was, he thought, doomed to fail: "Would the plays of Shakespeare be then interpreted as they should be? No, not even then. Not if the finest and most passionate actors in the world were to come together and attempt to perform Hamlet could the right representation of Hamlet be given, for I fear to represent *Hamlet* rightly is an impossibility."[25] We might here detect an echo of Polonius, who declares the traveling players in *Hamlet* "the best actors in the world" (2.2.392). To Edward Gordon Craig in 1908, "to represent *Hamlet* rightly," even with the best actors in the world, was "an impossibility."

Nonetheless, he was willing to try. In 1908, Konstantin Stanislavski invited him to collaborate on a production of *Hamlet* for the Moscow Art Theatre. Craig was to be the director, the designer, the *metteur en scène*. The production was delayed—Stanislavski was sick, Craig was designing in Italy and transmitting his sketches and ideas to the actors and carpenters long distance. When the play was finally produced in 1912, the difference between the two men's visions inevitably led to conflict.

Craig's controlling concept was that the play was Hamlet's dream, the events seen through the eyes and the imagination of the main character. In early sketches, Hamlet was seen in shadows, downstage, with the brightly lit court at the rear. Stanislavski described Craig's production as "the monodrama of Hamlet. He sat on the forestage, near the stone balustrade of the palace, sunk in his sorrowful thoughts, and he visualized the foolish, licentious, and unnecessary luxury of the court life of the King he hated." Craig himself wrote in his instructions, "He can be in the distance, lying, sitting, in front of the people acting, at the side, behind, but the spectator ought never to lose sight of him."[26]

The keynote of the marionette essay had been death. (The *übermarionette* will "aim to clothe itself with a death-like beauty while exhaling a living spirit," and when he returns to the theater, "once more will Creation be celebrated—homage rendered to existence—and divine and happy intercession made to Death.")[27] When he came to design his production for the Moscow Art Theatre, Craig proposed that the figure of Hamlet be accompanied always by a companion figure, "Daemon death," who would—in classic Expressionist mode—represent the split in Hamlet between the wish for life and the wish for death. The figure of death "in the guise of a woman" would appear during the "To be or not to be" soliloquy, where the choices of life or death are debated, and would accompany Hamlet throughout the play.[28] Stanislavski found this concept unstageable, and it was never implemented, but it is a window into Craig's vision of *Hamlet* the play, and Hamlet the character.[29] Craig proposed to Stanislavski that everything in the play should be "conveyed without words, to which Stanislavski replied, presciently, 'Yes, but that would not be Shakespeare's *Hamlet*. It would be a new art founded on the theme of Shakespeare's *Hamlet*.' "[30]

Craig spoke no Russian, and Stanislavski no English. They communicated in what has been described as an "Anglo German *lingua franca*" and a "kind of Volapuk of Russian and German."[31] Craig was the spokesman for a new symbolic theater, and Stanislavski the famous proponent of a new psychologically informed acting style. The collaboration was fated to have problems, and these increased when Craig drew designs for the stage and left Stanislavski to try to build and implement them. His famous screens, huge, tall, transparent and reversible, covered with light gray fabric, had a tendency to topple over—although even this was a matter of dispute between Stanislavski and Craig, with Craig contending that the screens never fell during performance and demanding that Stanislavski remove this allegation from his published account. (Stanislavski retained the anecdote in print but privately acknowledged to Craig that the problem only happened during rehearsal and was the fault of the stagehands, not the designer.)[32] Craig's belief was that the production was a failure, and that it proved his contention that *Hamlet* was unactable.

With what appears to be a certain perverse satisfaction, Craig added a footnote to his "First Dialogue":

> since this was written . . . I have myself attempted to produce *Hamlet*—the *Hamlet* of Shakespeare—at Moscow. Knowing it was impossible, why did I attempt it? There are many reasons: I wanted to strengthen my belief—I wanted people to realize the truth. Also, I wanted to "face the music,"—and I wanted to exercise my faculties as stage director (for I had not produced a play for many years). Added to this, I wanted to do what my friends wanted me to do.
>
> Was I satisfied? Yes. I am more thoroughly convinced than ever that the plays of Shakespeare are unactable—that they are a bore when acted.[33]

Yet Craig continued to be obsessed by *Hamlet*, even as—or perhaps because—he believed it could not be staged. In a short-lived plan for a "School for the Art of the Theatre," sponsored by his admirers Yeats and Pound, he toyed with the idea that the school would "produce ONLY *Hamlet*" (although in so varied and imaginative a way that the production "will be able to be visited many times without the audience being able to say 'we have seen it before' "). The play was to be *repeated*, with a difference, over and over again. World War I put an end to these plans; the space was requisitioned for another purpose, and the model stages dismantled.³⁴ This left the Kessler *Hamlet*, the Cranach Press *Hamlet*, as the only form in which Craig would realize his ideal "production" of the play.

Craig's drawings for Stanislavski had included his famous "black figures," cutout characters in dramatic poses, included in photographs as three-dimensional cardboard or wooden miniatures, designed to communicate with the actors for the Moscow *Hamlet*.³⁵ Intrigued by the black figures, which looked uncannily like woodcuts, Count Harry Kessler, who had long been his patron and promoter in Germany, proposed that Craig might illustrate something for the Cranach Press: perhaps *Antony and Cleopatra*, or Milton's *Comus*. To which Craig is said to have replied that they might as well do *Hamlet*.³⁶

This might be the moment to recall that little anecdote about the rivalry between Henry Irving and Ellen Terry, with its memorable punch line, "there must be only one black figure in this play, and that's Hamlet!" In the Cranach Press *Hamlet*, Craig's "black figures" took center stage. The Moscow screens and the *doppelgänger* "daemon" are generously represented in the illustrations. The title page shows a dreaming Hamlet seated on a cushion: all that follows is, we might think, his dream. The black figure is Hamlet, and Hamlet is Edward Gordon Craig. As his biographer Christopher Innes points out, "Craig began working on this edition immediately after the [Moscow Art Theatre] production, and considered it his definitive interpretation of the play."³⁷ Indeed, the Cranach edition was imagined as a way to "'make good' on what had been missing in the Moscow production."³⁸ The Cranach *Hamlet* was to be Craig's aesthetic revenge.

"DULL" REVENGE

To this point, I have described the Cranach *Hamlet* as if it were principally a collaboration between Edward Gordon Craig, the artist, and Count Harry Kessler, the patron. On the level of the book's design there were, of course, many other contributors to the beauty and singularity of the volume, including the calligrapher, the letter-cutter, the papermakers, and so on.

In a discussion of the interesting and persistent problem posed by works that are both text and performance—a problem felt especially acutely in Shakespeare studies—Stephen Orgel provides a sumptuous description of the Cranach *Hamlet*, its design, typeface, and images, observing that the deployment of Craig's woodcuts on the page "resembles more the format of the Nuremberg Chronicle than any illustrated scholarly edition of drama: the images are not contained by the typography, but are in full partnership with it, and sometimes even seem in control." Noting that the Craig–Stanislavski collaboration for the Moscow Art Theatre was "not a success," Orgel sees the Cranach Press *Hamlet* as a project that—by contrast—successfully rethinks the relation among drama, text, and image: "It reconceives the book of the play as a performance and completes the play as a book."[39] This "complete" *Hamlet* was thus not only a visual and sensory achievement but also, and importantly, a text edition of Shakespeare's play, taken from the second quarto of *Hamlet*, "According to the True and Perfect Coppie." The textual editor for the English edition was the Shakespeare scholar John Dover Wilson, described by Kessler in a letter to Craig as "the greatest living authority on Shakespeare."[40] And it is Dover Wilson who is my next example in the trajectory of *Hamlet*, repetition, and revenge.

Alexander Pope had famously complained of "the dull duty of an Editor" when completing his own, eighteenth-century edition of Shakespeare's plays.[41] Hamlet, equally famously, rues the fact that all occasions "do inform against me / And spur my dull revenge" (4.4.32–33). Dover Wilson, as we will see, found neither activity dull, and indeed conceived that part of the duty of an editor was the opportunity, or obligation, to exact a kind of critical revenge.

When Dover Wilson published his book, *What Happens in "Hamlet"* in 1935, he described it as "the third volume in a *Hamlet* trilogy."[42] The first two were *The Manuscript of Shakespeare's "Hamlet"* (1934), an expansion of his textual notes in the Cranach Press volume, and an edition of the play published in 1934 for the New Cambridge Shakespeare series, of which Dover Wilson had become general editor.[43] Terence Hawkes describes the article and edition as "two major salvoes" in the *Hamlet* wars.[44] *What Happens in "Hamlet"* would be the third and final assault. It was prefaced by a lengthy and tendentious "Epistle Dedicatory" to a rival scholar, Walter Wilson Greg.[45] Repetition and revenge.

Dover Wilson recounts in his "Epistle" that the initial provocation for his interest in *Hamlet* was the fact that he had read, on a train en route to northern England, an article published by W. W. Greg in the October 1917 number of the *Modern Language Review*. The article,

"Hamlet's Hallucination," argued that the ghost in the play was a figment of Hamlet's imagination, that the message it delivered had no authority, and that the idea of poisoning through the ear was suggested to Hamlet by his memory of the play *The Murder of Gonzago*, so that instead of catching the conscience of the king the play performed at court merely indicated the source of Hamlet's own fantasy, or hallucination.[46] (It is intriguing to note that Stanislavski had proposed a similar theory six years previously, in rehearsals for the Moscow Art Theatre production—that the Ghost should be invisible to the audience, existing only as Hamlet's "inner vision, an hallucination"—but this interpretation was rejected by the Theatre board as contrary to the "convention of Shakespeare's tragedy.")[47]

Dover Wilson's response to Greg's article, as he himself describes it, was an immediate impulse to reply, and the language he uses, however genial—from the perspective of eighteen years' distance—is the language of revenge. "From the first," he writes, echoing Hamlet, "I realised that I had been born to answer it" (compare Hamlet's "The time is out of joint. O cursed spite/That ever I was born to set it right" [1.5.196–97], which is uttered, perhaps significantly, right after Hamlet has seen and spoken to the Ghost). "Your theory," Dover Wilson wrote in his "Epistle Dedicatory" to Greg, "raged 'like the hectic in my blood', and my first anxiety was lest some one should slip in and cross swords before I could have at you."[48] ("The hectic in my blood" is a quotation from Claudius, longing for "the present death of Hamlet," and sends him off to England with a sealed letter asking the king there to "do it" [4.2.68–69].) The minute Dover Wilson arrived at the station, he mailed off a postcard to the editor of the *Modern Language Review* that read as follows: "Greg's article devilish ingenious, but damnably wrong. Will you accept a rejoinder?"[49] "Damnable" is also a Hamlet echo, and indeed a call to revenge, spoken by Hamlet in the middle of the play within the play (*The Murder of Gonzago*): "Begin, murderer. Leave thy damnable faces and begin. Come, the croaking raven doth bellow for revenge" (3.2.246–48). So Hamlet—the text of *Hamlet*—haunts Dover Wilson's memory of this occasion. Whether he felt so at the time or not, the repetition of these incidents keeps touching on revenge.

The entire "Epistle Dedicatory" is full of symptomatic language of this kind. For the most part, it is conscious raillery. "You and I had hardly finished our passage of arms over the meaning of the dumb-show and the objectivity of the Ghost," he writes to Greg, "when a fresh group of critics entered the lists."[50] "Before I could write this book I had to qualify myself by settling the text of *Hamlet* and by wrestling with the meaning of every word and sentence."[51] Later, he encounters another Shakespeare scholar, the theater manager Harley Granville-Barker, amiably here called a "fresh antagonist," and Dover Wilson reports to Greg that "we have fought backwards and forwards over almost every line of [the play scene] as violently as ever Hamlet and Laertes passed at foils."[52]

Of course, there needs no ghost come from the grave to suggest that literary scholarship and textual editing are themselves species of revenge. We have only to look at the jousting of eighteenth-century editors, each annotating and refuting the opinions of their predecessors. The greatest poem of the eighteenth century, Alexander Pope's *Dunciad*, is an attack by one Shakespeare editor on another, staged as a manifest—and successful—act of revenge. Shakespeare editor Lewis Theobald had published in 1726 a book called *Shakespeare Restored: Or, a Specimen of the Many Errors, as Well Committed, as Unamended, by Mr. Pope in His Late Edition of this Poet.*[53] For this public rebuke of Pope, Theobald was enshrined in the first version of *The Dunciad* as the King of Dunces and the personification of Dulness.[54]

Similar pointed enmities developed between the Shakespeare editors Steevens and Malone, Collier and Dyce, Furnivall and Halliwell-Phillips. Greg himself was celebrated, among other things, for the unusual amity of his relationship with other Shakespeareans, among them his friends R. B. McKerrow and A. W. Pollard, a "triumvirate" described by one commentator (perhaps inevitably) as "a happy band of brothers." Dover Wilson's rhetorical jousting with Greg about the Ghost in *Hamlet* was "spirited" but not personal—the two men later became friends, although they continued to disagree.[55] His mode is one of courtly collegiality, the objective to hoist the enginer on his own petard. "I often wondered whether the present book, begun in 1917, would ever get finished," he writes. "Let me gratefully acknowledge in passing that you were yourself, unconsciously and most wholesomely, the chief cause of the delay."[56] Not only the *delay* here, but even the question of *wholesomeness* leads back to the crisis of Hamlet and the Ghost, for the word *wholesome* appears five times in the play, almost always associated with Old Hamlet and his times, or with Hamlet's status before he heard the Ghost's message (1.1.167, 1.5.70, 2.2.440, 3.2.313, 3.4.65). "If the reader would catch something of the initial—and final—excitement," Dover Wilson continues, "let him plunge straight into Chapter V and begin asking himself the question with which you first sent me mad."[57] In this recasting, Greg and the "hallucination" essay stand in the place of the Ghost, while Dover Wilson is—of course—Hamlet. And Greg's "hallucination" essay is demonstrated to be itself a hallucination.

LAWFUL ESPIALS

Both the Cranach *Hamlet* and Dover Wilson's *What Happens in "Hamlet"* were productions of the period between the two world wars, and both were affected by politics and current events. Dover Wilson's career-changing encounter with Greg's article on *Hamlet* took place, as Terence Hawkes notes, on a train taking him to the site of a trade union dispute, and at a time—November 1917—when the Bolshevik Revolution in Russia was very much in the news.[58] Dover Wilson himself had noted in his published letter to Greg, "For some reason or other, the War acted as a stimulus to the study of *Hamlet*."[59] He meant the 1914 war, when a number of important books and articles on *Hamlet* had been published. But it seems to me that an even more interesting moment is this interwar period, the volatile decade of the thirties. For it is in this decade that issues like treason, espionage, propaganda, double agents, and cryptography become a focus of interest for literary, as well as military, experts.

Just as Hamlet is a detective, investigating clues, setting up sting operations, easily identifying the double-agent stool pigeons Rosencrantz and Guildenstern, verifying the testimony of the Ghost who is both victim and eyewitness to the crime, so literary critics and textual editors are detectives, tracking evidence in the form of repeated phrases, printing errors, spelling preferences, inconsistencies between quarto and quarto, quarto and folio. The clue, the trace, the compulsion to repeat—all these are hallmarks of both revenge tragedy and scholarly investigation.

It may not therefore come as a surprise to learn that textual editors, critics, and bibliographers in the thirties, during World War II, and in the Cold War years that followed were employed by the governments of Britain and the United States as highly skilled cryptanalysts. Fredson Bowers, an eminent American bibliographer, was "given secret instruction as a cryptanalyst in a naval communications intelligence group being formed at the university [of Virginia]" in the years immediately prior to U.S. entry into World War II.[60] During the war, Bowers, the author of such works as *Principles of Bibliographical Description* and "Hamlet as

Minister and Scourge," moved to Washington "to supervise an intelligence unit working on deciphering enemy codes."[61] Bowers's code-breaking group included a number of prominent literary and bibliographic scholars, including Charlton Hinman, whose Hinman Collator, later used to collate copies of the Shakespeare First Folio, was inspired by the military intelligence practice of "comparing successive photographs of enemy fortifications."[62]

The link between code breaking and Shakespeare studies emerged in part from the persistent belief that someone other than the man from Stratford had written the plays. Francis Bacon, an accomplished Elizabethan diplomat, was known to have written in cipher, and a cottage industry of cryptographers grew up around the Bacon-is-Shakespeare claim. In the early twentieth century, the American millionaire George Fabyan founded a think tank, Riverbank Laboratories, to explore Baconian ciphers as clues to Shakespeare's real identity and published a book on the topic in 1916. Two of his top cryptographers, William F. Friedman and Elizabeth S. Friedman, cracked German and Mexican codes in the First World War, helped Scotland Yard to expose anti-British agents in North America, and trained the first generation of officers for the U.S. Army's Cipher Bureau. William Friedman became America's top code breaker, leading the team that cracked Japanese codes in World War II; his wife did similar work for the Coast Guard and the Treasury Department. In 1957, the Friedmans published their own book on the Shakespeare authorship controversy, *The Shakespearean Ciphers Examined*.[63]

In Britain the "double-cross system," the World War II antiespionage and deception operation that turned German spies into double agents working for the British, was headed by J. C. Masterman, an Oxford don (later Provost of Worcester College) who was also an eminent cryptographer. Among the various agents with code names like GARBO, BISCUIT, BRONX, TRICYCLE, ARTIST, and SNOW who worked under his supervision in 1942 was a double-cross agent known only as HAMLET (described as "an Austrian ex-cavalry officer, a Jew, a businessman, and an exploiter of various commercial patents") who was a member of the *Abwehr*, the German secret service.[64] Masterman, whose British counterintelligence unit worked with the U.S. Office of Strategic Services, was himself also something of a literary double agent. In 1933, he had published an acclaimed detective novel titled *An Oxford Tragedy*, which began the fashion for Oxford-based crime fiction.

It is in this context of spies, counterespionage, code breaking, learned textual scholars, and *Hamlet* that the mystery writer Michael Innes published his own detective novel *Hamlet, Revenge!* in 1937. The book centers on an amateur production of *Hamlet* at the fictional Scamnum Court, the greatest stately home in England, where the cast includes the Duke of Horton, the owner of Scamnum (as Claudius); the Lord High Chancellor of England (as Polonius); a celebrated Shakespearean actor (as Hamlet); and many others of the great and the good. The director of the production is a young Oxford don and scholar of Elizabethan literature, who writes best-selling detective novels under a pseudonym. The fictional scholar, Giles Gott, shares this double identity with his creator; "Michael Innes" was the pseudonym of the Elizabethan literary scholar J. I. M. Stewart, the author, among other works, of a book called *Character and Motive in Shakespeare*. Gott's ambivalence about his double identity and his worry lest scholars think less of him for writing detective fiction mirror those of Stewart, whose academic career took him from Leeds to Adelaide to Belfast and finally back to Oxford. As we will see shortly, this worry on Stewart's part (as on the fictional Gott's) proved to be unfounded.

The murder in *Hamlet, Revenge!*—for of course there is a murder—is committed in the middle of the performance; the victim, the Lord High Chancellor, is killed just when Hamlet would have killed Polonius. When a document vital to national security is found to be missing, a detective from Scotland Yard is called in. The action involves the receipt of messages heralding "revenge" (in famous quotations from Shakespeare and other Elizabethan dramatists) delivered in a variety of methods, from telephone, telegram, and radiogramophone to a crumpled piece of paper dropped into the back of an open limousine.

The plot features spies (domestic and Russian) and a range of significant technologies, old and new, including transcription, photography via hidden camera, painting from life, speech recording on a linguist's sophisticated Dictaphone machine, and two quite different cultural traditions of memorization (one practiced by a charmingly otherworldly visitor from India and the other by a village postmistress). To these, we might compare the equally varied information technologies in Shakespeare's *Hamlet*, a play closely concerned with messages and foiled communication: the Ghost's report, the players, Reynaldo set to spy on Laertes, Polonius and Claudius as "lawful espials" (3.1.32), Ophelia loosed on Hamlet in the lobby, the players as "abstract and brief chronicles of the time" (2.2.525), Rosencrantz and Guildenstern as untrusty messengers, Polonius hidden behind the arras in the Queen's closet, the King's sealed—and doctored—commission commanding Hamlet's death, Hamlet's "father's signet" (5.2.49) used to sign a forged document—not to mention the "Mousetrap" play or, indeed, the soliloquies.

But for a novel entitled *Hamlet, Revenge!* (the phrase is itself a quotation from an Elizabethan writer who seems to have seen a lost precursor to Shakespeare's play),[65] what is chiefly intriguing is the sheer, and competing, number of detectives at work. In addition to the official detective on the case, there are a psychoanalyst, a linguist, a gossip journalist, a doctor, two academic Shakespeareans with very different research methodologies, a novelist, an advertising copywriter, and the young Oxford scholar (and mystery writer) directing the play.

The denouement offers two competing solutions to the mystery: the first, ingenious and based on a kind of clever orthographic code breaking, is offered by Gott, the amateur sleuth; the second is provided by his friend, the young Scotland Yard detective John Appleby, who will go on to be the star of some forty more Michael Innes mysteries. In this case, it is the professional, not the overingenious amateur, who has the right answer.

As a young man, Stewart had studied psychoanalysis in Vienna for a year in 1929 before beginning his career as a literary scholar. One of the most intriguing figures in *Hamlet, Revenge!* is an urbane and articulate psychoanalyst, who the young academic-and-novelist Giles Gott wrongly identifies as the culprit in his public exposition of the case. To make matters worse, the analyst, once exonerated, holds no grudge: "It's all a matter of scientific interest to him," Giles reports ruefully. "I don't believe, ideologue though he be, that he's capable of one flicker of enmity toward any living creature."[66]

A distinctly nonfictional psychoanalyst hovers in the wings here, in the person of Ernest Jones, Freud's student and disciple. Jones was the author of one of the most influential theories about *Hamlet* in the period, expressed in articles published in 1910 and 1923 and later expanded into a book, *Hamlet and Oedipus*, in 1949.[67] Jones, following Freud, suggested that Hamlet's famous delay, his inability to act, was caused by what Claudius had done, what Hamlet himself, in fantasy, had wished to do: kill the father and marry the mother. Stewart's response to Ernest Jones—or rather, Michael Innes's response to Jones—first took the form of a Hamlet-themed radio play entitled *The Hawk and the Handsaw*, in which a character he describes as a "Freud-cum-Jones" appears. The play poses the hypothetical question, "How would Hamlet have reacted had he been able to read Jones's notion of him?" This infolded time-travel fantasy, involving a flashback psychiatric session between the young prince and a visiting Scottish doctor, may be the ultimate in repetition as revenge. (Hamlet "rejects with some eloquence the Oedipal explanation of his conduct" but promises to give it more thought on his way to England.)[68] I should add that my own infolded tale here contains one more reflexive turn, for in addition to his mention of Jones, Michael Innes singles out for special praise in his introduction Greg's essay on "Hamlet's Hallucination"—the very essay that had prompted such a powerful and sustained response from Dover Wilson.[69]

As Stewart describes it in his memoirs, however, the production "had an odd sequel." Riding home on a late-night train (shades of Dover Wilson's Sunderland journey), Stewart was suddenly visited by the strong conviction that Ernest Jones would regard him as having both "pillaged" from his work and held him up to ridicule. Great was his consternation when a letter from Jones duly arrived, written in "a neat medical hand." But Jones was writing just to say that he had missed the first half of the radio play and would like to receive a copy. Stewart sent it, and received in return an offprint of one of Jones's papers on Hamlet, published in the *International Journal of Psycho-Analysis*.[70] Years later, Stewart, having "under [his] own name" reviewed Jones's three-volume *Life of Freud*, was invited to give the Ernest Jones Memorial Lecture at the British Psychoanalytical Society. As he recalled the event, he handed over the single extant copy of his lecture text to the secretary of the society after the lecture, and never saw it again.

Édition de luxe; critical study; mystery novel. All are appropriate forms for the revisitation of the scene of the crime, the mastery that, as Freud clearly saw, came with repetition, the talking cure, and the transference. And all are, as we have seen, thematically related to *Hamlet*, a play in which the mad Hamlet makes his first onstage appearance "*reading on a book*" (2.2.168 sd). Edward Gordon Craig, as we saw, took his revenge on actors and directors of Shakespeare's play by putting his finest creative energies into a magnificent folio book. But the quintessential literary forms of repetition and, or *as*, revenge may well be, in academic life, the "new preface" to a previously published work and, in general writing, the autobiographical memoir. As it happens, this narrative, my tale of three *Hamlet*s, includes an abundance of such material, including several "new prefaces," and memoirs by both the indefatigable John Dover Wilson and the urbane J. I. M. Stewart.

As the success of *What Happens in "Hamlet"* led to a second and then a third edition, Dover Wilson, repeating the practice that had been so effective in his "Epistle Dedicatory" to W. W. Greg, added to each edition a new preface that enabled him to joust with new antagonists and rivals and put them in their (subsidiary) places. One such rival, indeed, was Ernest Jones, whose 1923 article and 1949 book on Hamlet, Oedipus, and Freud had garnered a great deal of interest. Dover Wilson acknowledged the "charm and persuasiveness" of Jones's style in the preface to the third edition of *What Happens in "Hamlet,"* while determining that to accept Jones's arguments required a "willing suspension of disbelief." Jones's interpretation of Hamlet's character as if he were a "case in the psychoanalytic clinic" rather that as an element in an "elaborate dramatic composition" was, he felt, "wrong in method and futile in aim." Moreover, Jones had misunderstood Dover Wilson's own book: "when he gathered . . . from these pages that I believed 'personality' in *Hamlet* to be 'consistent,' I realized that my chapter VI had been written in vain, as far as he was concerned, and that we must go our several ways each convinced he is being misunderstood by the other."[71]

This is Dover Wilson at his most magisterial, writing in 1951. But I want to draw your attention to a slightly earlier moment, the publication of the second edition of *What Happens in "Hamlet,"* which came out in 1937. The book had been well received and seriously discussed and debated. Its author was in a cheerful mood. So after some renewed jousts with the admired Harley Granville-Barker, with his "first antagonist, Dr W. W. Greg," who had replied "in a delightful and characteristic essay . . . in which generosity and scepticism were judiciously mingled," and with the annual conference of the Modern Language Association (where, he writes, the book was "publicly butchered . . . to make an American holiday"), Dover Wilson turns casually via a footnote to another *Hamlet* publication of 1937 to which I have referred.[72]

There had been, it seems, a production of *Hamlet* at the Westminster Theatre[73] in July 1937 designed "to try out the notions set forth in this book." It ran for a fortnight but unfortunately Dover Wilson, whose book had inspired the production, was unable to attend anything but the first half of the dress rehearsal. "After which," reads the footnote, "I was—not poisoned by Lucianus for sacrilege, as Mr. Michael Innes, author of *Hamlet, Revenge*, might perhaps surmise, but—obliged to leave England for the continent."[74]

This explanation falls curiously flat, both as an excuse for missing the entirety of the production's run and as a reference to *Hamlet, Revenge!* No one in Michael Innes's mystery novel is poisoned, and the scene in which Lucianus appears, the Mousetrap scene, the play-within-the-play, is not described in the novel. In fact, the mention of Michael Innes's popular fictional account is a diversionary tactic (of a kind not unlike the ones Dover Wilson proposes, in his own book, for the production of the Mousetrap scene). The entertaining thriller is here remanded, not only to a footnote, but also to an aside within that footnote, a dependent clause: "as Mr. Michael Innes, author of *Hamlet, Revenge*, might perhaps surmise." This is masterly. The upstart thriller is put in its place, genially, at the foot of the page, while the eminent editor and critic slips out and heads for the continent. "Half the dress-rehearsal" would have taken him, indeed, just about up to the time of the play within the play, and the entrance of Lucianus, nephew to the King. In fact, we may surmise, Dover Wilson may have risen and taken his leave at about the same time that Claudius does in *Hamlet*.

Yet "Mr. Michael Innes" continued to write mystery novels and J. I. M. Stewart continued to write criticism and fiction, and half a century later Stewart published an autobiographical memoir called *Myself and Michael Innes*. In that memoir, he revisits the ambivalent frame of mind that he shared with his *doppelgänger* protagonist, Giles Gott. Having taught for a decade in Australia, Stewart was eager to return to the northern hemisphere, but he felt that his scholarly production had been slight. Moreover, he was worried, like Giles Gott, that his second career might undercut his first. Here is how he describes both his state of mind at the time and a subsequent piece of information that altered his understanding of the situation.

> And on the debit side of the ledger also—for so I conceived it—were all those detective stories. It still didn't occur to me that, if they were satisfactory in their kind, such things might earn the favorable regard of the good and the great in academic life. Only many years later did I learn—from the *Proceedings of the British Academy*—that Sir Walter Greg, the most eminent Shakespeare scholar of the time, had read *Hamlet, Revenge!* again and again, submitting it to "the same kind of scrutiny he gave to the variants in the first quarto of *King Lear*."[75]

Walter Wilson Greg, it will be remembered, was the scholar and bibliographer—later the author of "The Rationale of Copy-Text" (1950) and

The Editorial Problem in Shakespeare (1951)—whose 1917 essay on Hamlet had provoked such an immediate and passionately competitive response from J. Dover Wilson. It was this same Greg whose essay "Hamlet's Hallucination" Michael Innes had praised in 1950 in the introduction to his radio entertainment based on *Hamlet*, calling it a *tour de force*. Here, we find Greg studying up on the plot details of a mystery novel and treating its contents, if we may believe the *Proceedings of the British Academy*, with the same kind of comparison and care that goes into a scholarly edition of a Shakespeare play. The transitory piece of detective fiction remanded to a mere footnote by the scholar J. Dover Wilson had, it turns out, inspired multiple readings by the most eminent Shakespeare scholar of the time. What goes around comes around. Or, as Michael Innes so aptly expressed it in his title, *Hamlet, Revenge!*

REPETITION AS REVENGE

In "Hamlet's Hallucination," Greg had contended, provocatively, that the ghost was a product of Hamlet's imagination, produced not by any supernatural agency but by Hamlet's subconscious memory of the old play he then recommends to the traveling players—so that, in the nice redaction of Michael Innes, "the latter prompts the former!" and "the apparition . . . is not the cause, but a consequence, of his disordered intellect."[76] My argument here has taken a similar tack, suggesting that *Hamlet* the play itself becomes an uncanny engine or motor of the cycle of revenge—what I have called "the *Hamlet* effect"—whether what is at stake is fine printing and book making, editing and criticism, detective fiction, or indeed the career of an artist like Edward Gordon Craig.

In the spirit of what-goes-around-comes-around, or what might be described as the recursive revenge motif in literary structure, I want to return to the text with which we began, the book that made my heart beat faster, the Cranach Press *Hamlet* and the idea of *Hamlet* itself as an infolded narrative of repetition and revenge.

At the conclusion of his textual notes included in the Cranach *Hamlet*, Dover Wilson sounded, once again, the note of "revenge," this time explicitly and in connection with the editing process itself. While he allows some room for learned scholars to disagree with him on the basis of textual evidence, Dover Wilson has no patience for readers who will simply find his edited text different from the one they have "grown accustomed to from childhood." Such readers are, he says like the players who "took their revenge for Hamlet's officious advice on how to speak their lines, by removing wholesale the delicate punctuation which would have helped them to follow it, and by scores of careless or high-handed verbal alterations."[77]

This offhand remark, the very last sentence of Dover Wilson's "Note on the Text," sits in interesting relation to Edward Gordon Craig's role in the production of the volume. For Craig, as we have seen, identifies himself with Hamlet the dreamer, and with Hamlet the controller of the scene. In his "First Dialogue," he deplores any changes or cuts that might be made to the Shakespeare text, while in his dealings with Stanislavski he made it clear that it was his vision, and not that of the actors or the director, that should dominate the production. Stanislavski was willing to agree, while conceding failure. (And here it is striking to compare the technological resources of the theater today with the situation as Stanislavski lamented it a hundred years ago.)

> What a huge difference there is between a designer's and a director's dream and actually bringing them to be on stage! How crude all the existing technical means for achieving that! . . . The radio, electricity, all kinds of rays perform miracles everywhere, but not for us, in the theatre, where they might discover a completely new form of beauty and banish forever the vile paint and size, the papier mâché, the props. . . . Craig, like me, wanted perfection, an ideal, i.e., a simple, profound, inspiring, artistic, beautiful expression of human feeling. I could not give it to him.[78]

Craig wanted perfection. Stanislavski could not give it to him, but Count Harry Kessler could. And the testimony for that comes from no other source than J. Dover Wilson.

In his own memoir, entitled *Milestones on the Dover Road*, Dover Wilson describes his role as textual editor for the Cranach *Hamlet* as a stroke of good fortune offered him by a man he calls "the German millionaire Count Harry Kessler." He praises the title page, the paper, the typography, the binding in red calf, the sources printed in the margins. "Kessler was content with nothing but the best." He charts, as well, the fortunes of the volume, impeded in its sales by the untimely arrival of the depression in America ("Kessler could hardly have sold the copies he expected to sell to millionaires over there") and the even more untimely arrival of Hitler and the Nazis, "which led to the expulsion from Germany of Harry Kessler. . . . His press was ruined and he died in poverty in

Paris."[79] What goes around comes around, we may again be tempted to reflect, in the wake of this somber report.

Dover Wilson writes that "seven copies were printed on vellum, fifteen on imperial Japanese paper, and three hundred on hand-made paper, plus one especially printed for me." Almost as if abashed by his own pleasure in all this opulence, he has brief recourse to the defensive aggressiveness of donnish wit. "How many copies were sold I do not know, but it cannot be regarded as a text easily available to students." Nonetheless, the book itself was unique, and uniquely beautiful: "the finest edition of *Hamlet*, I dare say, in the world."

It is Dover Wilson's specific praise of Edward Gordon Craig that may serve as the last word here. For the Cranach Press *Hamlet*, he writes, contains "the marvelous woodcuts of Gordon Craig, each a piece of dramatic criticism of a high order."[80] So Craig the actor who banished actors, the director who displaced Stanislavski, now becomes the artist who is also the preeminent critic, upstaging even the critic and editor whom Kessler had called "the greatest living authority on Shakespeare." For just as Stanislavski had acknowledged the limits of his own medium, the theater, so Dover Wilson here tacitly does the same with respect to critical writing. The editor's learned notes in closely printed columns of text are located at the back of the volume, easy to skip or ignore, while the "marvelous woodcuts," Edward Gordon Craig's "dramatic criticism," dominate page after breathtaking page of "the finest edition of *Hamlet . . .* in the world."

The upshot is an uncanny dramatization of the wartime counterintelligence plan I cited in my epigraph, in which agents with code names like ARTIST and HAMLET were deployed to infiltrate the enemy: "It was agreed that we should use ARTIST to the full for this purpose and not attempt to use HAMLET, who had also been suggested as a possible source of information."[81] In the Cranach Press book so lovingly produced by Count Harry Kessler, the ARTIST, Edward Gordon Craig, takes center stage and center page: used "to the full," he is actor, director, and critic in one. As for HAMLET—Shakespeare's *Hamlet*—it remains a dangerous and risky ally, a "possible source of information" but also a potential double-agent, never wholly under control, always on the verge of turning or being turned, the vehicle of repetition as the instrument of revenge.

CHAPTER FOUR

Shakespeare in Slow Motion

The last several decades have seen a sustained interest on the part of literary scholars in the contexts of Shakespeare's plays, from political, social, religious, and cultural history to biography. Studies of the court, of the "middling sort," of women in early modern England, of witchcraft, of race and exoticism, of travel, of economics, of philosophy and theories of personhood and power, of affect and emotion in the period—all these have come increasingly to occupy the attention of scholars. Textual studies have often focused on the history of the book and the book trade, as well as on questions of editing, bibliography, authenticity, and textual variants. Stage history and the history of productions, film, and adaptation offer another kind of context through the permutations of material culture.

My objective in a course called "Shakespeare in Slow Motion" was to slow down the move to context, if not reverse it altogether, by redirecting attention to the language of the plays, scene by scene, act by act, moment by moment, word by word. Let *Shakespeare* be the designation we give to the author of the plays published under his name. Let us not speculate on his personal or professional motives, his inner thoughts, his relationships with his wife or his children, his cultural aspirations, his finances, his religion, or his attitude toward the reigning monarch. Let us discuss not "the opinions or creed of the being whom we sometimes oddly call 'Shakespeare the man,'"[1] to quote A. C. Bradley, writing skeptically about such matters a little more than a hundred years ago—but rather the text of the play and what it tells us.

The concept of "Shakespeare in Slow Motion" was drawn from a 1959 essay called "Reading in Slow Motion" by Reuben Brower,[2] but its energy comes in part from the description offered by one of Brower's teaching assistants, who was struck by the "critical, even subversive, power of literary instruction" that could emerge from a rigorous process of close reading. Here is an account of this process, as recalled more than twenty years later by the literary theorist Paul de Man:

> Students, as they began to write were not to say anything that was not derived from the text they were considering. They were not to make any statements that they could not support by a specific use of language that actually occurred in the text. They were asked, in other words, to begin by reading texts closely as texts and not to move at once into the general context of human experience or history. Much more humbly or modestly, they were to start out from the baf-flement that such singular turns of tone, phrase, and figure were bound to pro-duce in readers attentive enough to notice the and honest enough not to hide their non-understanding behind the screen of received ideas that often passes, in literary instruction, for humanistic knowledge. This very simple rule, surpris-ingly enough, had far-reaching didactic consequences. I have never known a course by which students were so transformed.[3]

The passage hints at the radical nature of close reading, achieved through the analytic rigor of attention to the philological or rhetorical devices of language. The results of this pedagogical decision were startling, de Man reported.

> Mere reading, it turns out, prior to any theory, is able to transform critical discourse in a manner that would appear deeply subversive to those who think of the teaching of literature as a substitute for the teaching of theology, ethics, psychology, or intellectual history. Close reading accomplishes this often in spite of itself because it cannot fail to respond to structures of language which it is the more or less secret aim of literary teaching to keep hidden.[4]

This statement is tendentious, but also suggestive. What does it mean to close read Shakespeare in the twenty-first century, after the most recent period of attention to historical, cultural, and religious context? To explore this question in the classroom, I decided to spend each meeting time on a single act of the play, assigning no literary or historical criticism. This exercise of focusing on "the way meaning is conveyed rather than on the meaning itself"[5] is harder than it may seem, perhaps para-doxically more difficult for Shakespeare scholars than for beginning stu-dents. I anticipated that our discussions would generate theories of reading and of language as well as theories of Shakespearean meaning, that Shakespeare in slow motion, like a frame-by-frame analysis, would offer some unpredictable and counterintuitive insights. Participants were not expected to forget what they knew about "Shakespeare" or his time, but they were invited to put pressure on the language before presuming any sense of its meaning and to expect to be surprised as they returned to the text of the play.

I have taught "Shakespeare in Slow Motion" both as an English department seminar that brought together college freshmen, English majors, and graduate students in English, comparative literature, and law and as a faculty seminar on literary studies hosted by the National Humanities Center in the Research Triangle Park, North Carolina (NHC). The participants on this second occasion were assistant professors of English, whose own professional training took place during the years when historicism was the unstated but assumed basis of much though not all academic literary study. The ground rules were simple. In each case we read slowly, one act of a play per session. For the NHC faculty seminar, I purposely did not specify in advance the play to be read—indeed, I didn't select it until shortly before the group was scheduled to meet. A few weeks before our session, the participants received a packet containing the Brower and de Man essays and some readings on slow motion and visuality; the play text was sent to them, under separate cover, a day or two before we convened as a group. Instead of studying the play in advance, they were asked to think about slow motion as a theoretical practice. My suggestion to the participants in these seminars, whether they were published scholars or first-time readers of the plays, was to read until they were halted by something contrary to their expectation—something "wrong," something that stopped them in their tracks, something they did not already "know" from their cultural consciousness of what Shakespeare had said, written, intended, or meant in the play.

Brower's essay had used the phrase *slow motion* as a metaphor. The phrase appears in his title, and is explicated once ("a method that might be described as 'slow motion,' by slowing down the process of reading to observe what is happening, in order to attend very closely to the words, their uses, and their meanings"),[6] but elsewhere it is shortened to *slow reading*, both in the text ("why a course in slow reading?"[7] "the family reading circle, where books were read aloud and slowly, has all but disappeared,"[8] and "let me now attempt to describe Literature *X*, a course in slow reading")[9] and in a footnote of acknowledgment ("my colleagues will best know how much I owe to their ingenuity and their cheerful support in making experiments in slow reading").[10] But for all its literary references, justifying and amplifying the process of "slow reading," there is nowhere a reference to film, photography, visual art, dance, or performance. The motion of "slow motion" in Brower's essay is simply that of the eyes on the page, of the voice reading aloud, and of the contemplative mind. What would happen if the idea of slow motion were taken more literally, or more historically, or, more precisely, to accord with developments in the visual field?

"UNCONSCIOUS OPTICS"

Slow motion, "the technique of filming a scene at a faster speed than normal so that when it is projected the action will appear to be slowed down,"[11] was invented in 1904 by August Musger, an Austrian physicist and priest. Musger's experiment in cinematic time, space, and vision was preceded by the work of the French scientist and chronophotographer Etienne-Jules Marey and the English photographer Eadweard Muybridge. Muybridge's studies on animal and human locomotion began in the 1870s: one of his most famous early experiments was designed to prove former California Governor Leland Stanford's belief that a galloping horse had all four feet off the ground at once, a phenomenon known as "unsupported transit." What seemed to some impossible the stereoscopic cameras, taking pictures every one-thousandth of a second, demonstrated was true. In 1879, Muybridge invented a device called a zoopraxiscope, which projected images on rotating glass discs to produce the impression of motion, and at the World's Columbian Exposition in Chicago in 1893 this early version of a movie projector showed motion pictures to the paying public.[12]

At the same time that these advances in photography and optics were taking place, a parallel revolution was developing in the analysis of mental images and spoken language. Sigmund Freud's *Interpretation of Dreams* was published in November 1899, but the book bore the date 1900, ushering in the new century.[13] The following year Freud published *The Psychopathology of Everyday Life*, one of his most popular books, in which he demonstrated that the same unconscious activities that shaped the logic of dreams—displacement, condensation, over-determination, and compromise formations—were also at work in commonplace daily events like forgetting, slips of the tongue (and slips of the pen), misreadings, screen memories, and the belief in chance or fate. Freud's examples included some from Shakespeare: Portia's slip of the tongue in *Merchant of Venice* 3.2 ("One half of me is yours, the other half yours,—/Mine own I would say, but if mine, then, yours,/And so all yours"),[14] a similar slip in *Richard II* 2.2.100, and a fatal coincidence of names in *Julius Caesar* 3.3.117–18. Suddenly everyone, not just neurotics, were found to make these "mistakes": the unconscious, like the camera, saw more than the waking or conscious mind, or the unaided eye, could ever see.

The connection between these two developments, slow-motion photography and unconscious mental processes, was noted by Walter Benjamin in his essay "The Work of Art in the Age of Mechanical Reproduction," first published in 1936. The immediate analogy that came to his mind was between film and psychoanalysis.

> The film has enriched our field of perception with methods that can be illustrated by those of Freudian theory. Fifty years ago, a slip of the tongue passed more or less unnoticed. Only exceptionally may such a slip have revealed dimensions of depth in a conversation which had seemed to be taking its course on the surface. Since *The Psychopathology of Everyday Life* things have changed. This book isolated and made analyzable things which heretofore floated along unnoticed in the broad stream of perception. For the entire spectrum of optical, and now also acoustical, perception the film has brought about a similar deepening of apperception.[15]

Benjamin was particularly taken with the close-up, which appeared to expand space, and with slow motion, which appeared to extend movement. He wrote,

> Slow motion not only presents familiar qualities of movement but reveals in them entirely unknown ones, "which, far from looking like retarded rapid movements, give the effect of singularly gliding, floating, supernatural motions." Evidently a different nature opens itself to the camera than opens to the naked eye—if only because an unconsciously penetrated space is substituted for a space consciously explored by man. Even if one has a general knowledge of the way people walk, one knows nothing of a person's posture during the fractional second of a stride.[16]

"The fractional second of a stride" recalls Muybridge's studies of the male and female figures in motion. The internal quotation about "gliding, floating, supernatural motions" is taken from Rudolf Arnheim's

Film as Art, where the phenomenon had led Arnheim to suggest, "Slow motion should be a wonderful medium for showing visions and ghosts."[17] Noting these effects, Benjamin concluded, in a phrase that became foundational for our discussions in "Shakespeare in Slow Motion," "The camera introduces us to unconscious optics as does psychoanalysis to unconscious impulses."[18] "Unconscious optics"—trying to see what the eye has missed—underscored the importance of reading not only slowly but against the grain of expectation.

To the avant-garde filmmaker Maya Deren, slow motion offered a similar confluence of the visual and the affective.

> My own attention has been especially captured by the explorations of slow-motion photography. Slow-motion is the microscope of time. . . . [It] can be brought to the most casual activities to reveal in them a texture of emotional and psychological complexes. For example, the course of a conversation is normally characterized by indecisions, defiances, hesitations, distractions, anxieties, and other emotional undertones. In reality these are so fugitive as to be invisible. But the explorations by slow-motion photography, the agony of its analysis, reveals, in such an ostensibly causal situation, a profound human complex.[19]

Deren's list of these latent conversational performances is both an index of ordinary psychopathologies and a lexicon for actors (an actor playing Macbeth or Hamlet, for example, would presumably deploy all of these in performing the role). Deren's attention to slow motion was not principally metaphoric, however: as a filmmaker, film theorist, poet, and choreographer, Deren saw its specific visual potential.

> A running leap has, with slight variations, a given tempo; slow-motion photography creates of it a reality which is totally unnatural. But a use of slow-motion in reference to a movement which can, in parts, be even more creative . . . one creates a movement in one tempo which has the qualities of a movement of another tempo, and it is the dynamics of the relationship between these qualities which creates a certain special effectiveness.[20]

As with Benjamin's citation of the stride, Deren's initial reference point, the running leap, seems to tie her imagination of slow motion to photographic sequences like those of Muybridge. The formal analogy she drew was between film and poetry—or, rather, between the practice of filmmaking and the practice of poetry: "Just as the verbal logics of a poem are composed of the relationships established through syntax, assonance, rhyme, and other such verbal methods, so in film there are processes of filmic relationships which derive from the instrument and the elements of its manipulations."[21]

It was precisely a set of logics like these—dramatic, visual, verbal, even specifically Shakespearean—that I thought reading Shakespeare in slow motion would permit participants to explore and derive.

"A SEEING WHICH IS ALSO A READING"

The logic of slow-motion photography and film, like the logic of the dream, can sometimes seem alogical, or counterintuitive. For Shakespeare such incertitude was not merely an occasional effect but also a fundamental technique. "This dream is all amiss interpreted," says the conspirator Decius Brutus, brushing aside the prophetic dream of Caesar's murder dreamt by Calpurnia and substituting his own, plausible reinterpretation: both come true (*Julius Caesar* 2.2.83). Malvolio finds a letter thrown in his path and interprets it as a love missive sent to him by his employer, the lady Olivia. Macbeth compels the witches to speak to him, though they warn that he should "seek to know no more" (*Macbeth* 4.1.103): inevitably what he takes from them is a fatally partial message, the dangerous and slippery echo of his own desire. Errors in reading are not only semiotic and syntactic but also visual and observational: Iago shows Othello a tableau in which Desdemona seems to flirt with Cassio; Claudio watches while his beloved and virginal Hero seems to be engaged in dalliance with another man. Here the logic is that of the mistake or sometimes of the double take, a term that developed in early-twentieth-century film and theater practice.[22]

To say that these misreadings are evidence of character flaws (Othello's self-doubt, Claudio's lack of sexual experience, Malvolio's vanity) is necessary but not sufficient: what is being performed here is not only character but language, and in many cases the spectator or listener makes, at least briefly, the same "mistake." If King Lear were immediately to reward Cordelia for her plain speaking, not only would there be no play, there would also be no role for language. In *The Merchant of Venice*, the choice of three caskets would have no dramatic value if the first chooser chose the right casket. The bad choosers here can be retrofitted with character flaws and psychic blindnesses that keep them from seeing right, but the logic that animates their choices comes as well from other kinds of agency. The impetus could, for example, be generic (the fairy tale), narratological (the play requires its own continuation), affective (the audience, like the audience of a thriller or a horror film, desires a negative outcome), or gendered (the woman's choice is inscribed by her father). Reading Shakespeare in slow motion resists the idea of determination by character and motive unless these elements can be descried in a particular linguistic formation. Puzzles and loose ends remain as puzzles and loose ends, instead of being neatly tied up. (Lady Macbeth's "I have given suck" [1.7.54] produced a famous set of exchanges on this topic, as has, more recently, Viola's abandoned plan—or Shakespeare's textual false start—to appear as a eunuch in Orsino's court [*Twelfth Night* 1.2.55–56].) Character and motive, in fact, are revealed or produced as critical fantasies—which is not at all the same as saying that they do not exist.

But when the text is read in slow motion in a legal context—to determine guilt or innocence, to impute character and motive—such fantasies, and such existences, may become determinative. Slowing down a film or video can exhibit not only unconscious optics, but also unconscious (or even conscious) politics. Judith Butler's essay on the Rodney King case and the use of videotape in court to exonerate the arresting officers of the charge of police brutality brings this issue vividly to mind.[23] The events took place in Los Angeles in 1991; Butler's essay was published in 1993. It is instructive to quote some excerpts from her analysis.

> The video shows a man being brutally beaten, repeatedly, and without visible resistance; and so the question is, How could this video be used as evidence that the body being beaten was *itself* the source of danger? . . . How was this feat of interpretation achieved?
>
> That it was achieved is not the consequence of ignoring the video, but, rather, of reproducing the video within a racially saturated field of visibility. If racism pervades white perception, structuring what can and cannot appear within the horizon of white perception, then to what extent does it interpret in advance "visual evidence"?[24]

> From these two interpretations emerges . . . a context within the visual field, a crisis in the certainty of what is visible . . .[25]

> The defense attorneys broke the video down into "stills," freezing the frame, so that the gesture, the raised hand, is torn from its temporal place in the visual narrative. The video is not only violently decontextualized, but violently recontextualized; it is played without a simultaneous sound track which, had it existed, would have been littered with racial and sexual slurs against Rodney King. In the place of reading the testimony alongside the video, the defense

attorneys offered the frozen frame, the magnification of the raised hand as the hyperbolic figure of racial threat, interpreted again and again as a gesture fore-shadowing violence, a gesture about to be violent, the first sign of violence . . .[26]

This is a seeing which is a reading.[27]

This last phrase, like Benjamin's "unconscious optics," came to represent for the Shakespeare seminars both the opportunity and the necessity posed by reading in slow motion. The video required, Butler asserts, an aggressive counterreading—one that "the prosecutors failed to perform." Instead of that counterreading, there interposed a set of terms from liter-ary and narrative analysis, foremost among them "intention." By what Butler calls "a transposition and fabrication of dangerous intention,"[28] it was King, the unarmed black man, not the police officers armed with Tasers and batons, who was said to pose a threat that had to be subdued by force. The essay's insistence on the activity of reading (the essay was first published in a collection called *Reading Rodney King / Reading Urban Uprising*) brought deconstructive logic together with psychoanalysis, describing the use and abuse of the videotape in court as "a form of white paranoia which projects the intention to injure that it itself enacts."[29]

Some seminar participants, struck by the forcefulness of this argu-ment, wondered whether it put in question the value of reading in slow motion. Wasn't it true that by slowing down the videotape and breaking it into freeze frames the defense attorneys secured acquittal for their guilty clients? Couldn't one make the visual text, and the play text, say anything one wanted it to say, by such acts of decontextualization? The response to this, it seemed to me, was not an answer but, again, an examination of the process. Like the prophecies of the witches in *Macbeth*, the videotape was a medium: although it was sutured to interpreta-tion, no single interpretation could sustain or encompass all its latent and manifest meanings. The point was not that reading in slow motion would disclose the singular truth but that many readings are not readings at all but prior identifications with meanings already there, a literary practice that projects an intention to mean. Whether such readings were historicist (based on a supposed historical referent or cause), generic (based on expectations of what a tragedy or a comedy was or should do), or characterological (making claims about personality and psychology and motive), or indeed whether they developed out of the sheer weight and preexistence of so much prior commentary on Shakespeare, each had a narrative to offer. Small details that seemed to interrupt or contradict the narrative could be, and often were, ignored or set aside.

"I . . . SLOW . . . IT . . . DOWN, AND THEN SOMETIMES ISPEEDITUP"

The Rodney King video was an instance from life, transformed into techne, "art" or "craft," for purposes that were forensic and political. But video art and live theater have also made use of slow motion in recent years to expose and critique what we think we see. Such art practices query issues of mimesis and representation, on the one hand, and determinate meaning, on the other.

A good example is the work of Bill Viola, an artist whose use of ultra-slow-motion video has become an identifiable signature of his work. In a series called *The Passions*, Viola allows the viewer to linger in the moment of seeing, exposing a gap or disruption just at the point where the extra time would seem to offer certainty. For pieces like *The Quintet of the Astonished* (2000) and *Observance* (2003), he gave detailed instructions to the actors. For *Quintet*, each actor was assigned a different emotion and a point on which to fix his gaze; they were then free to invent gestures and expressions; no actor knew the instruction given or the emotion assigned to another. In *Observance*, the actors respond to an unseen object with a series of powerful expressions of grief and loss.[30] Most of the works in Viola's *Passions* series were shot on 35mm film at a very high speed, then slowed down and transferred to video. John Walsh, a curator, describes the effect.

> In *The Passions* the familiar and the unfamiliar are tightly bound together. Slow motion is thoroughly familiar from movies and sports replays and MTV, but not as a means to observe the movements of people's faces and speculate on their feelings. . . . We know the ordinary-looking people on the screen to be actors, and we know their emotions are feigned, or at least produced at will; yet their appeal is apt to be stronger than we imagine possible. . . . Viola's pieces, in short, are charged with the peculiar energy of consistent contradiction.[31]

We might compare the effect of slow motion in video and installation art to the work of the avant-garde stage director Robert Wilson. Wilson's theater is famously concerned with time and space, stretching out moments and movements so that the plays become palpably visual as well as verbal. As a director, he suggests that actors should themselves avoid too much interpretation, leaving the ambiguity and richness to the audience—precisely what is often said that directors and actors, unlike literary scholars, cannot or should not do. "There's so much going on in a line of Shakespeare," he has said, "that if the actor colors the voice too much, the audience loses too many other colors."[32] Wilson sets aside questions of naturalism, realism, and psychology in favor of openness, the "emptying out" of meaning, and the pleasures that come with *not* understanding a play. As he told the critic Mel Gussow in an interview, "Often I take much more tiiiiime than one would normally take to do something. I . . . slow . . . it . . . down, and then sometimes Ispeeditup."[33] The performative language here, as transcribed by Gussow, offers a compact model for what it might mean to understand reading in slow motion in a literal, and also a theatrical, way.

What would happen if that process were directly explored in the performance of Shakespeare's plays? A good example from contemporary theater practice occurred in Rupert Goold's 2007–8 production of *Macbeth*, with Patrick Stewart in the title role. The banquet scene in which Macbeth sees Banquo's ghost was staged twice, once before the intermission, once after.[34] In one version the audience sees events through Macbeth's eyes, with the ghost of Banquo an intrusive and terrifying presence. In the second version, visualized from the point of view of the guests, Macbeth's terror is inexplicable, since no ghost appears. In the withering phrase of his wife, "When all's done./You look but on a stool" (3.4.66–67). In another staging of the same play in 2009, the British company Punchdrunk converted a forty-four-room school building outside Boston into an immersive theater space through which audience members were invited to wander at will, choosing what they watched and where they went. In this production, entitled *Sleep No More*, two particular moments made explicit use of slow motion as a stage device. In the banquet scene, here performed in silence and in extreme slow motion, actors seated at a long table raised above floor level ate, drank, flirted, and whispered, moving their arms and bodies in big, sweeping gestures, while at the head of the table Macbeth, glimpsing the ghost, tried to hide his dismay. By contrast, a scene in which Macbeth encounters the witches was illuminated by strobe lights, generating a jerky, flickering sense of hyperreality, both slow and fast at once, freeze-frame modulating to frantic energy, as the witches stripped, danced, grew goat heads and horns. Whether read as a drug trip, a fantasy, or an encounter with the supernatural, the visual effect of slow motion here induced a disorienting sense of nightmare.

"MERE READING"

Neither Reuben Brower nor Paul de Man could have predicted the twenty-first century's profound shift toward the visual that has come with the spread of the Internet, digitization, cell-phone cameras, and video culture. Slo-mo, as it is now called, is used today as much in sports and motion technology as it is in cinematic or installation art. (Sports technology now makes use of high-definition cameras that allow judges to "see" what cannot be seen by the naked eye, changing the outcomes of races that are decided by a fraction of a second and making visible formerly invisible distinctions.) But Brower's idea of "reading in slow motion" and de Man's assessment of "mere reading" as an activity with the capacity to be "deeply subversive" seem as perceptive and as necessary now as they did then. De Man wrote, in a highly characteristic sentence, "Close reading accomplishes this often in spite of itself because it cannot fail to respond to structures of language which it is the more or less secret aim of literary teaching to keep hidden." Participants in the seminar were quick to see that the rhetoric of this sentence ("in spite of itself . . . it cannot fail to respond," "the more or less secret aim . . . to keep hidden") itself performs the signature double take of slow motion, staging its function as mirror image, counterlogic, and internal resistance.

Initially developed as a technological advance with intriguing implications for the world of film, creatively deployed at mid-century by a literary scholar as a figure for a certain kind of close textual reading, slow motion today describes a practice of inventive artists, a popular mode for re-viewing key moments in sports, and a revelatory and potentially still deeply subversive mode of teaching. Whether it will have what de Man aptly called "far-reaching didactic consequences," as he said of Brower's course, will depend upon the rigor of the next generation of teachers, readers, artists, and performers—and their commitment to remain open to consternation, contradiction, resistance, and surprise.

CHAPTER FIVE

The Shakespeare Brand

Call the roller of big cigars,
The muscular one . . .
  —Wallace Stevens, "The Emperor of Ice-Cream"

Sometimes a cigar is just a cigar. But what if its name is Shakespeare? Created in 2002 by Robert "Shakey" Shakespeare and his son Scott, and incorporated in 2003, Shakespeare Cigars advertises itself with a tagline from sonnet 15: "Everything that grows holds in perfection but a little moment." A logo of the *playwright's* classic signature, not the founders', appears on the corporate website, and the site is also adorned with a coat of arms and a rather sullen, colorized version of the Droeshout engraving. What's of special interest to me, though, is that the business platform name of the company is the "Works of Shakespeare." Cigar aficionados will know that Shakespeare is not the first brand to be associated with the Bard of Avon. Since 1875 Romeo y Julieta has been providing handmade cigars to the rich and famous. The brand logo is a version of the famous balcony scene. Alas, neither of the famous lovers is pictured smoking a cigar.

We could multiply these instances if we wanted to take the time. *Shakespeare* is the brand name of a high-end kind of fishing equipment, *Falstaff* the name of a famous "light-hearted" beer, and so on. Advertising is dissemination, and name recognition sells products. So it is not surprising to find Shakespeare quoted in the book *How to Build a Corporation's Name and Project Its Image*, although the selected quotation, "A rose by any other name would smell as sweet," seems oddly contrary to the message ("Changing a company's name is the most serious change you can make in its identity").[1] My interest here, however, is not in the association of the Shakespeare name with other products, but with the concept of branding as it pertains to Shakespeare the author, and the plays and poems often metonymically referred to as "Shakespeare" (or, indeed, "the works of Shakespeare").

We hear a great deal these days about branding, and the concept of the brand, as it applies to politics, politicians, corporations, and personality types. In the 2008 election in the United States the "Republican brand" in particular came in for some bashing, both from the left and from the right. "If the Republican party is to survive, the brand will have to be rebuilt," intoned one columnist,[2] and many others agreed. Bush "has killed the Republican brand," opined a Virginia congressman,[3] as the election neared. John McCain was repeatedly said to have established a successful brand for himself as a maverick. Tim Russert insisted that McCain had a "maverick brand" with the public, and *New York Times* columnist John Harwood concurred, saying that the "maverick brand" was "intact" despite McCain's flip-flopping on some basic issues.[4]

Now, a maverick is, in fact, an *unbranded* calf or yearling. The term derives from Texas politician and rancher Samuel Maverick, who owned a huge herd of cattle, many of which were unbranded (and thus strayed into other herds where they were promptly branded and dubbed "mavericks").[5] So the concept of a "maverick brand" is thus in a way a contradiction in terms, which has, of course, not kept it from becoming both a media truism and an actual brand name for bicycles, blue jeans, soft drinks, a meat grinder, and a line of discount cigarettes.

Meanwhile, the word *brand* as a figure of speech has become virtually ubiquitous. Angered at the support given by the Mormon Church in the defeat of California's Proposition 8, activists targeted "the Utah brand," calling on skiers to choose another state for their winter vacations, and urging filmmakers not to exhibit at the Sundance Film Festival.[6] Food critic Gael Greene, fired from *New York* magazine, issued a news release calling herself "the brand name of restaurant journalism."[7] A headline on the front page of the *New York Times* read "Kennedy Brand Leaves a Rival Feeling Stymied."[8] Nowhere in the article was the word *brand* glossed or explained; there was no need to do so. The term has crossed over into common language as a doubly-displaced figure: the word *brand* is now a metaphor for economic success in the free market.

But this was not, of course, always the case. Consider Shakespeare's sonnet III.

O for my sake do you with fortune chide,
The guilty goddess of my harmful deeds,
That did not better for my life provide
Than public means which public manners breeds.
Thence comes it that my name receives a brand,
And almost thence my nature is subdued
To what it works in, like the dyer's hand.

In this sonnet the speaker imagines himself bearing a "branded" name because—presumably in his career as an actor on the public stage—he sought out "public means" and therefore developed "public manners," a free and easy familiarity rather than an aristocratic reserve. In Shakespeare's time, criminals were still often branded with the sign of their crimes: (*V* for vagabond, *F* for "fraymaker" or brawler, *M* for malefactor).[9] In the next sonnet the speaker continues the figure, invoking "th'impression . . . Which vulgar scandal stamped upon my brow" (112:1–2). In *Hamlet*, Laertes refers offhandedly, if feelingly, to a harlot branded between the brows, and Hamlet himself fears the possibility of leaving behind him a "wounded name" (*Hamlet* 4.5.115–16; 5.2.349). Our modern word *notoriety*, often mistakenly conflated with *fame* or *celebrity*, is probably related to the Latin *nota*, or "brand," the mark inflicted by Romans on erring slaves, as well as the mark of censure placed next to the *names* of persons guilty of immorality.[10]

Today Shakespeare, who wrote so feelingly about the "brand" of ignominy that was his lot because he sought out "public means," has become the most powerful brand name in English studies. In fact *Shakespeare*, the name, the brand, the taglines and occasionally the works, has come not only to signify, but also in many ways to replace, the study of literature and the humanities today.

The decline in the number of students who decide to major in literature in colleges and universities might be attributed to a number of factors, among them the focus on pre-professional training; the tilt toward the sciences and social sciences on the part of students, educational institutions, public interest and the media; and the emphasis in many fields on "fact," "data," and "metrics" over interpretation and speculation. Where once a liberal arts education in college was considered an excellent platform for a future in medicine, law, diplomacy, or politics, these days it is far more likely that programs in pre-law, pre-med, or some other pre-professional course of study will be recommended to, or elected by, undergraduates.

A cumulative result of these disparate factors has been a reduction in the "must-have" (or "must-know") list of authors. Homer, Virgil, Spenser, Pope, Milton, Wordsworth, Dickens, Joyce, and both of the canonical Eliots (George and T. S.) are often cultural *references* rather than familiar bodies of *work* to modern readers. But one figure stands out as an exception to this trend, a figure who, at least in the United States, has increasingly come to be substituted for *literature* or *literary culture*: the figure of Shakespeare. I use the word *figure* here advisedly, rather than *author, playwright,* or *poet,* because Shakespeare has become a figure for our time—not only a personage but a *figura,* a figure or type.[11] His name, his image, his collected works (each of these, in context, designated as "Shakespeare") signify something different from, and virtually transcending, literary authorship.

The phrase "American exceptionalism" is a familiar one to political theorists, historians, lawyers, and sociologists, and has been the topic of some lively—and heartfelt—debates.[12] In the realm of literature and culture there is a cognate concept, one that we might call *Shakespearean exceptionalism*: the idea that Shakespeare is unique among authors, and that therefore to know Shakespeare is to possess—in one compact and convenient package—the best and the brightest of the literary canon.

In this context we might consider three kinds of public offering: the myth, the tattoo, and the brand. These modes of public display—what I call Public Displays of Shakespeare (on the model of the old "Public Displays of Affection")—are not a developmental sequence—that is to say, we have not grown out of one mode or into another. Rather, they exist concurrently in different markets and subcultures. Each is a kind of writing effect, a kind of inscription. The Shakespeare myth might be regarded as a metaphor, the Shakespeare tattoo as a demotic rhizome, and the Shakespeare brand as an effect of metonymy. Each depends upon a different mobilization of Shakespearean exceptionalism. And it is Shakespearean exceptionalism, I suggest, that has ultimately used the brand name *Shakespeare* to corner the market, relegating many other authors to the status of *generics*: that is, literally, those who write in genres, especially the genres of which Shakespeare is thought to be the name brand (genres like comedy, tragedy, history, romance, and the sonnet, and also meta-genres like drama and poetry).

Let me begin, though, not with the brand but with the myth.

The phrase "the Shakespeare myth" was used in the first half of the twentieth century in the titles of a number of books about the authorship controversy (the question of who "really" wrote the plays).[13] This dispute—represented by books like *The Shakespeare Myth and the Strat-ford Hoax*, published in 1937 by the Bacon Society—actually reinforces the myth, since it leaves the "works" in a position of enviable attain-ment. Arguing about who wrote them doesn't question their value; it inflates it.

But it was in the latter half of the twentieth century that the concept of a "Shakespeare myth" became the object of theoretical analysis. In 1988, during the last years of the reign of Margaret Thatcher, a collection of essays called *The Shakespeare Myth* was published in the Cultural Poli-tics Series of the Manchester University Press under the general editor-ship of Jonathan Dollimore and Alan Sinfield. Graham Holderness, who edited the collection, introduced it by explaining that a myth was "a real and powerful form of human consciousness," and that the Shakespeare myth, held together by "the institutions of bardolatry and quasi-religious worship," had produced "Shakespeare as culture hero, as transcendent genius and omniscient seer." This Shakespeare was the consummate individual author who—the collaborative practice of the early modern theater notwithstanding—wrote plays that expressed his profound inner thoughts and meanings, and in so doing founded the field of English literature. His shrines and temples, from "The Birthplace" to the Shake-speare Theatre, were places of reverence and pilgrimage. His image graced the currency. And his life story—and mysterious identity—fit, with uncanny precision, the typical pattern of folklore, Bible story, and fairy tale in which the hero's true parentage is always a mystery: "he is never the person he appears to be."[14]

The book bore an epigraph from Roland Barthes's *Mythologies*—"myth is a type of speech chosen by history"—but it could readily have cited other observations from the same text: "myth is depoliticized speech," for example, or Barthes's succinct statement of "the very princi-ple of myth: it transforms history into nature."[15] Myth, he argued, was a second-order semiological system: "driven to having either to unveil or to liquidate [a] concept, it will *naturalize* it," so that mythical speech is "not read as a motive, but as a reason. . . . Everything happens as if the picture *naturally* conjured up the concept, as if the signifier *gave a foun-dation* to the signified."[16]

In the decades since the publication of *The Shakespeare Myth* in 1988, a good deal has changed, both in the world and in Shakespeare studies. Just to give one emblematic example: the twenty-pound note bearing the image of Shakespeare, a famous centerpiece of materialist analysis, was withdrawn from circulation in 1993. The most recent twenty-pound note, first issued in March of 2007, features, instead, the Scottish economist Adam Smith (the first Scot to appear on an English note). An emblem of myth is replaced by the emblem of the market.

But the Shakespeare myth has scarcely gone away. Indeed (why should this surprise us?) it is particularly alive and well in the United States, and—what is central to my argument here—is tied to the paradoxical situation of a *dwindling* interest in the humanities and in reading. For "Shakespeare," the name and the image, has increasingly become the emblem (or token) of American national literacy. In a program that began in 2003, the National Endowment for the Arts joined forces with Arts Midwest to sponsor "Shakespeare in American Communities," bringing professional companies—and "educational resource kits"—to schools, and educators, nationwide. The program's poster looks like a postage stamp in color, iconography, and proportions: Shakespeare—again, the Droeshout engraving version from the First Folio—posed against a rippling American flag. The publicity materials announce that "All the world's a stage . . ." but this image declares that Shakespeare is an American playwright.

The example that Roland Barthes gives in his essay "Myth Today," a photograph of a black soldier in a French uniform saluting the tricolor, seems to me in some ways uncannily similar to this blithely confident Shakespeare, in his ruff and doublet, standing—like an Elizabethan George W. Bush?—in front of an enormous, rippling American flag. Barthes read this image—which had appeared on the cover of *Paris Match*—three times, first as an empty signifier (the saluting black soldier is the *symbol* of French imperiality), the second time as a full one (the saluting black soldier is the *alibi* of French imperiality), and the third time as a mythic signifier, resisting ambiguity, combining meaning and form (the saluting black soldier is the *presence* of French imperiality). So, likewise, in our image, Shakespeare is the symbol of American cultural literacy, Shakespeare is the alibi for American cultural literacy, and Shakespeare is the presence of American cultural literacy—present, please note, in "American Communities," which is code for "places other than San Francisco, Los Angeles, or New York."

If myth is a mode of ideology, tattooing is a mode of appropriation and resignification. There is both too much and too little to say about the explosion of tattoo art in recent decades. Early modern branding of the body has been described strikingly coterminous with "print culture."

Is the postmodern tattoo a sign of the long-foretold "death of the book"—or of its dissemination? (Everyman his own Kindle?) What was once a *legibody*, the body marked by stigma (*V* for vagabond, *F* for fraymaker) is now, we might say, a *logobody*, the tattoo chosen by the bearer (a term I prefer to *wearer*). Etymologically, *logo* comes not only from word but also from riddle, an anagram or enigma. It will not, perhaps, surprise you that Shakespeare, bodied forth in image and in text, is omnipresent in the world of the tattoo—and on the Internet. The tattooed body, in effect, becomes a mode of postmodern commonplacing.

When there are quotations, they are, as so often in today's "public Shakespeare," misquotations, the misquotations themselves so commonplace as to almost represent a mode of conjectural re-editing: what Shakespeare should have said. I've commented elsewhere on the tattoo on the shoulder of actress and model Megan Fox: described as a quotation from *King Lear*, it reads "We will all laugh at gilded butterflies." *Lear* adepts will know that the word "all" is an interpolation that radically changes the sense, since the line in question, from act 5, scene 3, is Lear's desperate fantasy of a life for himself and Cordelia in prison: "we two alone will sing like birds i' th' cage,": "so we'll live/And pray, and sing, and tell old tales,/And laugh at gilded butterflies." The fantasy, of course, does not come true: "take them away," says Edmund, curtly, and Cordelia is killed offstage. Megan Fox's optimistic revision ("we will all laugh at gilded butterflies") makes of this tragic duo a merry throng. But her tattoo is always described as a quotation from Shakespeare's *King Lear*.[17]

Other modifications are more predictable, like the change from "What's past is prologue" to "What is past is prologue." (Everyone, even the National Archives Building in Washington, D.C., seems to resist Shakespeare's contractions as somehow un-Shakespearean.) A number of visual variations of Polonius's "to thine own self be true" (on the arm, shoulder, chest, and décolletage) posit the commonplace cliché, spoken by a Shakespearean windbag, as a visible Shakespearean truth. In one case the text is divided, "To thine own" tattooed on a man's right side, and "self be true" on his left: the quotation is thus designed to be read by the audience, from stage left to stage right. Likewise, "To be . . . or not to be" appears on either side of a man's head, "tomorrow and tomorrow and tomorrow" around a woman's waist, and so on. The *loci communes*, the common "places," are now—as in old style memory systems—also places on the body.

As with other modes of Shakespearean quotation, the speaker, the speech-prefix, falls away. A temporary tattoo (so captioned) on the chest of a young woman pictures a skull and the words "Alas, poor Yorick." She comments, "Mine is a Shakespeare quote since I'm an English major n all." Shakespeare here, as so often, *equals* English major. I found one Dickens tattoo on the Web (the entire first paragraph of *A Tale of Two Cities* inked on the inner forearms of the subject: "It was the best of times, it was the worst of times . . .") but Shakespeare is far and away the favorite canonical author among the online inked set—another manifestation of the phenomenon of "Shakespeare love," or Public Displays of Shakespeare. An earlier generation of tattoos often exhibited the bearer's love for "Mom" or for a romantic partner whose name might appear within a heart. But what would happen if, having inscribed his lines on the body, you fell out of love with Shakespeare? Tattoo Erase, or the addition of marginal commentary? Absence, or more presence? Either would offer an embodied way of putting Shakespeare under erasure.

Individualized, localized, occasionally oppositional, hand-designed and inked by hand, a tattoo today would seem to be something like the converse of a brand, although both historically describe the marked (and stigmatized) body. Yet the brand is also imagined as declaring an identity—the identity of the *corporate* person.

As we've noted, the most powerful rhetoric in marketing and communications right now is this language of branding, or rebranding. Brand management, as it is called, involves developing a "personality" or an "image" for a product or service (and, lately, for entities like political candidates and universities). Within this area there is attention to a number of factors—for example, "attitude branding," which takes account of feelings toward the brand that may not have anything to do with the product or service (e.g., Starbucks; Nike; Apple's iPods, iPhones, and Macs); aspirational brands, desired by more of the "exposure audience" than can afford them (Mercedes-Benz; BMW; the Hermès Birkin bag); brand loyalty, brand penetration, brand share, and branded environments. There is also an intriguing category called evangelism marketing, in which customers come to believe so strongly in a particular product or service that they actively recruit others to buy and use it.

Viewed through this optic, Shakespeare is the perfect product. Aspirational, attitudinal, inspiring a level of brand loyalty to rival that of Coke or Disney, promoted by word of mouth as well as by direct marketing and retail (i.e., classroom) sales. The word *Shakespearean* has become a recognizable, all-purpose adjective, often paired with a word like *proportions* or *dimensions*. The Shakespeare logo—some version of the First Folio Droeshout engraving—is everywhere. Taglines from the plays are used to sell other products ("Out, damned spot!") as well as to ornament speeches, sermons, headlines, book titles, and movie scripts.

Contrast the success of the Shakespeare brand with that of comparable generics. Renaissance drama, Elizabethan sonnets, verse tragedies, verse comedies, revenge plays—these are all highly respectable, and respected, genres, and each category indeed contains a number of other brand name authors (Marlowe, Spenser, Lyly, Middleton, Webster, and so on). But an interest in, and an admiration for, Shakespeare is not swappable for other items within these categories, at least not without the advance consent of the consumer (whether that consumer is a student, a teacher, a theater goer, or the departmental curriculum committee). Thus many educational institutions (my own included) require every English major to take a course in Shakespeare. No other single author has such market share.

Marketers have developed the idea of the Q score, or Q factor, in estimating the fame, success, or "likeability" of a person or product. Among the categories rated are TV Q, Cable Q, Performer Q, Dead Q (measuring the current popularity of dead celebrities), Sports Q, Cartoon Q, Product Q, and Kids Product Q.[18] I think probably the time has come for a category called Shakes Q. Such is the popularity and ubiquity of Shakespeare; in fact, we might consider replacing the *Q* with an *S*, and merely discussing the S score of various authors, playwrights, performers and other cultural figures. (Would Marlowe get an S score of 7 or 8? What about Sidney? Fulke Greville?) If he were a gymnast, Shakespeare would have been a perfect 10, before Olympic inflation made that score attainable.

A score of 10 is appealing, needless to say, to investors. But those of us who work in literary studies might ask ourselves, is this conflation of the myth and the brand good for business? When one brand so monopolizes the market that it comes to stand—metonymically—for the whole?

It's not at all surprising that the drop in readership for many other authors and works in the literary canon should be concurrent with a rise in the cultural citation of Shakespeare. The concept of "cultural literacy," like the idea of the "public intellectual," uses the modifying adjective as a way of qualifying, rather than exemplifying, the noun. *Public* intellectual as contrasted with mere, and perhaps suspect, intellectuality; *cultural* literacy as contrasted with literary knowledge or literariness.

Shakespeare, in fact, has now himself become a Public Intellectual. An eloquent "communicator" who seems to offer powerful ideas about social problems, ethics, politics, human relations, and categories of knowledge and behavior. A figure whose work is actively and extensively cited in leadership institutes and executive training programs, as well as in the speeches of congressmen and senators. (On a recent episode of *The Simpsons*, Shakespeare was to be found in "celebrity heaven," together with George Washington, John Wayne, and John Lennon.)[19] Shakespeare's "exceptionalism" can here be seen as a crossover quality, transcending the genres of drama and poetry, and moving into the realms of philosophy, sociology, cultural anthropology, and political theory—to name only a few of the areas in which Shakespeare is now a designated expert. "Shakespeare says" or "as Shakespeare says" or "as Shakespeare puts it" are common locutions, far beyond the confines of literary criticism. Shakespeare's dramatic characters and famous speeches or phrases have become detached from their original contexts, floating free in the world of sound bites and taglines. They too have become cultural exemplars, instances of cultural literacy.

The success of the Shakespeare brand today seems unquestionable. Under the banners of "Shakespeare festivals" and "Shakespeare theatres," productions of other playwrights—both early modern and postmodern—are mounted and merchandised. In an academic job market down 20 percent in literary studies, it is presumed that a Renaissance candidate, no matter what her dissertation is on, will be able to teach Shakespeare—and will be called upon to do so. (Indeed it may be that Americanists, medievalists, and Victorianists enhance their credentials by having a little Shakespeare to offer on the side.) But when *Shakespeare* becomes not only a metonymy for English studies but also the only required author (or period) for English majors, we may have reached a tipping point.

The cliché about the exception that proves the rule is one of the few such bromides in common usage that *cannot* be traced to Shakespeare. (In fact the word *exception* in the plays is almost always used in another sense, as in "taking exception" to a statement or proposal.) The original concept, first articulated by Cicero and later adopted into medieval Latin law, says *exceptio probat regulam in casibus non exceptis* ("the exception proves the rule in cases not excepted")—which is to say that in order for something to be noted as an exception, there must be a rule, somewhere, to which it *is* an exception.

But is Shakespeare the exception that proves the rule? And if so, what is the rule? Here it may be instructive to return to the idea of a *canon*, a word that indeed *means* "rule." By the logic of the Ciceronian precept, Shakespeare would be the exception that proves the existence of a (literary) canon. In the current case, though, what this would mean—and what seems accurate—is that the love, or veneration, or ideology that attaches to Shakespeare seems to justify, in some compensatory way, the *neglect* or *sidelining* of the literary canon by, on the one hand, gesturing toward the existence of such a canon, and, on the other hand, suggesting that Shakespeare transcends it, and thus that by reading, studying, and "knowing" Shakespeare we have done due homage and obeisance, due diligence, to literature.

If there were no concept of "great literature" then Shakespeare's greatness would be more difficult to categorize. But once that category is acknowledged, even as a list of "great books," then the claim that Shakespeare is an exception, a unique "genius"—in the spirit of Kant's declaration that "genius gives the rule to art"[20]—allows the rest of the canon to fall into place, decorously, behind him. Appropriated, disseminated, inked, and reliably bankable (even in these uncertain times), Shakespeare has provided modern life with social plots, character psychologies, quotable phrases, and business school case studies—the entire fundamental architecture of culture. But his supposed exceptionalism, the effective aspirational monopoly of the Shakespeare brand, gestures reassuringly toward the existence of the literary canon while at the same time providing a reason—or an excuse—not to read it.

CHAPTER SIX

Translating F. O. Matthiessen

The life and work of F. O. Matthiessen seem very vivid and timely these days, given recent political developments. A lifelong supporter of left politics and political engagement, Matthiessen might well have found great interest in the election of Barack Obama. Himself under attack during the so-called Red Scare and the repressive period of McCarthyism and the blacklist, he might have noted, with concern, the loose talk during the political campaign about Obama "palling around with terror-ists," and the accusatory tactic—so familiar from those Red Scare years of the 1940s and still with us today—of "guilt by association." And as a man who lived quietly in a loving relationship for twenty years with another man, decades before gay rights or the increased acceptance and visibility of same-sex partnerships, Matthiessen might well have been concerned, as others have been, by the defeat of Proposition 8 in Califor-nia, which repealed the right of same-sex couples to marry. This was a right he was so far from envisaging that he wrote to his companion, the painter Russell Cheney, a month after they met, that he considered their relationship to be a marriage.

> Marriage! What a strange word to be applied to two men! Can't you hear the hell-hounds of society baying full pursuit behind us? But that's just the point. We are beyond society. . . . In the eyes of the unknowing world we are a talented artist of wealth and position and a promising young graduate student. In the eyes of the knowing world we would be pariahs, outlaws, degenerates. . . . And so we have a marriage that was never seen on land or sea. . . . It is a marriage that demands nothing and gives everything.[1]

The brave optimism of this assertion of difference would, over time, be mitigated by a concomitant sense of exclusion from the "serene" comforts of the law. A few months later he wrote to Cheney that their other friends had wives, and that "in their love for them lies their refuge and serenity. But we have been alone. . . . In order to be full and spontaneous, to grasp life fully, I need to be close, close to you."[2]

What I have to say here will touch on the ways in which Matthiessen's scholarly, activist, and private worlds may be read together, even though he kept his own scholarship—as he thought—quite distinct from his political and personal life. Yet such stories always intertwine. And as a Shakespearean, as well as someone who has written on gender and on cultural politics, I am particularly fascinated that Shakespeare and the Elizabethan period offer a way into the interconnections between Matthiessen's public and private lives.

Let me begin with an intriguing fact: F. O. Matthiessen did not invent the title of his most famous book, *American Renaissance*. The title was suggested to him by a colleague and former student who became an equally celebrated professor and critic, Harry Levin. Matthiessen at first wanted to give his big book on American writers a different title—*Man in the Open Air*—a title he would ultimately use within the book for his chapter on Whitman. But the publisher, apparently, found this phrase from Whitman too diffuse and indirect, and requested "something more descriptively categorical."[3] So Levin, who had followed the progress of the manuscript "from draft to draft," suggested another phrase, a phrase that would become the unquestioned description of the era from Emerson to Whitman: *American Renaissance*.

As an undergraduate in Harvard College, living, like F. O. Matthiessen, in Eliot House, Harry Levin had been one of Matthiessen's first students. But, as Levin wrote many years later, his intellectual curiosity was not then focused on the new field of American literature that Matthiessen would do so much to promote. "My interests then, I must confess, were all too narrowly bound to the classical and the European," he said. What then brought these two literary scholars together? Levin explained, "When our minds met, it was usually upon the common ground of the English Renaissance."[4]

By the time he came to write this, in 1958, Harry Levin was on his way to becoming a celebrated scholar of the English Renaissance, publishing books on Christopher Marlowe (1952), on *Hamlet* (1959), and on *The Myth of the Golden Age in the Renaissance* (1969). And when he first joined the English faculty at Harvard in 1929, Matthiessen was an English Renaissance scholar, steeped in the study of Shakespeare, having written his dissertation, in 1927, on Elizabethan translations (Hoby's *Courtier*, North's *Plutarch*, Florio's *Montaigne*, and the translations of Philemon Holland).[5] The revised manuscript was published by the Harvard University Press, in 1931, as *Translation: An Elizabethan Art*.

I will return later to this question of translation, and how it might be taken as a powerful emblem of Matthiessen's life and work. For now, though, I want only to note two things: that F. O. Matthiessen came to his American authors fully versed in the work of Shakespeare and English Renaissance literature, and that *American Renaissance* is chock-full of discussions of English Renaissance poetry and especially, of Shakespeare. Shakespeare appears both as the conscious authority cited by authors like Emerson and Melville, and as Matthiessen's own template for understanding literature, culture, and the passions.

Harry Levin tells about his diffident suggestion of a title for Matthiessen's great book on "art and expression in the age of Emerson and Whitman" (to cite the subtitle of *American Renaissance*) in the preface to *The Power of Blackness*, Levin's own book on Hawthorne, Poe, and Melville. The influence of Matthiessen, as teacher, scholar, colleague, and friend, was so pervasive that Levin, the dedicated scholar of the English Renaissance, found himself, some years later, writing about the American canon his mentor had created.

Matthiessen graduated from Yale in 1923, studied at Oxford on a Rhodes Scholarship, did his graduate work at Harvard, and then began his teaching career at Yale. He returned to Harvard in 1929, attracted by the opportunity to teach in the new Department of History and Literature and to focus on tutorial work. "It is time for the history of American literature to be rewritten," he declared in a review essay on "New Standards in American Criticism," published in the *Yale Review* in March 1929[6]—a pronouncement that is often taken as the beginning of his pathbreaking work on American studies. But at Harvard he continued to teach the English Renaissance and, especially, Shakespeare. He wrote to his partner, Russell Cheney, in October of his first teaching term at Harvard: "I woke up to the realization that I have to talk about Hamlet on Saturday—have to put it all into an hour—which means a fearful amount of work."[7]

The previous day he had tutored a Radcliffe student on the poetry of John Donne and a Harvard student on Shakespeare and Plutarch. In

November of that year he advised a precocious Harvard freshman who had come to him with a paper psychoanalyzing Hamlet according to the theory of the Oedipus complex,[8] and by December he had been asked by the English department to teach courses the following year in Elizabethan literature and American literature of the South and West.[9] What we think of as very different academic specializations today—English Renaissance literature and Shakespeare, on the one hand, and American literature, on the other—were combined both in Matthiessen's mind and expertise, and, indeed, in the expectations of the Harvard English department. In his acknowledgments to *American Renaissance*, Matthiessen singles out in particular two colleagues, Harry Levin and C. L. Barber, both English Renaissance scholars, as "readers whom I have in mind as the kind of audience I most wanted to satisfy."[10]

The pages of Matthiessen's landmark book on American writers are studded with nuanced and knowledgeable accounts of English Renaissance poetry and drama: Edmund Spenser's importance to Hawthorne; the value of the Metaphysical poets to Emerson; evocations of John Donne and Andrew Marvell, of George Herbert and Richard Crashaw, of Sir Walter Raleigh and Sir Thomas Browne, of Christopher Marlowe and Ben Jonson. In one compelling paragraph Matthiessen discusses the moment in *Moby-Dick* in which Captain Ahab looks over the side of the ship at the head of the dead whale suspended there, "re-enact[ing] a scene that had been an Elizabethan favorite from *Hamlet* to Tourneur— the soliloquy to the skull."[11]

Shakespeare is everywhere in *American Renaissance*. As the literary critic Jonathan Arac has pointed out, Shakespeare occupies more lines of the index than does Thoreau.[12] In Nathaniel Hawthorne's writing, for example, Matthiessen detected many devices that were "a far-off echo of Shakespearean drama: the habit of dividing his characters into groups and of carrying along the actions of each group separately; the way of developing his plot by means of a few spot-lighted scenes, with speeches of an exalted pitch . . . the occasional interweaving of oddities of low comedy."[13] A character in Hawthorne's *The Marble Faun* has "something of the shattered majesty of a Lady Macbeth."[14] Hawthorne's title, *Twice-Told Tales*, suggested to Matthiessen that he was thinking of the line from Shakespeare's play *King John*, "Life is as tedious as a twice-told tale."[15] Elsewhere in the book he noted that Hawthorne "often wrote as though he had set himself to answer Lear's question, 'Is there any cause in nature that makes these hard hearts?' "[16] It may be considering too curiously to think that these lines from Shakespeare ring bells for Matthiessen, as well as for Hawthorne (the tediousness of life; the ubiquity of hard hearts). What is clear, though, is that he lived and thought through Shakespeare, just as, he claimed, nineteenth-century American writers did.

This becomes especially evident in *American Renaissance* when Matthiessen moves away from the specific author he is discussing and toward a kind of philosophical generalization. Thus we find, in the Hawthorne chapter, the following freestanding observation:

> Tragic power springs not from the mind's recognitions, but from the depth to which the writer's emotions have been stirred by what he has recognized, from the degree to which he has really been able to comprehend and accept what Edgar meant by saying,
>
> Men must endure
Their going hence even as their coming hither:
Ripeness is all.[17]

Written by a scholar who had been hospitalized for suicidal depression in the course of the composition of his book (and who would indeed, much later, commit suicide), this wise and apparently disinterested utterance may, in retrospect, give the reader pause. Shakespeare is the conducting text here, and he, or it, functions as something like the unconscious of *American Renaissance*.

In his chapters on Whitman, Matthiessen describes the poet as a journalist who went to the theater free of charge and had what was "beyond question the fullest aesthetic experience of his life" there.[18] The theater, he says, enabled Whitman to "satisfy his eagerness to have his impressions of Shakespeare reinforced by immediate embodiment." Whitman read through each play the day of the performance "and could never conceive of anything finer than the energy of Junius Booth's voice as he gave himself up to Richard III, Lear, or Iago."[19] Later, in a footnote, Matthiessen traces echoes of Shakespeare in Whitman's poetry: "it seems probable that . . . some of the richest sounding archaic words in *Leaves of Grass*—were suggested to Whitman by the plays."[20]

But the most sustained attention is given to what Matthiessen calls in his book's introduction "Melville's extraordinary debt to Shakespeare."[21] Herman Melville had compared the moment of artistic awakening among American writers of his own time with "the number of dramatists that surrounded Shakespeare," and Matthiessen remarks that "his choice of the Elizabethan drama as an example was not accidental, for he had just begun to meditate on Shakespeare more creatively than any other American writer ever has."[22] Melville, thought Matthiessen, had come to his profound understanding of tragedy through Shakespeare. "This was the charge that released *Moby-Dick*, and that carried him in *Pierre* to the unbearable desperation of a Hamlet."[23]

Tracing this development, Matthiessen hears every echo, since he himself knows the Shakespeare texts so well. The adviser of his PhD thesis had been John Livingston Lowes, the legendary Harvard professor who exhaustively traced the echoes and references in Coleridge's "Rime of the Ancient Mariner" and "Kubla Khan" in his tour de force of a book, *The Road to Xanadu*. In *American Renaissance*, Matthiessen borrowed that methodology and improved upon it, turning the record of a writer's reading habits into a powerful commentary about American literature and American writers.

Thus, for instance, noting that Melville felt the necessity for thought as well as sensation, even though "thought was painful," Matthiessen includes a footnote to explain what he means: "It is significant that [Melville] checked the note, in his edition of Shakespeare, on Enobarbus's answer to Cleopatra at the moment of the rout of her forces: 'What shall we do, Enobarbus?' 'Think, and die.'" The note said, "To *think* or *take thought*, was anciently synonymous with to *grieve*."[24] In a later footnote Matthiessen, characteristically, names and thanks the researcher who located Melville's copy of Shakespeare, with markings on every page that were "heaviest in *Antony and Cleopatra* and *Lear*."[25] The seven volumes with Melville's handwritten marginal notes are, he says, "now in the Harvard College Library" (as they are still, although they have been relocated to the Houghton Rare Book Library for safekeeping).

Matthiessen was aware that Shakespeare could play the role of a literary unconscious, though he refers to Melville's unconscious, and not his own:

> [Melville's] liberation in *Moby-Dick* through the agency of Shakespeare was almost an unconscious reflex. . . . He did not find a valuable clue to how to express the hidden life of men, which had become his compelling absorption, until he encountered the unexampled vitality of Shakespeare's language.[26]

The word *almost* seems for a moment to be a gesture of denial, but by the next page Matthiessen's magnificent language is in full spate: Melville's "possession by Shakespeare went beyond all other influences"; "Melville meditated more creatively on Shakespeare's meaning than any other

American had done"; "Shakespeare's phrasing had so hypnotized him
that often he seems to have reproduced it involuntarily."[27] Specific examples from *Hamlet, King Lear, The Merchant of Venice*, and *Othello* follow
immediately: "the borrowed material has entered into the formulation of
Melville's thought." A "hidden allusion" (detected by Matthiessen) to
Hamlet's "bourn" from which "no traveler returns" serves "to increase
our awed uncertainty" about the fate of the ship's crew.[28] And so on.

Matthiessen is here using the technique he learned from J. L. Lowes,
tracing the reading of a writer so as to follow the movements of his
mind and his creative imagination. But as he does so, Matthiessen is
simultaneously providing, for us as readers, evidence of his own possession, his own meditation, his own borrowing, his own use of Shakespeare
as an unconscious reflex, a way of thinking. And often in these pages
what is meditated upon is death.

Another passage from Matthiessen on Melville brings more of these
issues to the surface. Matthiessen is discussing "an oddly transformed
allusion" in which Captain Ahab offers a "recombination of some of
Hamlet's words to the Ghost." Matthiessen wants to show "how deeply
Shakespeare's words had entered into Melville's unconscious," and here
is the relevant passage:

> An important contrast between such allusions and those of our age of more
> conscious craft, those in *The Waste Land* or *Ulysses*, is that Melville did not
> intend part of his effect in this scene to depend upon the reader's awareness of
> his source. Indeed, from the way he handles the source here, he seems to have
> been only partly aware himself of its pervasive presence.[29]

Matthiessen then discusses more of Melville's pencil underlinings in his
Shakespeare edition: from *Measure for Measure, Othello, Richard II, Lear*.
But the double-reading he performs (watching Melville reading; detect-
ing the "hidden allusion" and the "oddly transformed allusion" of which
Melville was "only partly aware") is also a technique that can be used in
double-reading Matthiessen's *American Renaissance*. Just as Melville is
"only partly aware" of what Matthiessen sees more fully, so Matthiessen
is "only partly aware" of the double story he is telling, tracing Shakespearean echoes in the writings of his American authors, and adding (as
if they were not significant evidence of his own associations and his own
unconscious, his own thinking) illustrative passages from Shakespeare's
plays.

I have gone into such detail about Matthiessen's use of his authors'
use of Shakespeare for two related reasons. One is simply to stress, in a

way that is partly nostalgic and partly a glance toward a possible future, that the teaching of literature at Harvard (and elsewhere) was done by interested, well-prepared, deeply committed generalists who did not self-identify as Americanists or Renaissance scholars or modernists but who rather—like Matthiessen, Harry Levin, and Theodore Spencer, and others—wrote serious, well-researched books and articles about all of these topics, about the literature and culture of their own time and also about the literature and culture of the past, about America and about England. Matthiessen's Shakespeare informs his American studies, as his study of American authors moves him to rethink Shakespeare. The English Renaissance is alive and well in *American Renaissance.*

My second reason for noting this returns us to the question of translation, understood broadly as working within established codes and finding ways of saying things without saying them, or of saying them in a way that speaks differently to different segments of the audience or the reading public. At the outset I mentioned that Matthiessen's PhD dissertation and the book that emerged from it in 1931 were about Elizabethan translation. I now want to return to that topic, to say something about the role of what might be called "translation" in Matthiessen's own life.

The word *translation* actually occurs in *American Renaissance* in the final section on Emerson. Discussing Emerson's book *Representative Men* (which contains a chapter on Shakespeare, along with accounts of Plato, Napoleon, Swedenborg, and other emblematic figures) Matthiessen writes that

> Where he was at his best in *Representative Men* was in translating Plato into Concord . . . Elsewhere, as in "Self-Reliance," he often said, "Where is the master who could have taught Shakespeare? . . . Every great man is unique." But here he saw that "the rude warm blood of the living England circulated in the play, as in street-ballads." He went even further and declared: "What is best written or done by genius in the world, was no man's work, but *came by wide social labor, when a thousand wrought like one, sharing the same impulse.*"[30]

This "impulse" was Matthiessen's own commitment to left social politics, from his support of the Harvard Teachers Union and the ACLU to his controversial travels in and writings about Czechoslovakia in the Cold War. He often declared that he was a Christian, not a Communist, but his interest in democratic socialism and his willingness to bond with other progressive intellectuals led to his being branded a "fellow traveler." In 1939 he was one of four hundred signatories to an open letter "denouncing 'the fantastic falsehood that the USSR and the totalitarian states are basically alike' "[31] He was active in popular front causes, fought censorship of works banned in Boston, traveled and lectured in Eastern Europe, and spoke out on the question of the United States' potential entry into World War II. Matthiessen was a member of (by one count) some twenty-eight political organizations described as "fellow-traveling and Communist front."[32] These activities put him in jeopardy: the Smith Act of 1940 made it a crime to "advocate, abet, advise or teach the duty, necessity, desirability or propriety of overthrowing the Government of the United States," a statute that was used as an excuse to hunt down and prosecute socialists, labor union organizers, and members of the Communist Party USA.

The Red Scare was also a Lavender Scare, targeting homosexuals because they were thought of as susceptible to blackmail and thus were security risks.[33] The very culture that created a need for secrecy about same-sex relationships could then accuse those in such relationships of having, and harboring, secrets—and of being potential traitors. Translating a same-sex relationship into the simulacrum of an asexual "friendship," or hiding it completely, produced the very "evidence" that suggested, to Senator Joseph McCarthy, the existence of a "homosexual underground." We may recall that Matthiessen's original title for his book on "the age of Emerson and Whitman" was *Man in the Open Air*—a quotation from Walt Whitman, whose own sexuality (and its relationship to his work) would be written about, far more openly than Matthiessen could or would do, much later in the twentieth century. The closet was in every way the opposite of "man in the open air."

In an essay on Hawthorne, Melville drew a strong comparison between Hawthorne and Shakespeare, whom he described as "masters of the great Art of Telling the Truth," but "covertly, and by snatches."[34] Both writers were characterized, Melville said (in a phrase that Matthiessen quotes approvingly in *American Renaissance*) by their "short, quick probings at the very axis of reality."[35] Shakespeare was able to insinuate things, through the mouths of his "dark characters," that were so painfully true that "it were all but madness for any good man, in his own proper character, to utter, or even hint of them." It was a temperamental "blackness in Hawthorne," Melville thought, that made him "a man, as yet, almost utterly mistaken among men."[36]

The aesthetics of the hint, the indirect insinuation or covert admission, was the only way Melville or Hawthorne could approach the articulation a difficult truth. Elsewhere in *American Renaissance* Matthiessen

noted Emerson's attraction to the idea of indirection ("As he expressed
it in a favorite figure, 'The gods like indirect names and dislike to be
named directly'")[37] and identified a similar interest in Whitman ("the
expression of the American poet," Whitman wrote in his first preface,
"is to be indirect and not direct").[38] In this use of indirection as an art
of disclosure that is simultaneously an art of concealment, we may find
an uncanny anticipation of Matthiessen's own "translations," his deployment of allusion as a mode of telling the truth, though "covertly, and by
snatches," in his work and in his life. He was conscious of being "a man,
as yet, almost utterly mistaken among men."

In his early years, certainly, he thought of his homosexuality as something to be hidden, "translated" into a more acceptable mode. He wrote
to Cheney, as he struggled to finish the revisions on his book, that the
"falseness of my position in the world" made the "prolonged chore of
the manuscript" even more difficult. "Consciousness of that falseness
seems to sap my confidence of power. Have I any right in a community
that would so utterly disapprove of me if it knew the facts?" A remem-
brance of their love temporarily cheers him up ("together we can con-
front whatever there is") but the letter then returns to the "false
position" he feels put in by the need to conceal his sexuality and his
private life: "damn it! I hate to have to hide when what I thrive on is
absolute directness."[39]

"An act of translation," wrote the critic George Steiner, "is an act of
love. Where it fails, through immodesty or blurred perception, it tra-
duces. Where it succeeds, it incarnates."[40] *Traduce* comes from the same
root as the Italian *traduttore* ("translator"). It means "to translate" or
"render," but often with a pun on another sense, "to defame, malign, or
slander."[41] Steiner is very likely here remembering, and half citing, for
the cognoscenti, a familiar adage about translation and treason. *Traduttore, tradittore*, goes the adage in Italian: literally, "translator, traitor."
Any translation alters the original text—and in fact, as some work in the
recent field of translation studies suggests, puts the question of an original itself in question. Is a translation supposed to be faithful, as we put
it, word by word? Or is it supposed to capture the spirit, essence, tone,
and nuance of the original through a creative act, an act of infidelity or
treason, that translates (literally, carries across) the experience of the work
into the new (foreign, alien) language.

Traduce, in English, is an uncommon word, now obsolete. Its most
famous appearance comes in act 5 of Shakespeare's *Othello*, where the

beleaguered hero, affirming his loyalty to Venice, tells an audience of ambassadors that when a "malignant" enemy "beat a Venetian and traduced the state" he took him by the throat "and smote him—thus!" (5.2.351–4). On the word *thus* he stabbed himself. The hero's suicide is, paradoxically, both a sign of his despair and loss, and a final affirmation of his loyalty and love.

For F. O. Matthiessen, writing at the beginning of a remarkable career that touched many lives, the decision to write about Elizabethan translation seems uncannily apt. "The translator's work was an act of patriotism," Matthiessen wrote on the first page of his book. "He too, as well as the voyager and merchant, could do some good for his country: he believed that foreign books were just as important for England's destiny as the discoveries of her seamen, and he brought them into his native speech with all the enthusiasm of a conquest." And later on the same page, "An important thing to remember from the outset is that the Elizabethan translator did not write for the learned alone, but for the whole country."[42]

The translator's work was an act of patriotism. The Elizabethan translator did not write for the learned alone, but for the whole country. Here, in this early work by Matthiessen, published in 1931, a decade before *American Renaissance*, we find a prophetic expression of Matthiessen's own credo, and an allegorical vision of his life story—personal, professional, political. As the literary critic William Cain has observed, "In describing translation, Matthiessen is also describing patriotism—the ways in which the literary imagination is vitally connected with the desire to rally and serve one's country."[43] This art of the Elizabethans became, for him, a conducting practice of life.

The "foreign books" whose importation into his "native speech" Matthiessen would later trace were—among others—the works of Shakespeare. *American Renaissance* can be seen as a record of the translation of English Renaissance literature into an American idiom. And the "translations" Matthiessen performed himself in his political and personal life—translations made urgent and necessary by a repressive cultural climate—were acts that touched his teaching, his private life, his politics and his career. "The translator," he would conclude at the end of that early book, "must either suppress his personality and produce a scholarly work, faultless, but without life; or, if he enters creatively into his work, he runs the almost certain risk of adding elements which the next generation will consider a clouding of the spirit of the original." The translators he wrote about "all sinned in this second way," he wrote approvingly, "and yet their work has endured."[44] So we may say of his own.

CHAPTER SEVEN

Good to Think With

An invitation to speak in a Modern Language Association Presidential Forum on the topic of "The Humanities at Work in the World" led me to reflect on a number of moments in my own career, as well as on a set of relevant—and disparate—literary texts. Before I turn directly to the implications of my title, "Good to Think With," I will therefore frame my argument, first with a personal anecdote, and then with a fairy tale. It should be immediately evident that these two narratives are versions of the same story.

When I was in college, I was seized with the idea that I needed to be doing something more important and meaningful than studying English literature. It was the sixties, after all. So I looked up the address of an agency in New York City that arranged for American students to emigrate and do work in another country. I was full of idealism, optimism, energy. I arrived for my appointment and sat across the desk from a woman who was organizing such arrangements. My idea was to get closer to the soil, perhaps, and to the people. So I burst out with my ideas about farming, building, and clearing the land. "Do you have any experience with these things?" she asked. (At this distance I can't recall whether she asked gently or pointedly—but in any case I began, dimly, to get the point.) "Have you ever worked on a farm, or built a house?" No, I confessed. Not yet. But I could learn. "What *do* you know how to do?" she asked. "I study English literature," I said, rather haltingly. Poetry and novels and plays. But I could learn to do useful work, I was sure of it . . . I could contribute to the work of the world. "We need English teachers," she said.

All the way home on the train I thought about this advice, which was surely both gentle *and* pointed. I had assumed that my liberal-arts training, my interest in literature, my interest, even, in criticism and scholarship, were things to be got past on my way to entering the world.

I wanted to work in the world, to do good in the world, to make the world a better place. My interest in, penchant for, obsession with the humanities and the arts seemed to me, at the time, an indulgence, a self-indulgence. What I learned from this experience was that the humanities were my work and that they were already in the world.

That was the anecdote. Here is the fairy tale.

In *The Blue Bird*, a symbolist play by the Belgian writer Maurice Maeterlinck,[1] two children search the world for a special blue bird. The brother and sister, who live in a woodcutter's cottage, have been told that Father Christmas will not come to them this year. On Christmas Eve, as they are peering out the window, watching the rich children next door receive toys, cakes, and fruit, a fairy appears to them in the form of an old woman of the neighborhood and demands that they find the bluebird, which she needs to cure her little girl, who is very ill.

The children set out on their journey. In the space of what they think is a year but what turns out to be a long Christmas night's dream, they travel to the Land of Memory, the Palace of Night, the Graveyard, and the Kingdom of the Future, but although they often glimpse a bluebird, they can never quite capture it. "The one of the Land of Memory turned quite black," laments the young boy, "the one of the Future turned quite pink, the Night's are dead and I could not catch the one in the Forest. . . . Is it my fault if they change color, or die, or escape? . . . Will the Fairy be angry and what will she say?" "We have done what we could," is the answer. "It seems likely that the Blue Bird does not exist or that he changes color when he is caged."

Returning home—or, depending upon your reading, awakening from their dream on Christmas morning—they discover that their own pet turtle dove, a caged bird they have undervalued and overlooked, is in fact colored blue: "Hullo, why it's blue! . . . it's much bluer than when I went away! . . . Why, that's the blue bird we were looking for! . . . We went so far and it was here all the time!"

Our modern cliché about the "bluebird of happiness" comes from this play, which was first performed in 1908 at Constantin Stanislavsky's Moscow Art Theatre. As you can see, it is a close relation of J. M. Barrie's *Peter Pan*, written at about the same date. (Barrie's first book about Peter was in fact called *The Little White Bird*.) But what I want to underscore here is that the children of this story needed to travel around the world, and to the worlds of the past and the future, in order to recognize that what they had been seeking was at home with them all along. They had neglected or failed to value it, because it seemed so ordinary.

Their bluebird, when they finally put it to work in the world, giving it to the neighbor's child and curing the child's illness, ultimately escapes. At the end of the play, one of the children addresses the audience, charging them with the task of finding and returning the bluebird: "If any of you should find it, would you be so very kind as to give it back to us? . . . We need it for our happiness, later on . . ." Curtain.

Whether this play is a parable about empty signifiers, the return of the repressed, the unattainability of desire, or the spirit of Christmas depends on the reader, the context, and the performance. The very phrase "bluebird of happiness," which does not appear in the play, seems to foreclose a decision; the search remains open. But let me draw our attention first to the neglect and then to the escape, of the bird. Where has it been all along? Where does it go? Which is the home, and which is the world?

*

In 1962, the French structural anthropologist Claude Lévi-Strauss coined the phrase that is now regularly rendered in English as "good to think with." It has been so successful that it is now, arguably, almost meaningless, something between a tautology and a cliché. Among the concepts, objects, theories, practices, and organs that have been recently declared by scholars to be "good to think with" are feminism, science, architecture, taxes, the body, food, hypertext, networks, the liberal tradition, capitalism, and the brain. Scholars and theorists are drawn to this phrase, I suspect, because it has certain validating power: it explains, or purports to explain, why we do what we do and why it matters. It seems, that is to say, to explain the work of the humanities to the world—as if the humanities were not in the world, not the same as the world, not the language of the world. No phrase I know of has been more consistently footnoted to a list of secondary sources. That it's not only attributed to Lévi-Strauss but also often as quoted by someone else is a sign not of its elusive nature but rather of its ubiquity.

The actual citation is in Lévi-Strauss's book *Totemism*, first published in French in 1962 and translated into English the following year. The context is a discussion of what would come to be a central practice of structuralism: "How to make opposition, instead of being an obstacle to integration, serve rather to produce it."[2]

This formulation is the primal scene of the binary opposition. It comes to Lévi-Strauss as he is reading the work of another anthropologist, A. R. Radcliffe-Brown, on the persistently interesting and puzzling question of the totem. The key examples from Radcliffe-Brown are two bird clans, the eaglehawks and the crows. Lévi-Strauss claims that "the animals in totemism" serve an intellectual and speculative function. They are not, or not only, objects of symbolism or identification, much less objects of culinary desire, but part of a structure of thinking. Here is the passage, in Rodney Needham's translation:

> The animals in totemism cease to be solely or principally creatures which are feared, admired, or envied; their perceptible reality permits the embodiment of ideas and relations conceived by speculative thought on the basis of empirical observations. We can understand, too, that natural species are chosen not because they are "good to eat" but because they are "good to think."[3]

Bon à penser. Animals, Lévi-Strauss said, are "good to think [with]." This phrase is not really a maxim about animals (or science, or feminism, or hypertext, or any of the other things critics have said are "good to think with")—it is not about the referent, the thing in the world; it is a celebration and a validation of thinking. Thinking that may have its initial impetus in "empirical observations," those vital signs of the social sciences, the physical sciences, or the life sciences, but its payoff is in speculation, which is then reattached to, embodied in, or reembodied in the objects, concepts, or beings that gave rise to it. Now the empirical (or edible) facts reemerge as figures of speech or, more precisely, figures of thought: metaphors, metonyms, personifications, allegories, categories, oppositions, analogies—the work product of the humanities.

For Lévi-Strauss this opposition was central because it allowed one to categorize and interpret elements of culture. The next move, which has proven equally important to theoretical work in the humanities, is to question the boundary between the terms of the opposition, and to use that questioning as a way of thinking beyond an impasse.

What impasse can Lévi-Strauss's opposition ("not because they are 'good to eat' but because they are 'good to think'") help us to think beyond? In our case, it is the demand that the humanities be useful, that they demonstrate their utility, either in terms of dollars and cents or of power, be it ethical, moral, religious, therapeutic, or ameliorative. This is one meaning, though not the only meaning, of "the humanities at work in the world."

Are the humanities "good to eat" or "good to think with"? Before we can refuse this opposition, we should at least examine it.

"Some books are to be tasted, others to be swallowed, and some few to be chewed and digested," Francis Bacon famously wrote.[4] His explanation of this aphoristic statement is less often cited, though it follows immediately: "that is, some books are to be read only in parts, others to be read, but not curiously, and some few to be read wholly, and with diligence and attention." Bacon was a courtier, a politician, a diplomat, a philosopher, and a scientist before that word was invented. His notion of a digested book is the opposite, we might suppose, of the excerpted snippets in a modern-day digest—not only the *Reader's Digest*, still the best-selling consumer magazine in the United States, but also the executive summary, talking points, and PowerPoint presentations of today. Indeed the most modern sentiment in Bacon's essay ("Of Studies") may be his acknowledgment that "some books also may be read by deputy, and excerpts made of them by others."[5]

For another exploration of whether the humanities are "good to eat" or "good to think with," we might turn to a poem by Ben Jonson—where we encounter another set of totemic birds. Jonson's poem "Inviting a Friend to Supper," written in imitation of a poem by Martial, makes it pretty clear that the main focus of the meal will be poetry and conversation. There might be a "short-legged hen/If we can get her," but the enjambment makes it less than certain, and the grand bill of fare is full of ifs.

> . . . though fowl, now, be scarce, yet there are clerks
> The sky not falling, think we may have larks.
> I'll tell you of more, and lie, so you will come:
> Of partridge, pheasant, woodcock, of which some
> May yet be there, and godwit if we can:
> Knat, rail, and ruff too. Howsoe'er, my man
> Shall read a piece of Virgil, Tacitus,
> Livy, or some better book to us,
> Of which we'll speak our minds, amidst our meat;
> And I'll profess no verses to repeat.[6]

The godwit, knat, rail, and ruff are all birds. Even the wine to be served at this supper is bird themed—a "pure cup of rich canary" (the sweet wine of the Canary Islands; though the etymology of *canary* refers to dogs, not birds: the Canaries were the "Isle of Dogs"). But notice that these edible birds are all supposititious meals, not real ones ("a hen if we can get her"; "godwit if we can"; "we may have larks"; "some may yet be there"; "I'll . . . lie, so you will come"). The only certain nourishment will come from books: Virgil, Tacitus, Livy. Good to think with. This is a banquet, or symposium, for two (plus a literate servant), but the avian fare is elusive. The godwit of happiness—or the partridge, pheasant, woodcock or lark—may or may not be captured. (The woodcock was proverbial for its stupidity and thus easy to catch. The godwit, wrote Sir Thomas Browne, was the "daintiest dish in England.")[7] But what is promised on this occasion is history, poetry, the classics—the humanities. A better kind of sustenance.

That was then; this is now. Are the humanities good to eat or good to think with? The concern today would seem to be that there is not enough of either kind of nourishment within what are sometimes now called, in a kind of back-formation, "the academic humanities," a term presumably coined to distinguish them from the applied humanities, the public humanities, and the national humanities initiatives—all of which are more evidently examples of "the humanities at work in the world." Let me briefly describe each of these, since each in a different way interrogates the relation between the humanities and the world, and each offers an opportunity and a challenge for us to rethink our teaching, scholarship, and training.

First, the concept of the applied humanities already exists in academic institutions, and indeed such fields are flourishing: medical humanities, humanities and justice (or justice studies), law and literature, journalism and media studies, applied ethics. They seem to be both good to eat and good to think with, promising a material payoff: a changed policy, an improved world, or a well-paying and influential job. Universities are scrambling to add such programs, since there is great student demand. But there are problems as well as opportunities here— not the least of which is the idea that humanistic works can be reduced to case studies of human decision making and human character. Part of the question is who is applying the humanities to issues of medicine, law, war, ethics, leadership, and management. Often the instructors come from another or partner discipline—law, business, medicine, public service. Increasingly, applied humanities programs are also being established outside universities, in independent leadership institutes and executive training sessions "based on the insights and wisdom of the Bard."[8] (Is Falstaff a good decision maker? What makes Henry V an effective corporate leader?) It's one of the more intriguing paradoxes of our time that executives pay big bucks to attend sessions on topics they didn't think relevant in college. And it's simply not the case that college teachers in the humanities are theory heads or stuck-in-the-archives historicists who don't know how to bring these texts alive in the classroom. The problem is cultural, not pedagogical.

Second, humanities outreach programs for the public are sometimes run by colleges and universities and feature lectures and symposia as well as arts festivals, performances, and postperformance conversations—events designed to bring together what was once called, rather quaintly, "town and gown." The intended audiences are not college students, but people "in the world" (children, working adults, alumni, retired persons). There are political, public-relations, and even financial benefits to the universities in presenting or partnering with such programs. But the presenters are often tenured faculty and emeriti. Here is a situation in which younger, emerging scholars—assistant professors and graduate students—might be given an opportunity to address a wider audience. As every writer knows, explaining a current research or writing project to an interested group of nonspecialists can be extraordinarily clarifying, about both the goals and the stakes of such research.

Last, the National Endowment for the Arts sponsors initiatives like Shakespeare in American Communities, Poetry Out Loud, and the Big Read—the last is a program that describes itself as "designed to revitalize the role of literature in American popular culture and bring the transformative power of literature into the lives of its citizens."[9] I would like to know how many MLA members, and indeed how many college and university teachers of literature, have been asked to contribute to these projects and to aid in their design. "American communities," "American popular culture," and "American citizens" are all located inside as well as outside universities and colleges. What we do, what we have chosen to do, what we train ourselves and our graduate students to do is precisely to revitalize the role of literature in our classes and our writing, and to address—or question—ideas like "the transformative power of literature." (I can't resist pointing out here that one of the first books showcased in the Big Read is Harper Lee's *To Kill a Mockingbird*. Good to eat, or good to think with?)

National prescriptions for the humanities and the arts do not always, I believe, take into serious-enough consideration the commitment of college and university teachers, scholars, and critics. They tend to work around us rather than with us, as if they think (or think that we think) that the humanities in the world is not our business, that educators are not the same as college professors.

So here is my real question: Why should we accept the dichotomy between academe and the world? between our workplace and the world? Isn't the university part of the world, not only in its outreach capacity, but in its everyday life? Isn't the classroom part of the world? If we draw a line between our work in the world and our work as college professors, or if we allow others to draw it for us, we encourage students to think that such a line inevitably exists.

I began with the personal, and it may be useful now to return to it, because there are ways in which my own career as a scholar has always had this binocular, stereoscopic view.

I'm a peripatetic writer. Many of topics on which I've chosen to write seem to be in the world and to be in it in a timely way: cross-dressing, sexuality, dogs, houses, the relation of the humanities to academic culture. I've just finished a project on the arts and the ambivalent relation that contested category has with the university and to the world (including the so-called art world). As a result of the restlessness in my work, which is always moving sideways, associative and metonymically, I've had a chance to speak to a wide range of audiences, from the Fantasia Fair in Provincetown to high-end realtors in New York City, to dog breeders, Shakespeareans, literary theorists, actors, artists, Oprah, and Geraldo. But my books are not principally about the referent (golden retrievers, say, or real estate) but about the argument. They are books about ideas. If love is one of their principal preoccupations—and it is, from dog love to house love—my writing, my work, is enabled by the fact that these elements in the world are themselves good to think with. This kind of work emanates from the university, belongs in the university, returns to the university and to the classroom. It's a place to which I always come home—and home to me means not only the university but also Shakespeare.

In summer 2007 I taught Shakespeare in my university's summer school. The preponderance of the summer students were in secondary school, though some were in their forties and fifties, and a few were in college. The mix made for invigorating teaching. That fall I taught also

Shakespeare in the Extension School, part of the Division of Continuing Education. The typical age of an evening-school Shakespeare student was over fifty, though there were younger people present as well. Many of the evening students were lawyers, doctors, psychoanalysts, businesspeople.

The humanities are now a lifelong learning business, starting young, going on through and past retirement. We need to expand our notion of the world not just in space but over time, widening our sense of audience to include students of all ages. Those I taught in summer school may be back for more when they enter college in a year or two. Doctors and lawyers and high school teachers and other professionals, postcollege, return to the classroom with renewed commitment.

Before you say, "Oh, but Shakespeare is a universal language," I want to stress that both the summer school and the evening school are full of humanities courses—courses on the classics, on philosophy, and on fiction both old and new. Many of my colleagues teach these courses because they like the conversations with another age group, students who are there because they want to be and often at some personal cost. I have also taught an evening graduate course on contemporary literary theory and criticism, with a dozen students, some of whom came from quite far away and after full days of work at other jobs.

I would also like to note that this kind of "inreach" program is enabled by changing technology. I once thought that *distance learning* was an oxymoron, but I have learned in the last couple of years that it can be a vital resource. If we do not learn to handle these new technologies, they will handle us instead. We've become accustomed to using and exploring the tools of the Internet for research. The Internet, for example, allows electronic examination of many rare books. *Digital humanities* is now a common phrase and a favorite one of deans and administrators. But it is not only our research tools but also our students who are distributed across the globe. The world is coming home to the university.

The work of the humanities in the world can include links between universities and arts institutions, on campus and beyond: theaters, museums, galleries, orchestras, dance companies. Bringing the arts into productive relation with scholars and students on campus is a way of making the humanities at work in the university into the humanities at work in the world. Bringing the practice of the arts as well as their history and interpretation into the curriculum—through courses, departments, and programs in writing, art making, film, dance, and theater—is part of this vital project for the future.

Good to eat, or good to think with? The humanities at work in the world or in the classroom? One of my favorite passages from Wallace Stevens articulates the choice that is involved in refusing the terms of this dichotomy.

>   it was not a choice
> Between excluding things. It was not a choice
> Between, but of. He chose to include the things
> That in each other are included . . .[10]

"It was not a choice/Between, but of." The concept of the humanities at work in the world is like the quest for the bluebird: it gives pleasure, it provides exciting glimpses, and it may also lead us to recognize what we have overlooked at home. The idea of the humanities at work in the university may seem overfamiliar, a little drab, not quite blue enough, not the exotic thing we thought we were seeking. But the university and the world are part of a single structure. In both places, in all places, there is a lot of work to be done—work that we are trained to do, that we are training our students to do. We might consider what lies between the university and the world not a boundary but a continuum or a narrative: part of an ongoing and supervening plot, a *fort-da* structure, one of inevitable escape and return. Gone and there, loss and mastery: which is which?

And if what seems most desirable is always a little beyond reach—if the world seems the other of the university rather than its dream self—we might remind ourselves that this idea too is part of the quest narrative and that it underlies all research and writing, all the work that scholars and teachers do. The nearest bluebird may be right behind you, and it may not seem, at first, to be blue.

CHAPTER EIGHT

The Marvel of Peru

Another world was searched through oceans new
  To find the *Marvel of Peru;*
And yet these rarities might be allowed
  To man, that sovereign thing and proud,
Had he not dealt between the bark and tree,
  Forbidden mixtures there to see.
  —Andrew Marvell, "The Mower Against Gardens" (1681)

How can we assess the erotic, social, and political effects of cross-dressing at a remove of four centuries, in the context of a culture very different from our own, and as described in a Spanish-language text? The short answer, of course, is that we can't. In the fascinating and fantastic adventures of the Lieutenant Nun Doña Catalina de Erauso, who cross-dressed her way out of a Spanish convent and into the New World, what we read, what we find, is a version of ourselves.

When Catalina de Erauso fights duels, steals money, leads soldiers into battle, rescues a woman in distress, evades the marriage plans of hopeful widows and their daughters, and marches across league upon league of uncharted Peruvian terrain, it is tempting to see in her tale an allegory of early modern woman's emergent subjectivity. When, acting as a "second" for a friend whose honor has been insulted, she kills her brother unknowingly and inadvertently, it seems possible to see her as a version of Shakespeare's Viola in *Twelfth Night*, stepping into the shoes—and the clothing—of the brother she believes is dead. (It is a happy coincidence that her hometown in Spain is San Sebastian, the name of Viola's lost brother.) When Catalina flirts with two young women, "frolicking" and "teasing," it might seem intriguing to read this as lesbianism avant la lettre, an instance of female homosexuality or, at the very least, love play between women. Yet all these readings are allegorical—that is to say, they are readings of her story as a story *about something else*, readings that offer her life—as indeed saints' and others' lives have been offered in the literary annals of her time and ours—as exempla, as indications of deeper or higher truths.

Such modern readings are no more allegorical, it is perhaps needless to say, than the readings offered within the text itself: the search for the king on Holy Thursday that culminates in his discovery on Easter, the revelation that after all her adventuring (and horseback riding) the Lieutenant Nun remains *virgo intacta*, the close calls (or clothes calls? or close shaves?) in which she encounters first her father, then her mother, shortly after her cross-dressed flight from the confines of the convent, and neither parent recognizes her. She is already someone else. As a story about emergent subjectivity, male or female, early modern or postmodern, Catalina de Erauso's narrative is a description of self-fashioning in which, quite literally, clothes make the man.

We may ourselves mistake subject for object, or discourse for subjectivity, when we regard Catalina's "self" as stable, and her costumes and roles as shifting. One thing that is very striking about this memoir is the materiality of clothing, and its value. Recall that this is a time period far removed from the mass production of garments and the availability of ready-to-wear. Clothing was wealth, and even identity. Actors in the theater wore noblemen's hand-me-downs and were criticized for social climbing, a transvestism of rank or status as well as of gender. Catalina's payment from benefactors and employers is frequently a suit of clothes, and she describes such gifts with distinct pleasure and gratitude. They help to transform her, again quite literally, into another person, with a new status as well as a new gender. Clothes offer sensuous pleasure, wealth, status, and social roles.

Leaving the convent Catalina says she "shook off [her] veil" and spent three days and nights (the Christological interval is perhaps not inadvertent) remaking herself anew, cutting a pair of breeches from her blue woolen bodice, a doublet and hose from her green petticoat. Not long after this transformation, she describes herself finding work as a page and resembling "a well-dressed young bachelor."[1]

Pages are often described in Renaissance literature as beautiful young boys who looked (almost) like girls and could be regarded as sexual partners for men as well as women. Malvolio in Shakespeare's *Twelfth Night*

correctly "reads" Viola's "femininity" when she is dressed as the boy
Cesario, though he doesn't realize what he sees. A male page in *The
Taming of the Shrew* is dressed in women's clothes and pretends to be the
wife of the drunken tinker Christopher Sly. The fantastical Spaniard
Don Armado in *Love's Labour's Lost* rehearses his love discourse with a
page in the court of Navarre. In the Forest of Arden, Rosalind chooses
as her alias "no worse a name than Jove's own page" *(As You Like It,*
1.3.124), and the name she adopts is "Ganymede," a slang term in the
period for "boy lover" or "male prostitute." Since on the English public
stage during the Renaissance female parts were played by boy actors, a
complex eroticism attends these impersonations. Rosalind as Ganymede
at the height of the plot's foolery is a boy (actor) playing a girl playing a
boy playing a girl. "Madam, undress you, and come now to bed," says
Christopher Sly to the page he thinks is his wife, only reluctantly agree-
ing, at the last minute, to substitute a stage play for immediate love
play "in despite of the flesh and the blood" (*The Taming of the Shrew*,
introduction, 2.128).

In the "real life" situations of Renaissance courtesans and prostitutes,
who—for example, in Venice—often dressed as boys, the *frisson* of gender undecidability might be reversed, with provocative results for the
flesh and the blood. "You talk like a fair lady and act like a pageboy,"
wrote the sixteenth-century author Pietro Aretino approvingly to a cour-
tesan in the Italian town of Pistoia. Masculine clothing was stylish not
only in Renaissance Italy but also in England and in France, where in
the sixteenth century no less a personage than Marguerite de Navarre was
described as both handsomely and bewilderingly attired: "You cannot tell
whether she is male or female. She could just as well be a charming boy
as the beautiful lady that she is."[2]

In a later time period equally titillated by gender crossover, Lady Car-
oline Lamb sat for her portrait in the costume of a page and appeared in
that guise at the door of her lover, the romantic poet Lord Byron. "He
was a fair-faced delicate boy of thirteen or fourteen years old, whom one
might have taken for the lady herself,"[3] a visitor reported of the cheeky
young "page." In an instance of literature accompanying if not imitating
life, Byron's poem *Lara* centers on a male page who is revealed to be a
girl, with a hand "So femininely white it might bespeak/Another sex."

The cultural and erotic fascination with pages, their borderline gen-
ders and sexualities (together with the literary and sexual fantasy of
"turning the page"), continued on through the early twentieth century.

In the 1920s lesbian poet Renée Vivien, dressed as a page, posed for a photograph with her lover Natalie Barney. Pageboy haircuts were the standard feminine style for conventional women in the 1950s (the same period that favored so-called "little boy" leg styles on women's tailored bathing suits). Where the page was once a young man who could be taken for a young woman, he/she had become, by the early part of this century, a young woman who resembled an elegant if somewhat anachronistic young man.

But in the Catholic Spain of the seventeenth century, the cross-dressed woman might have other valences and associations besides, or instead of, erotic ones. While England banned women from the stage, permitted transvestite actors, and feared that cross-dressing might provoke homosexual desire, Spain allowed women on the stage, rejected the use of transvestite boy players, and punished homosexuality with death. Female cross-dressing seems to have been viewed with particular concern, since it was banned a number of times—for example, in 1600, 1608, 1615, and 1641. (The ban, obviously, proved ineffective, since it needed so frequently to be renewed.)[4] Pedro Calderón de la Barca's *La vida es sueño* (*Life Is a Dream*), a play dated around 1636, features a cross-dressed woman determined to avenge her own honor, in the tradition of *pundonor*. "As a man I come to serve you bravely/Both with my person and my steel," Rosaura tells the prince to whom she has revealed her true identity. "If you today should woo me as a woman/Then I should have to kill you as a man would/In honourable service of my honour."[5] The medieval Catholic example of Joan of Arc, the cross-dressed soldier and saint tried for transvestism by the Inquisition, is never invoked in the memoir, nor is the more distant but equally pertinent example of Saint Uncumber or Wilgefortis, known as Librada in Spain, the "redeemer of women from men," of whom it is said that, to protect her virgin status, she prayed for Christ's help and was immediately adorned with a moustache and beard; her intended husband, the pagan king of Sicily, declined to marry her, but her father had her crucified. Where Joan and Librada both differ signally from Catalina de Erauso, of course, is that neither ever tried to pass as a man.

In the course of her long career as an itinerant soldier of fortune, Catalina is once stripped and placed on the rack, and on several other occasions her wounds are tended by benevolent strangers. Why does she never express a fear of detection? Wouldn't the stripping reveal aspects of her female anatomy, her woman's body? For a modern reader, much of the suspense initially inheres in the constant risk that her "secret" will be discovered. But these are questions she does not explore and worries she does not manifest. (The episode on the rack seems to have produced no disquieting revelation, since on receiving a note urging clemency the justice instructs the torturers to "take the lad down.")[6] But Catalina de Erauso is much more concerned about self-exposure with people she *knows*: her mother, her father, her brother. It is these persons alone who can return her to an identity she has by now set aside, or moved beyond.

And what about her own erotic life? She says virtually nothing about it. From a modern perspective, gender disguise looks to many readers like a transparent narrative about sexuality and eroticism. But we have in the memoir no articulation of longing, no sense of entrapment in gender disguise, no relief at avoiding male attentions, no sustained temptation to engage in courtship or to take a lover or a mate. Catalina's story does not seem to be about "sex," at least as she tells it. No man ever suspects Catalina's female identity, or makes a pass at her either as a man or as a woman. The threat of marriage with a half-breed widow's daughter or an eager churchman's niece precipitates a little crisis, but it is only a crisis in *narrative*: "I saddled up and vanished." The flirtatious and overly familiar whores at the memoir's end are dismissed out of hand as "harlots" whose honor only a fool would defend. As she tells it, hers is the story of a loner who enjoys camaraderie with men, an adventurer who spends most of her peripatetic career in the New World, yet whose proudest claim to identity is not as a man or a woman but rather as a Spaniard.

*

In England, the Puritan pamphleteer William Prynne was one of many who inveighed against cross-dressing on the stage as a transgression sure to produce immoral desire. During his trial for sedition in the 1630s, Prynne's disparaging view of contemporary hairdressing styles was read aloud to the court. Identifiable gender markings, he had complained, were perversely undone by contemporary fashion. Men curled their long hair, while "our Englishe gentle-women, as yf they all intended to turn men outright, and weare the breeches, or to be Popish nunnes, are now growne soe farr past shame, past modesty, grace, and nature, as to clipp their hayre like men, with lockes and foretoppes."[7] Cutting their hair, English women became—or "intended to turn"—either "men" or "nuns." In either case, the strongly anti-Catholic Prynne maintained, they were behaving against nature.

Yet surprisingly, in the case of the Lieutenant Nun, who becomes *both* a "man" *and* a "nun" in the course of her adventures, no strong sense of moral outrage is expressed by those who learn her secret, no sense that she is "unnatural" or behaving "against nature." In Seville, she became a celebrity. Rather than cross-dressing, the sins for which she needs absolution are more likely to be fighting, brawling, gambling, and murder.

In my book *Vested Interests: Cross-Dressing and Cultural Anxiety*, I describe the literary and cultural phenomenon I call a "category crisis" and a related manifestation I call the "transvestite effect."[8] A category crisis is a failure of definitional distinction, a borderline that becomes permeable, permitting border crossings from one apparently distinct category to another. What seems like a binary opposition, a clear choice between opposites that define cultural boundaries, is revealed to be not only a construct but also—more disturbingly—a construct that no longer works to contain and delimit meaning. Some examples pertinent to Catalina's story might include male–female, black–white, gay–straight, Christian–Indian, Christian–cannibal, Old World–New World, master–servant, master–slave. The appearance of a transvestite figure in a text, I suggest—whether that "text" be an artifact of fiction, history, narrative, or visual culture—was almost invariably a sign of a category crisis *elsewhere,* not, or not only, in the realms of gender and sexuality, but also, and equally importantly, in registers like politics, economics, history, and literary genre. Since, from the point of view of a modern, twentieth-century readership, gender and sexuality are often regarded as a kind of "ground" of identity and identity formation, these transvestite figures mark the narratives in which they appear as narratives of a world under conceptual stress. And the more extraneous the fact of cross-dressing appears to be to the story the text seems to be telling, the more critical the "crisis" of category, the more blurred the boundary that is being, apparently, policed.

After Catalina is nursed to health by a lady she describes as a "half-breed" in Tucumán, "the daughter of a Spaniard and an Indian woman, a widow and a good woman," the stage is set for a category crisis. Indeed, she is remanded into the good woman's care by rescuers whose initial identity she doubts—"were they cannibals or Christians?" The woman's desire to have this apparently eligible young bachelor marry her daughter founders not only on the bachelor's "real" gender identity but also on questions of race and beauty. It is perfectly possible that among the non-narrated escapades of the memoir (Catalina will say much later that "a few other things happened to me. . . . but since they don't add up to much I omit them from these pages") is, or rather might have been, some evidence of (homo)sexual desire. But, as it stands, the resistance to marriage is more strongly marked by aversions of class, race, and nobility than by gender or sexuality. The transvestite effect is powerful in part because it seems both "the point" of the story and somehow something "beside the point."

Catalina de Erauso's Basque identity is another such border crossing. She and her family are proud that they come from the Basque country, a region on the borderline between Spain and France with its own distinct language and culture. More than once in the New World her escape from a tight spot is facilitated by a fellow Basquero. The disruptive gender identities (marked in the text by "masculine" and "feminine" pronouns) and geographical wandering between Spain and Peruare undertaken by a figure already exceptional and transgressive, whose nationality is as complex as her personal history.

Tensions between Old and New World, between Indians and Spaniards, between purebreds and half-breeds, and between the merchant class and the nobility put under increasing pressure by the *encomienda* system of settlement and fealty could be said to have produced a triumphant story of transvestite transgression—or, at least, to have produced a sympathetic audience for such a tale. "News of this event [her confession] had spread far and wide, and it was a source of amazement to the people who had known me before, and to those who had only heard of my exploits in the Indies, and to those who were hearing of them for the first time." Catalina's celebrity was not only a sign of personal distinction; it was, as she tells it, an effect of paradox, risk, and excess. If, as Michele Stepto has said in the introduction to Catalina's memoirs, "in Peru, as everywhere else in the Americas, abundance tended to dissolve ancient links between power and hereditary status,"[9] this was the very kind of category crisis for which a transvestite heroine (and, moreover, one both impeccably virginal and commendably patriotic) was emblematically ideal, a "marvel of Peru."

The poem by Andrew Marvell quoted at the beginning of this chapter is spoken by a mower who deplores the growing seventeenth-century taste in gardening, the desire to alter and "improve" on nature by grafting ("forbidden mixtures") and by importing flowers from the New World. (The "marvel of Peru" [*mirabilis jalapa*], also known as "beauty in the Night" and "four o'clock," a staple of modern gardens, was at the time an exotic flower.) This was a major topos in both seventeenth-century gardening and seventeenth-century poetry (in *The Winter's Tale*, Shakespeare's Perdita has a quarrel with the disguised King Polixenes along the same lines), and it was often taken, as the "garden" figure suggests, as a description of both an ideal and a desecrated Eden, with serious political implications.

In what are perhaps the best-known lines of the poem, the mower laments the ambition of "luxurious man."

> No plant now knew the stock from which it came;
>   He grafts upon the wild the tame,
> That the uncertain and adulterate fruit
>   Might put the palate in dispute.
> His green seraglio has its eunuchs, too,
>   Lest any tyrant him outdo;
> And in the cherry he does Nature vex,
>   To procreate without a sex.

The mower's conservative resistance to "forbidden mixtures" and "uncertain and adulterate fruit" (precisely the titillating transgressions that excited modern garden enthusiasts of the period) may be pertinently juxtaposed to the vogue for cross-dressing and cross-dressing narratives—on the stage, in the streets, and in the annals of popular culture. Were "forbidden mixtures" and the intergrafting of "wild" and "tame" the end of civilization as the old garden knew and embodied it, or the beginning of a brilliant and tumultuous new future?

The anxieties of "adultery," the power of the "eunuch," and the dark fantasy of procreation without a sex appear innumerous undercover forms in *Lieutenant Nun*, all translated into figures for economic as well as erotic violation. The chief insult is *cuckold*; the scenario for a fight is the gaming table. Questions of property rather than propriety are paramount. Catalina, miraculously herself still a virgin, eluding the claims of her "natural" parents and family, confounds the "forbidden mixtures" of gender, sexuality, class, and nation to emerge as a sign of Spain's—and Catholicism's—primacy in a changing and mysterious world. No wonder the king was willing to grant her a pension, and the Pope a dispensation.

A study of female transvestism in early modern Europe by Dutch scholars Rudolf Dekker and Lotte van der Pol records the stage popularity of plays about "the Spaniard Catalina de Erauso and the Englishwoman Mary Frith." As they note, female soldiers had a propaganda value—the monarch could show to the world that "even women rallied under his banners," and the example they cite is that of Catalina de Erauso who lived "a life as a conquistador in South America, where she not only had not behaved like a lady, but in fact not like a gentleman either."[10] Not like a lady and not like a gentleman: as this formulation suggests, gendered behavior in what likes to think of itself as polite society is not "natural" but rather a series of adaptive roles. Catalina, quite literally neither the one thing nor the other, carved out for herself the freedom to transgress, and—like the most successful gender benders of today's popular culture and the arts—was rewarded for her temerity, however briefly, with fame and money.

New World narratives that engage the question of cross-dressing tend to locate it within the practice of the Indians rather than the Spanish. "Cross-dressed bodies," writes Jonathan Goldberg (analyzing an early account of Balboa's visit to an Indian king whose brother and other young male courtiers were said to be dressed in "womens apparell"), "are the locus of identity and difference, a site for crossings between Spanish and Indians, and for divisions between and among them."[11] In the case of Catalina de Erauso, however, the cross-dresser is female, not male; virile, not effeminate; Spanish, not Indian; and virginal, not dissolute.

Accounts of women who dressed as men have proven to be engaging reading for a late twentieth-century public interested in, even obsessed with, the fluidity (and limits) of its own gender and erotic roles. Julia Wheelright's 1989 *Amazons and Military Maids*, for example, contained accounts of numerous English, Irish, American, and Russian women who "dressed as men in pursuit of life, liberty and happiness," serving as soldiers, sailors, and pirates from the eighteenth century to the twentieth.[12] Among them were Hannah Snell, who became James Gray, a British soldier and sailor in the eighteenth century; Christian Davies, an Irish publican turned soldier; Maria Bochkareva, the leader of the Russian Women's Battalion of Death; Deborah Sampson, who fought during the American Revolution while disguised as Robert Shurtleff; Angélique Brulon, a soldier in Napoleon's infantry; and Valerie Arkell-Smith, otherwise known as Colonel Barker. Mary Fleming Zurin's translation of the journals of a Russian officer in the Napoleonic wars, published in 1988 under the title *The Cavalry Maiden*, chronicled the story of Nadezhda Durova, a cross-dressed hussar officer who served in the cavalry for ten years as "Aleksandr Andrevich Aleksandrov." In her hussar role, Durova confesses herself "shy" before women and the butt of jokes from the wives and daughters of fellow officers, who "never miss a chance to make me blush by calling me *hussar miss* as a joke"—not comprehending that their "joke" is a kind of truth. "A woman has only to look fixedly at me to start me blushing in confusion," she writes. "I feel as if she sees right through me and guesses my secret from my appearance alone."[13] Like Catalina at the end of her story, Nadezhda was known in her female identity to the monarch, in this case Czar Alexander I of Russia, who granted her the commission.

Michele Stepto and Gabriel Stepto have enterprisingly opted to use the idiom of the American West in rendering Catalina's story, reminding the reader that "Peru was on the western frontier of Spain's New World empire." They cite Huck Finn as a rhetorical model.[14] Another obvious figure from the annals of "the West" might be the legendary cross-dressed American frontierswoman Calamity Jane, also known as Martha Jane Burke, whose raucous history in Deadwood, South Dakota, was entwined with that of Wild Bill Hickok. An even closer analogue, however—since Calamity Jane married and had a subsequent public career as a woman in Wild West shows—might be the kind of cross-dressed Western pioneer who lived as a man, like the eponymous hero/heroine of the 1993 film *The Ballad of Little Jo*.

Jo (played by Suzy Amis) escapes from her repressive Eastern family and a romance gone awry, donning men's clothes as a way of avoiding men's advances as she works her way toward a rough-and-tumble mining town in the West. Achieving acceptance as a man in a man's world, Jo also finds love and sexuality in a secret relationship with a Chinese-American man she takes on as a hired hand; his marginal status (Asian, itinerant, subservient) balances her own, and provides the set of category crises out of which the film crafts its possibility for boundary-breaking romance. As so often occurs in such stories, her "real" gender identity is publicly disclosed only after her death, when the undertaker comes to lay out the body.

The Ballad of Little Jo, directed by a woman, Maggie Greenwald, is ultimately a tale of female heterosexual independence, with far more in the way of love story than *Lieutenant Nun*. But another signature story of the American West with a similar dénouement (the autopsy surgeon discovers the female body) tells a slightly different tale. The story is that of Jack Bee Garland, writer, newspaperman, and social worker, who was identified on his death in 1936 as "the long-vanished" Elvira Virginia

Mugarrieta, daughter of San Francisco's first Mexican consul, grand-daughter of a Louisiana Supreme Court justice. "She wanted to go to the Philippines in 1899 to see the Spanish–American war front there," reported Elvira's sister. "She couldn't go as a woman, so . . . she put on men's clothes, went over on an army transport with a Colorado regiment, and served as a field hospital worker."[15] After her death—described with unconscious wit by the *Oakland Tribune* as "her passing"—reporters discovered that Jack Bee Garland had had another life in the 1890s as a woman called Babe Bean, an eccentric denizen of Stockton's high society who dressed in male clothing but made no secret of her gender, and was "accompanied by a male companion." Interrogated by the Stockton police, Babe said of her male clothing, "It is my only protection; I do it because I am alone."[16]

Jack Bee's biographer, transgender activist Louis Sullivan, describes him as "a female-to-male transsexual, even though such luxuries as modern-day male hormone therapy and sex reassignment surgeries were not available options during his lifetime."[17] One can almost imagine such a sentence being written about Catalina de Erauso, who ended her life as the Mexican mule driver Antonio de Erauso. But the degree of anachronistic dislocation involved in such a diagnosis—across centuries, cultures, and gaps in knowledge—should serve as a warning against any temptation to assimilate individual life stories toward coherent master narratives. We read from where we are, and from our own cultural and historical position. All our reading is in a sense misreading or overreading. What I want to emphasize here is that such over-determination is part of the pleasure of reading as well as part of its danger. *All* reading is *partial* in two senses—not *im*partial and not whole.

*

In this engrossing and elegantly translated memoir, the reader is afforded a glimpse into a world almost unimaginably alien and estranging. Yet it is at the same time a world whose insistent if limited analogies to modern (and postmodern) experience are seductively present. The effect of the first-person memoir, even mediated through the translators' text, is disarmingly engaging and direct. If self-consciously modern categories like race, class, gender, sexuality, nation, and religion are all at work in this narrative—and they are—their mutual interplay is far from predictable. What emerges is a clear and complex voice telling a story that can be read at once as autobiography and pilgrimage, picaresque and memoir.

Ultimately the question of gender as a category of analysis within seventeenth-century Spanish and New World culture remains a space of negotiation rather than a set of knowable answers. We might compare it to the memoir's constant repetition of the word *league*. In almost every chapter Catalina records her travels: "I left Tucumán . . . and made my way to Potosi some five hundred and fifty leagues away"; "I had no choice but to leave La Plata, and I headed for Charcas some sixteen leagues off"; "they flung me and my two companions out on the Paita coast, a good hundred leagues from Lima."[18] How long is a league? Land leagues of about 2.63 miles were used by the Spanish in early surveys of parts of the American Southwest, but the term *league* is extremely various and contingent in its definitions, ranging from 2.4 to 4.6 statute miles (3.9 to 7.4 kilometers) by some reckonings. In English-speaking countries, the league is often equivalent to three statute miles; in ancient Rome it was 1,500 paces; in the eighteenth century a league was defined as the distance a cannon shot could be fired at enemy ships offshore. In a modern lexicon in which *league* has taken on some aspects of the fantastic or the marvelous ("seven-league boots"), the league, a common Spanish measure, seems in Catalina's account of her progress both excessively precise and excessively general. Catalina's cross-dressing occupies, I want to suggest, the same double terrain of fact and fable. Its "truth" is both literal and allegorical. In *Lieutenant Nun*, Catalina de Erauso emerges as a figure at once male and female, enigmatic and familiar, resolute and endangered, abject and celebrated, elusive and recognizable—a figure, we might say, in a league of her own.

CHAPTER NINE

Third-Person Interruption

If the relation to the other presupposes an infinite separation, an infinite interruption where the face appears, what happens, where and to whom does it happen, when another interruption comes at death to hollow out even more infinitely this first separation, a rending interruption at the heart of interruption itself? I cannot speak of interruption without recalling, like many among you, no doubt, the anxiety of interruption I could feel in Emmanuel Levinas when, on the telephone, for example, he seemed at each moment to fear being cut off, to fear the silence of disappearance, the "without-response," of the other, to whom he called out and held on with an "*allo, allo*" between each sentence, sometimes even in mid-sentence.

—Jacques Derrida, *Adieu to Emmanuel Levinas*

Is interruption possible? Or is the continuity on which such a breach or stoppage is premised itself an enabling fantasy of being, order, and control? Is what we commonly call *interruption* a false construct, an assumption of sequence produced to ward off the fear of being, precisely, inconsequential? I consider the implications of this question here in the context not of ethics but of a recovered literary formalism, a formalism *otherwise*. In order to do so, I want very briefly to revisit one of the most canonical moments of apparent interruption in English literary history.

The most notorious scene of interruption in the English literary tradition occurs at the end of the text—or, alternatively as a replacement for the ending of the text—of Samuel Taylor Coleridge's poem "Kubla Khan." The passage is well known, but it will be useful to quote it here, since it is my intention to disrupt its rhetoric of what might be called interruptability. The poet, having retired to a lonely farmhouse between

Porlock and Linton, had taken an "anodyne" drug, opium, "in consequence of a slight indisposition." He fell asleep over a book, Samuel Purchas's *Pilgrimage*, and dreamed that he could have composed two to three hundred lines of a poem "without any sensation or consciousness of effort." Then came the unhappy denouement.

> On awakening he appeared to himself to have a distinct recollection of the whole, and taking his pen, ink, and paper, instantly and eagerly wrote down the lines that are here preserved. At this moment he was unfortunately called out by a person on business from Porlock, and detained by him above an hour, and on his return to his room, found, to his no small surprise and mortification, that though he still retained some vague and dim recollection of the general purport of the vision, yet, with the exception of some eight or ten scattered lines and images, all the rest had passed away like the images on the surface of a stream into which a stone has been cast, but, alas! without the after restoration of the latter![1]

Generations of skeptical critics, and others with writer's block, have wondered whether the "person" and his untoward interruption were Coleridge's exculpatory fictions—or, perhaps, part of the design of the finished–unfinished poem.

It was the twentieth-century poet Stevie Smith who made a kind of hero of Coleridge's "person from Porlock" and unforgettably tied him to the question of interruption, and, by implication, of the surcease of death. "I am hungry to be interrupted," she wrote.

> I am hungry to be interrupted
> For ever and ever amen
> O Person from Porlock come quickly
> And bring my thoughts to an end.

And again,

> Oh this Person from Porlock is a great interrupter
> He interrupts us for ever
> People say he is a dreadful fellow
> But really he is desirable.[2]

Coleridge was wrong, she declared, to call the "person" a curse, and wrong to blame the untimely visitor for the loss of his poetic vision in "Kubla Khan."

The "person" and his personified interruption have attracted a host of twentieth- and twenty-first-century writers, from Kurt Vonnegut to

Robert Pinsky. Works including A. N. Wilson's *Penfriends from Porlock*, Theodore Weiss Russell's *The Man from Porlock*, Louis MacNeice's *Persons from Porlock, and Other Plays for Radio*, Vincent Starrett's *Persons from Porlock, and Other Interruptions*, and Linda Lê's novel *Kriss: Suivi de l'homme de Porlock* have explored, in tones that range from the genial to the anguished, the vicissitudes of artistic creation, or what Lê calls the demons of inspiration. Pinsky, ruminating—in an electronic journal in 1996—on the pleasures of being interrupted ("like many writers, as soon as I am free from distraction, I begin feeling bitter nostalgia for it") invokes, in a way that now seems amazingly dated, the importunacy of the telephone: "the perfect Porlockian escape . . . With no answering machine here on vacation, I am its grateful slave, answering on the third ring at the latest." Less than ten years later, with cellphones ubiquitous and answering machines de trop, it seems even clearer than it did at the time that Pinsky's Porlock was not in fact an interruption at all but rather part of the *mise-en-scène* of writing. Procrastination, distraction, and time wasting are all standard elements of the writer's daily exercise regimen.

*

> Reports that say that something hasn't happened are always interesting to me, because as we know, there are known knowns, there are things we know we know. We also know there are unknown knowns; that is to say we know there are some things we do not know. But there are also unknown unknowns—the ones we don't know we don't know.
>
> U.S. Secretary of Defense Donald Rumsfeld, winner, for this observation, of the 2003 Foot in Mouth Award given by the Plain English Campaign

> Porlock Wins Best Village.
>
> Tourism information, Porlock and the Vale

In 2003, Porlock, situated at the juncture of Exmoor and the Bristol Channel, was named "Best Large Village" in Somerset. "A village with 1,188 people on the electoral role" (the advertisement did not say "persons," thus missing an obvious opportunity) was deemed "remarkable" by the judges for the range of activities available in what some would have characterized as just a tourist village. The most lauded of Porlock's initiatives, in this context, was its leadership in "a high profile campaign to attract visitors during the foot-and-mouth crisis that devastated rural economies across the country," and "left much of West Somerset a no-go area."[3] Foot-and-mouth disease is an ailment of cattle, although it can be spread to humans. Foot-in-mouth disease is a common affliction of humans, as the epigraph from Donald Rumsfeld makes clear.

For a village, even a large village, Porlock is well connected, with its own online dating service (albeit one that serves, by merely substituting the name of another village or hamlet, virtually all of the UK, town by town). "How many Porlock singles are there? More than one. Chances are that they are listed here in our Porlock personals. You might feel like the loneliest single person in Porlock, but there are so many more singles, and you can find them on our site."[4]

So here is a way to meet a person from Porlock, perhaps one who also regards himself, or herself, as the "loneliest single person in Porlock." A list appended offers "Adult Dating Sites in Porlock," "Porlock Swingers," "Gay in Porlock," and other ways of personalizing the personals. Or of personalizing the persons.

But what is a "person"? Here Freud's "antithetical sense of primal words" seems almost inadequate to cover the possibilities. A person is a dramatic character (the word derives from the Latin *persona*, "mask") and a "real" human individual, a man or woman of distinction or importance (a personage) and a man or woman held in contempt ("a person in trade"; "this person"; "this Pearl person"; "a sort of secretary person").[5] By the time of Lord Peter Wimsey's socially adept butler Bunter, a "person" was the clear opposite of a gentleman. Coleridge's interruptive visitor was "a person on business," and thus perhaps a first cousin to Fanny Burney's "person in trade."[6] Moreover, a "person" is also one of the three modes of the Holy Trinity (Father, Son, and Holy Spirit), and a grammatical class of personal pronouns (first person, second person, third person).

It is in this curious conjunction of triads, the three Persons of the Trinity and the three persons of grammar, that I think we may, oddly, find some speculative space for imagining a theory of interruption.

*

[Patients] seek to bring about the interruption of the treatment while it is still incomplete; they contrive once more to feel themselves scorned, to oblige the physician to speak severely to them and treat them coldly . . . no lesson has been learnt from the old experience of these activities having led instead only to unpleasure. In spite of that they are repeated, under pressure of a compulsion.

Sigmund Freud, *Beyond the Pleasure Principle*

What follows is speculation . . .

Sigmund Freud, *Beyond the Pleasure Principle*

In *Beyond the Pleasure Principle*, Sigmund Freud explores, in ways that have been influential for literary theorists and particularly for theorists of narrative, that impulse to continuity without undo excitation that he calls the death drive, and the sexual instincts that excite and disrupt that orderly process.

> They are the true life instincts. They operate against the purpose of the other instincts, which leads, by reason of their function, to death. . . . It is as though the life of the organism moved with a vacillating rhythm. One group of instincts rushes forward so as to reach the final aim of life as swiftly as possible; but when a particular stage in the advance has been reached, the other group jerks back to a certain point to make a fresh start and so prolong the journey.[7]

On this logic, interruption becomes the very stuff of life: human encounters, falling in love, eroticism, and sexuality are "interruptions" of the seamless, eventless process toward the inevitability of death.

Stevie Smith's poem seems to suggest a kinship between death and the Person from Porlock.

> O Person from Porlock come quickly
> And bring my thoughts to an end.

And

> Oh this Person from Porlock is a great interrupter
> He interrupts us for ever

Her phrase "a great interrupter" seems even, half-consciously, to echo Shakespeare's "death's a great disguiser." In the context of Coleridge's narrative, though, the person from Porlock, while he signals the end of one speculative progression (the recollection and writing of the dreamed or imagined poem), in fact signals, as well or instead, a shift in genre, from lyric to something very like drama. Why has the poem, in its supposedly half-finished state, excited so much interest among generations of critics, poets, and writers? Precisely because the "interruption" creates a new and compelling story, a story not absent but fully present in Coleridge's own prose account of the event. Who was the mysterious "person," and what did he come to say, and why was Coleridge willing, or alternatively compelled, to be "detained" by him for more than an hour—always supposing, of course, that there was any such visit, and any such interruption, at all.

Like Sophocles's "third actor," who comes to signal a reversal and a development in the plot, the person from Porlock is a "third person" who moves the narrative into the dimension of event. The first two "persons," grammatically speaking, I and you, are part and parcel of what might be called the lyric contract. Even though Coleridge's poem begins with a projection, an apparent third person in the personage of Kubla Khan, the structure of address is from speaker to reader, and the word *I* surfaces, twice, in the second stanza. The *you*, or the *thou*, is the reader, and perhaps also the literary trigger of the occasion, the volume of *Purchas his Pilgrimage* over which the poet drowses, in good medieval-dream-vision fashion, as its story comes to life in his mind, and in his poem. But the third person here is extrapoetic, though not extradiegetic. The hapless person from Porlock (an itinerant evangelist? a creditor? a dope dealer? a local tradesman?) shifts the story of "Kubla Khan" away from Kubla Khan and toward Coleridge, or "Coleridge," himself.

Viewed in this way, there is no "interruption"—that is to say, the interruption *is* the story, is the narrative, is the embedded drama. And, arguably, a better story than a two- or three-hundred-line versified version of *Purchas his Pilgrimage* is likely to be. We may note in passing that according to Coleridge it was Byron—"a poet of great and deserved celebrity"—who urged him to publish the poetical fragment.[8] Kubla Khan is a natural topic for the lush exoticism of a Byron. For Coleridge, we may perhaps borrow Samuel Johnson's remark about *Paradise Lost* and say that despite the poet's articulate distress at his loss, none (but Coleridge, and maybe J. L. Lowes) ever wished it longer than it is.[9] The supposed interruption is what we value, and what has made this fragment into a total, mixed-genre work of art.

I suggested that the peculiar structural homology offered in the dictionary definitions of the word "person" between the three grammatical modes and the three Persons of the Trinity might offer some unexpected insight into the question of thirdness and interruption. The complex theological discussions of the Holy Spirit or Holy Ghost have often focused on the role of what St. John called the Paraclete, variously translated as "comforter," "advocate," "intercessor," "teacher," or "helper." One who intervenes. There is a way in which such intervention or intercession may be understood as interruption. But once again it is perhaps equally well understood as something akin to what in psychology would be an event, and what in drama would be plot. The interruption is not an interruption, but a fulfillment.

Derrida speaks, in his eulogy for Levinas, of death as "a rending interruption at the heart of interruption itself," and of the "anxiety of interruption" exhibited by the ethical philosopher in the mundane and risible activity of speaking on the telephone. "He seemed at each moment to fear being cut off, to fear the silence of disappearance, the 'without-response,' of the other, to whom he called out and held on with an '*allo, allo*' between each sentence, sometimes even in mid-sentence." Levinas, that is, created his own interruption, "in mid-sentence," in order to ward off the possibility of another interruption from outside, from a place beyond control. But interruption is part of relation, not its outside: "the relation to the other presupposes an infinite separation, an infinite interruption where the face appears."[10]

What is this interruption that is not an interruption? Again Freud anticipates some of these questions in *Beyond the Pleasure Principle*, by invoking, toward the end of his long essay, the story told by the "poet-philosopher" Plato speaking through his character Aristophanes in the *Symposium*. Here again we have a triad, not a pair: "In the first place, the sexes were originally three in number, not two as they are now; there was man, woman, and the union of the two."[11] According to the fable, Zeus cut these double creatures in half—an act of divine interruption—and they have, in Freud's appropriation, "ever since endeavored to reunite through the sexual instincts."[12] So the life of mankind is an attempt, a plot, to restore what has been interrupted. Or, rather, to acknowledge that that myth of interruption is life itself.

Readers familiar with Freud's essay will know that I have somewhat falsified his conclusion here, by reporting it as if it were a statement, when in fact, in context, this entire speculation is deliberately framed as a question. "Shall we follow the hint given us by the poet-philosopher . . . ?"[13] This long and complex medical paragraph, evoking the "kingdom of the protista," the "protective cortical layer," and allusions to "a multicellular condition," is in fact entirely staged as a series of rhetorical questions, until the great psychoanalytic dramatist senses his moment.

> [Shall we venture upon the hypothesis] that these splintered fragments of living substance in this way attained a multicellular condition and finally transferred the instinct for reuniting, in the most highly concentrated form, to the germ-cells?—But here, I think, the moment has come for breaking off.[14]

Interruption, in all its rhetorical and theatrical splendor, intrudes upon the litany of scientific hypothesis.

Or so it seems. But once again interruption is an illusion, a dramatic event rather than a "real" one. Having opened the door to his own censorious and interruptive person from Porlock, Freud proceeds to demonstrate not only that this person is part of his persona, but also that interruption is not disruption but art and artifice.

> —But here, I think, the moment has come for breaking off.
> Not, however, without the addition of a few words of critical reflection . . .

So also Coleridge, having chronicled the fatal interruption of the person from Porlock, does not rest with his exclamation of loss: you will recall that in returning to his room the poet

> found, to his no small surprise and mortification, that though he still retained some vague and dim recollection of the general purport of the vision, yet, with the exception of some eight or ten scattered lines and images, all the rest had passed away like the images on the surface of a stream into which a stone has been cast, but, alas! without the after restoration of the latter!

Here, we might think, the moment had come for breaking off, but Coleridge thinks otherwise.

> Yet, from the still surviving recollections in his mind, the Author has frequently purposed to finish for himself what had been originally, as it were, given to him.

Thus the interruption, "not without the addition of a few words of critical reflection," has become the new narrative, at least as compelling as the old. The person from Porlock is the figure of and for the third person. His much-maligned and much-lamented visit—scorned not least because he comes on "business" to intrude on the world of art—is the infinite interruption that marks, and does not cancel or block, the relation to the other. We might call this third-order interruption: neither loss nor recuperation, but interruption as transformation and transference. Interruption is the ordinary business of living. "Interruption" is the ordinary business of art.

CHAPTER TEN

Our Genius Problem

When the fortunes of the New England Patriots took a dramatic turn for the better in 2002 after years of disappointment, the media became enamored with the word *genius*. As a sports reporter for the *Boston Globe* noted, an Internet search had matched *genius* with the Patriots' coach, Bill Belichick, "not once, but more than 200 times."[1] And when the Pats actually defeated the heavily favored St. Louis Rams in the Super Bowl, the *New York Times* headline for the Boston edition, in sixty-point type, read simply "DEFENSIVE GENIUS." The text of the article made it clear that this figure of speech had taken hold. Coach Belichick was likened to a "neighborhood tough guy in a dark alley" who "also has the I.Q. of a nuclear physicist."[2]

Belichick was hardly alone in this peculiar species of gridiron celebrity. The Rams' coach, Mike Martz, was touted as an "offensive genius," the Washington Redskins' newly designated coach, Steve Spurrier, as a "genius strategist," and so on through a parade of sports pages, until even the TV commentators began to call for an end to the hyperbole. And as Belichick's father, a ripe eighty-three years old (and himself a former coach), took time out to observe, *genius* seemed an odd appellation for "somebody who walks up and down a football field."

We live in a time in which all terms and traits are inflated, and even the standard size at Starbucks is a tall. But *genius* appears marked for special inflation, so much so that the term *overrated genius* has begun to seem like a tautology rather than a cautious qualification. What is a genius, anyway? And why does our culture have such an obsession with the word and with the idea?

Genius is fundamentally an eighteenth-century concept, though it has had a good long run through the centuries since. The genius was, and to some extent continues to be, the Romantic hero, the loner, the eccentric, the apotheosis of the individual. The further our society gets from individual agency—the less the individual seems to have real power to change things—the more we idealize the genius, who is by this definition the opposite of the committee or the collaborative enterprise. Indeed, some of the resistance to the idea that Shakespeare wrote his plays in collaboration with other playwrights and even actors in his company comes from our residual, occasionally desperate, need to retain this ideal notion of the individual genius. We prefer the myth. It was Watson and Crick who discovered DNA—not a whole laboratory of investigators. Edison invented the electric light bulb and the phonograph—never mind that he worked with an extensive team of technicians, mechanics, and scientists.

The pursuit of genius is the pursuit of an illusion. As illusions go, it's among mankind's happier ones—the idea that an individual might have an exceptional and intrinsic talent for art, music, science, mathematics, or something else beneficial to civilization and culture. There's no doubt that such individuals have lived among us throughout history and have bequeathed to us the legacy of their art and their ideas—but do they constitute an actual class called geniuses? And if so, how can we tell the real ones from the wannabes, the genuine articles from the poseurs?

Over the years we have increasingly tried to analyze, codify, and even quantify "genius," the post-Enlightenment equivalent of sainthood. This wistful quest has itself become a kind of secular religion. Saint Einstein, Saint Newton, Saint Darwin, and Saint Edison have replaced the healers and martyrs of the past, their "miracles" the discoveries of modern science and modern research: relativity, gravity, evolution, electricity.

Artists, musicians, and writers, too, look to the genius standard to separate the "timeless" from the time-bound or the merely timely. In the British novelist Ian McEwan's Booker Prize–winning novel, *Amsterdam*, a self-absorbed and slightly over-the-hill composer, struggling to write a commissioned symphony, reflects on his musical gifts.

> Clive stood from the piano . . . and had once more a passing thought, the minuscule fragment of a suspicion that he would not have shared with a single person in the world, would not even have committed to his journal, and whose keyword he shaped in his mind only with reluctance; the thought was, quite simply, that it might not be going too far to say that he was . . . a genius. A

genius. Though he sounded it guiltily on his inner ear, he would not let the word reach his lips. He was not a vain man. A genius. It was a term that had suffered from inflationary overuse, but surely there was a certain level of achievement, a gold standard, that was nonnegotiable, beyond mere opinion.[3]

As it turns out, Clive is mistaken. His Millennial Symphony, desperately written in high hopes of praise, is a "drone" of sound even to his own ears; later assessments will call it a "dud," and note that a melody at the end is a "shameless copy of Beethoven's Ode to Joy." A worldly conductor, praising Clive's past achievements in tacit contrast to his present ones, remarks with unconscious cruelty, "The inventiveness of youth, so hard to recapture, eh, maestro?"[4] The real barb here is that honorific "maestro": master. Clive has become a public figure and a society success story, but he is further away from genius than he was as a young man.

At this point in history, genius has become a commodity, an ambition, and even a lifestyle. Biographers, scholars, critics, and fans spend untold hours trying to nail down a concept that can't be nailed down, to identify a proof or a marker the way scientists identify genes. At the same time, they seek to "humanize" or "personalize" the story of cultural and intellectual achievement, to make the genius lovable, accessible, and ready for prime time.

Consider an emblematic pair of titles: *Shakespeare in Love* and *Einstein in Love*. The first was the film hit of 1998, with a witty screenplay co-authored by Tom Stoppard; the second was Dennis Overbye's 2000 biography of the young Albert Einstein. Both portray universally accepted, card-carrying geniuses in moments of offstage intimacy. The movie hypothesized (cleverly, although entirely at variance with the facts) that Shakespeare's gift for writing brilliant plays was jump-started when the playwright fell in love with a beautiful, elusive, and ultimately unattainable female aristocrat. Before, he was a hack; afterward, he was a genius. Overbye's book, more grounded in reality, traced the early life of the winning and self-sufficient Albert as he romances women and ideas. The timing of Einstein's two major scientific feats, the equation $E = mc^2$ and the general theory of relativity, coincided, respectively, with his marrying Mileva Marie, a Serbian physics student, and his subsequent struggle to divorce Mileva to marry his cousin Elsa.

Both of these accounts are to a certain extent charmed by, and charming about, their famous subjects. Each offers a "human" genius, one with quirks, flaws, and feelings. And signally in each case, the tag *in love* alludes, finally, not to the human object of passion but to art or science—to the theater or to the universe.

The later Einstein became a cultural icon, personifying genius in look and name. With his unruly shock of white hair, ambling gait, warm ("absentminded") smile, and penchant for going sockless, he was a celebrity easy to love, at least from a distance. The Einstein legend, fully established in the mathematician's lifetime, has persisted long after his death. Walter Matthau (in a fright wig) played him as a warmhearted matchmaker in a 1994 film called *I.Q.*; a photograph of Einstein, his tongue sticking out, adorns a popular T-shirt; and the famous head is the manifest model for "Chia Prof" in the Chia Head pottery-planter series. On many computers a shaggy-haired Einstein "office assistant" can be found ready to explain the mysteries of word processing.

Movies about geniuses, if not about genius, are reliably popular, from *Amadeus* to *Good Will Hunting*. Books such as James Gleick's *Genius: The Life and Science of Richard Feynman* and Sylvia Nasar's *A Beautiful Mind* become top sellers and beget stage or cinema versions. In those books, genius is intertwined with flamboyant eccentricity and iconoclasm. In Peter Parnell's play *QED*, Feynman, the inventor of quantum electrodynamics, acts in plays, performs on bongo drums, enjoys nude life-drawing and the company of many women between his work on the atom bomb and his famous diagnosis of what went wrong with the space shuttle *Challenger*. And the mathematician John Forbes Nash, a complicated personality described in Nasar's biography as having had a child out of wedlock and being attracted to men as well as women, was airbrushed in Ron Howard's film *A Beautiful Mind* into a heroic one-woman man who triumphed over his schizophrenia—a typical film example of the "tortured genius." In real life both men won Nobel Prizes; indeed, the transformation of Nobel medal into Oscar statuette seems like a new kind of theatrical alchemy.

Meanwhile, the concept of genius seems broader than ever and ubiquitous. A special end-of-the-millennium issue of *Esquire* (November 1999) was devoted to "genius" and featured articles on the hidden quirks of famous brains from Benjamin Franklin to the physicist J. Robert Oppenheimer, a "(This Is Not a) Genius Test," and a list of twenty-one inventors, creators, and thinkers ("profiles in brilliance") for the rapidly approaching twenty-first century. "We are lucky," *Esquire* declared, "to be living in an age of genius." And who are these geniuses? A computer scientist (Bill Joy), a designer (Tom Ford), an actor (Leonardo DiCaprio), a basketball star (Allen Iverson), a singer (Audra McDonald), a foreign-policy expert (Fareed Zakaria), a chef (Thomas Keller), a novelist (Richard Powers), an entrepreneur (Amazon.com's Jeff Bezos), a director (Julie Taymor). Their wealth of accomplishment is undeniable. But do they really deserve to be called geniuses?

At a bookstall in the Amsterdam airport I came upon a volume titled *Think Like a Genius: The Ultimate User's Manual for Your Brain*. Written by Todd Siler, a self-described visual artist, technology specialist, and founder of a company that specializes in innovative learning materials "for fostering integrative thinking in education, business, and the family," *Think Like a Genius* is made up of the short, punchy sentences that typify self-help books. This passage is from a section called "You Don't Have to Be a Genius to Think Like One":

> We have been taught that a genius is someone who knows how to think deeply and with originality, an advanced thinker with an expansive mind, such as Plato, Aristotle, or Leonardo da Vinci. We have not been taught that, alongside our most celebrated geniuses, there are legions of everyday geniuses. They're not people who are mental giants. Nor are they intellectual heroes. Their theories and inventions don't change cultures or civilizations. But they have all experienced flights of exceptional thinking, often in some highly practical way. Such is the genius behind the invention of paper, Velcro, staples, nails, steel, glass, cement, currency, and other remarkably "simple" but useful things.[5]

What is especially striking about this book—which carries a blurb from the CEO (not yet mayor) Michael Bloomberg and is studded with cartoons, line drawings, four-step exercises, and advice like "explore your life from a genius's perspective" and "customize some aspects of genius to fit your way of thinking"—is its suggestion that *genius* has become an achievable goal, one of spiritual and commercial value. Resistance to exclusivity and privilege is coupled with a can-do spirit. This, in effect, is a manifesto for genius without the geniuses.

WHAT IS "GENIUS"?

The word *genius* derives from the same root as *gene* and *genetic*, and meant originally, in Latin, a tutelary god or spirit given to every person at birth. One's genius governed one's fortune and determined one's character, and ultimately conducted one out of this world into the afterlife.

The thinkers of antiquity suggested that every person had two geniuses, one good and one evil, which competed for influence. This concept was alive and well in Shakespeare's day and survives in the expression "his better genius." The word *genius* soon came to mean a demon or spirit in general, as in the fairy-tale *genie* or *jinni*. Genius thus conceived was part of a system that would later be called psychology, because it was thought of as residing somehow both inside and outside the individual, and as motivating behavior. Through the Renaissance and well into the eighteenth century the most familiar meaning of *genius* in English was something like "temperament" or "disposition": people were described as having a "daring genius" or an "indolent genius."

Joseph Addison's essay "On Genius," published in *The Spectator* in 1711, laid out the terrain of genius as we use the term today, to denote exceptional talent or someone who possesses it. According to Addison, there were two kinds of genius—natural and learned (the greatest of geniuses were the natural ones, whose inborn gifts freed them from dependence on models or imitation). Homer, Pindar, and Shakespeare were his examples of the first category; Aristotle, Virgil, Milton, and Francis Bacon of the second. In general terms this dichotomy—brilliant versus industrious—still underlies our notions of genius today, but despite Thomas Edison's oft quoted adage "Genius is one percent inspiration and ninety-nine percent perspiration," it's the inspiration that we dote on.

In Addison's day, the idea of the scientific genius was still for most people a contradiction in terms. Science, then and for years after, was more perspiration than inspiration. Genius was precisely what could never be quantified. As Immanuel Kant contended in his *Critique of Judgment*, genius is a talent for art, not for science, since "it is quite ridiculous for a man to speak and decide like a genius in things which require the most careful investigation by reason." The spontaneous generation of ideas that apparently characterizes genius seemed fundamentally at odds with the painstaking labor and analysis that characterize research. "We can readily learn all that Newton has set forth in his immortal work on the Principles of Natural Philosophy," Kant declared, "however great a head was required to discover it, but we cannot learn to write spirited poetry."[6] But in England, in the novel *Tom Jones*, Henry Fielding had already poked fun at the notion of unschooled genius.

> As several gentlemen in these times, by the wonderful force of genius only, without the least assistance of learning, perhaps, without being well able to read,

have made a considerable figure in the republic of letters; the modern critics, I am told, have lately begun to assert, that all kind of learning is entirely useless to a writer; and, indeed, no other than a kind of fetters on the natural spriteliness and activity of the imagination, which is thus weighed down, and prevented from soaring to those high flights which otherwise it would be able to reach.[7]

It was with the Romantic period that the true cult of the natural genius emerged. At the beginning of the nineteenth century, poets and critics such as Coleridge and Shelley, perhaps self-interestedly, staked out genius as the territory of the poet. Shakespeare—or at least the Romantic period's fantasy of Shakespeare—was the quintessential genius, his brilliance and his inventiveness the results of attributes and resources that were innate rather than learned. "Sweetest Shakespeare, fancy's child, warbl[ing] his native woodnotes wild," Milton had called him, and this portrait of untutored genius had an enormous effect on critics in the centuries that followed. The less Shakespeare had been taught, the more genius he had—so ran the thinking then, and so, to a certain extent, it continues today. Thus some scholars exulted over Shakespeare's supposed lack of formal education: he attended only a rural grammar school, not a university; he had, as his admiring rival Ben Jonson indelibly phrased it, "small Latin and less Greek"—though in point of fact the curriculum of the Stratford grammar school, rich in history and mythology, offered a solid training in the classics.

The Romantics differed among themselves in their estimation of Shakespeare's style and his degree of learning, trying in various ways to explain the causes of the poet's supposed barbarisms, separating what they judged his timeless genius from the unfortunate fact that he lived and wrote in a cruder age. William Hazlitt, an influential critic and essayist, catalogued the playwright's imperfections, including his irritating fondness for puns and wordplay and his unaccountable willingness to alter chronology and geography to suit his dramatic purposes. But these flaws did not detract, in Hazlitt's view, from what he deemed Shakespeare's unique genius: "His barbarisms were those of his age. His genius was his own."[8]

Coleridge, on the other hand, argued in a lecture forthrightly titled "Shakespeare's Judgment Equal to His Genius" that the plays were more than "works of rude uncultivated genius." Their form, he thought, was "equally admirable with the matter; the judgment of the great poet not less deserving of our wonder than his genius."[9] Here the word *wonder* underscores Shakespeare's quasi-miraculous achievement. Judgment—in his case, unlike so many others—is not an element that contradicts genius but, rather, a virtue, equally unfathomable, that serves as its complement.

The cult of genius inherited from these Romantic writers, one that still has enormous force today, tells us that ordinary mortals can achieve many things by dint of hard work, but the natural and effortless gifts of a true genius (like Shakespeare) will forever elude the diligent over-achiever. By this logic, genius, and geniuses, cannot be made, only born.

GENIUS AND ABERRATION

The Romantics found genius not only in the supposedly wild and uncultivated Shakespeare but also in the poets and personalities of their own period—in the extravagant Byron and the intense and charismatic Shelley. The perhaps inevitable next step was for an artist to announce his own genius, as did that great self-promoter and fearless breaker of cultural taboos, Oscar Wilde. Flush with celebrity as London's leading "aesthete," Wilde arrived in New York in January of 1882 for a triumphal tour of the United States; he is said to have announced to customs officials, "I have nothing to declare except my genius."[10] Thus genius became not merely a synonym for exalted intellectual power but a performed role. With his ostentatious clothing, his green carnations, his witty epigrams, and his flair for publicity, Wilde became the avatar of self-proclaimed genius.

Where Wilde dared to tread, others followed. Gertrude Stein, with a personality as obtrusive in its way as Wilde's, would claim the mantle of genius for the so-called "lost generation" of Americans who had taken up residence in Europe during the early years of the twentieth century. As Stein wrote in her autobiography, ventriloquized through the voice of her companion and secretary, Alice B. Toklas, "The geniuses came and talked to Gertrude Stein and the wives sat with me. How they unroll, an endless vista through the years . . . geniuses, near geniuses and might be geniuses, all having wives, and I have sat and talked with them, all the wives and later on, well later on too, I have sat and talked with all."[11] On one occasion Stein proclaimed that the Jews had produced "only three originative geniuses—Christ, Spinoza, and myself," a remark recorded in Robert McAlmon's memoir, titled *Being Geniuses Together.*[12]

Over the years there have been pockets of resistance to throwing the term around lightly. "Among scientists," James Gleick writes in his biography of Feynman, "it became a kind of style violation, a faux pas suggesting greenhorn credulity, to use the word *genius* about a living colleague."[13] But in her biography of Nash, Sylvia Nasar uses it relentlessly and unselfconsciously, on page after page, to refer to a whole bevy of mathematicians. Her book includes references to "Nash the mathematical genius," to "the two geniuses" (Nash and his fellow scientist John von Neumann), to Norbert Wiener as "a genius who was at once adulated and isolated," and to the "group of geniuses" in mathematics and theoretical physics who came to the United States from Europe in the years before and during World War II. Not only does Nasar revel in using the word, but she delights in summoning up the attributes and symptoms of genius. She writes that Nash's "arrogance was seen as evidence of his genius," that "a profound dislike for merely absorbing knowledge and a strong compulsion to learn by doing is one of the most reliable signs of genius," and that "Nash picked up the mannerisms of other eccentric geniuses" at MIT, appropriating as his own Wiener's gesture of running his finger along grooves in the tiled walls of the corridors. She also cites D. J. Newman's condemnation of music after Beethoven, Norman Levinson's dislike of psychiatrists, and Warren Ambrose's impatience with conventional social greetings.[14]

For Nasar and other true believers, the bona fide genius solves problems whole, with spontaneous outbursts of inspiration, rather than working them through step by step, or equation by equation, like the rest of us. Nasar often describes Nash as brooding intensely over a topic before finally approaching it from an unexpected angle, startling his colleagues. She writes that he seldom read the works of other mathematicians or engaged in any preparatory research, preferring to come at problems afresh.

The eccentric genius is especially familiar to readers of detective fiction, in which such titans as Sherlock Holmes and Nero Wolfe best their plodding competitors by sheer force of mind and gift for idiosyncrasy. Holmes, with his pipe, his violin, his cocaine habit, his melancholy, his diverse and erudite publications (on topics from motets to shag tobacco, from the ancient Cornish language to bee culture), his avoidance of women, and his disdain for ordinary police work, is a classic embodiment of the genius, as is Wolfe, a portly polymath, didact, gourmand, beer drinker, and orchid fancier, who also avoids women and the ordinary investigative methods of the police. "I have no talents," Wolfe declares with customary insouciance. "I have genius or nothing."[15]

Eccentricity has become such a strong identifying mark of genius that the very notion of a non-eccentric genius seems like a contradiction in terms. Thus in the genius sweepstakes we are drawn to Eugene O'Neill over Arthur Miller, Emily Dickinson over Felicia Hemans, Edgar Allan Poe over Henry Wadsworth Longfellow, and, of course, Mozart over Salieri. General Leslie Groves was delighted to find that his top scientist on the Manhattan Project, Robert Oppenheimer, was fluent in Sanskrit. "To physicists, Oppenheimer's command of Sanskrit seemed a curiosity," James Gleick writes in his biography of Feynman.[16] "To General Groves, it was another sign of genius." *Esquire*'s "genius" issue included a list of "eccentricities" gleaned from pop biographies of "seven bona fide geniuses," in which readers learned, for example, that Orson Welles supposedly wanted to play the lead in the rock opera *Tommy*, that Miles Davis wore his underpants backward, and that Oppenheimer, after he lost his security clearance, drank lead paint to "make [himself] stupider." Sometimes the element of eccentricity seems to crowd out everything else, including the subject's actual achievements—threatening to make genius almost entirely a theatrical role.

The growing perception in the nineteenth century of an inextricable link between genius and eccentricity led some to speculate about a possible connection to a darker form of anomaly: insanity. The English eugenicist Francis Galton expressed deep concern about such pathological undercurrents in his 1869 book *Hereditary Genius*.

> If genius means a sense of inspiration, or of rushes of ideas from apparently supernatural sources, or of an inordinate and burning desire to accomplish any particular end, it is perilously near to the voices heard by the insane, to their delirious tendencies, or to their monomanias. It cannot in such cases be a healthy faculty, nor can it be desirable to perpetuate it by inheritance.[17]

Another British physician who took the insanity question seriously was Havelock Ellis. In his *A Study of British Genius* (1904) he classified geniuses in a number of different ways: those who were insane during a considerable portion of their lives (John Clare, William Collins, William Cowper, Christopher Smart); those who were either briefly insane or died young, sometimes by suicide (George L. Fox, Charles Lamb, Dante Gabriel Rossetti); those who became insane only at the ends of their long lives, suffering from senile dementia (Robert Southey, Jonathan Swift);

and those who exhibited "marked eccentricity not amounting to insanity" (James Boswell, Laurence Oliphant). Ellis paused over the case of William Blake, noting a contemporary doctor's view that if the story of Blake's sitting naked in his summer house with his wife was to be believed, "he was certainly insane." In the end, however, Ellis's findings seemed to refute the notion of an ineluctable tie between genius and insanity. According to his tabulations, only 4.2 percent of his "men of genius" could be counted as insane by any of his criteria. "We must put out of court any theory as to genius being a form of insanity," he concluded.[18]

While the likes of Galton and Ellis were investigating the relationship between genius and insanity, others were looking closely at geniuses for different forms of aberration. The Italian criminologist Cesare Lombroso, best known for alleging (in *The Criminal Man*, 1876) that certain physical types were "born criminals," followed up this study of human transgression with a parallel study of human achievement, *The Man of Genius* (1888), in which he asserted that genius was related both to moral degeneracy (manifested variously as apathy, impulsiveness, sexual excess, morbid vanity, excessive mutism or verbosity, the tendency to put mystical interpretations on the simplest facts) and to certain physical characteristics (prominent ears, deficiency of beard, shortness of stature, left-handedness, pallor, stammering, sterility).

Sixty years later the British physician W. R. Bett devoted an entire volume to what he called "the infirmities of genius," with geniuses and their afflictions neatly paired: "Percy Bysshe Shelley: Neurosis and Genius"; "Algernon Charles Swinburne: Epilepsy and Genius"; "Honoré de Balzac: High Blood Pressure and Genius"; "Charles Baudelaire: Syphilis, Drugs, and Genius"; "Robert Burns: Rheumatic Fever and Genius"; "Lord Byron: Lameness and Genius," and so on. Lafcadio Hearn was called "The Disfigured Genius Who Worshipped Beauty." In his preface Bett announced his project in an uncompromising way: "This book is almost exclusively concerned with abnormal people—with the psychopathology of genius."[19]

QUANTIFYING GENIUS

With the invention of the intelligence quotient, or IQ, came the idea that genius could be quantified. Not surprisingly, this undermined the traditional Romantic vision of the genius as a different kind of being; it was the end of genius's aura.

It's not surprising either that IQ was the invention of an American—Lewis Terman, a psychology professor at Stanford who thought up this device for the scientific assessment of mental capacity at the beginning of the twentieth century. The French psychologist Alfred Binet had in 1905 developed a test for measuring the ability to think and reason, apart from education in any field. He gave the test to Paris schoolchildren, and arrived at the idea of a "mental age," which was based on the percentage of people who could pass a particular test geared for that age. Terman, adapting Binet's method, divided a test taker's mental age by his actual age times one hundred to arrive at the intelligence quotient. The idea was that the population might be sorted by intelligence and funneled into appropriate levels of schooling, suitable jobs, and so forth—all this decades before Nazi science made such categorizations invidious. Inductees into the U.S. Army during World War I were routinely given IQ tests. Britain's "11-plus exams," adopted in 1944, were an attempt to track students by intelligence and merit, and thus to contravene the old class system.

In 1921 Terman and his research team, through statewide testing in California, identified a group of 1,528 high-testing youngsters, whom newspapers called the "1,000 Gifted Children" or the "little geniuses" or, inevitably, the "Termites." Studied over the next eight decades, this group revealed a median IQ of 147, with some scores above 190. It included descendants of Benjamin Franklin, John and John Quincy Adams, Henry Wadsworth Longfellow, P. T. Barnum, Harriet Beecher Stowe, and Mark Twain. It also included Terman's two children. The results of the study were in some ways underwhelming. "There wasn't a Nobel laureate," Terman's successor, Albert H. Hastorf, a former Stanford provost, reported. "There wasn't a Pulitzer Prize. We didn't have a Picasso. It's my guess that Terman was a little bit disappointed."[20] Many in the group went on to become doctors and lawyers, but the label *genius* eluded them as adults. Perhaps the most famous members were the Hollywood director Edward Dmytryk; the creator of *I Love Lucy*, Jess Oppenheimer; and the physiologist Ancel Keys, inventor of the portable meal called the K-ration, who was the only one of the "little geniuses" to wind up on the cover of *Time* or *Life*.

Nonetheless, the notion that there was such a thing as an IQ—and, indeed, such a thing as a "genius-level IQ"—had taken hold in the popular imagination. Thus the gossip columnist who writes a weekly feature called "Walter Scott's Personality Parade" for *Parade* magazine referred to George H. W. Bush's chief of staff John Sununu as "a brilliant academician with a genius-level IQ." But, as the *Washington Post* noted, Sununu's IQ seemed to be constantly on the increase: it was reported as 170 when he was governor of New Hampshire and as "a genius IQ of 176" at the time of the Bush inaugural; William Safire described Sununu as a "quasi-genius, reportedly with an intelligence quotient of 180." The 180 was subsequently invoked by almost every commentator in the press.[21] If an abrasive and strong-willed politico like Sununu, whose IQ score was said to have been based on his responses to a quiz published in *Omni* magazine, was a new type of genius, what did that say about the transcendent cachet that seemed formerly to have attached to that troublesome, enigmatic, and increasingly elusive term? The idea that genius could be quantified and placed on a continuum with ordinary intelligence—that the genius was just like everyone else, only smarter—was at odds with the Romantic notion of the genius as fundamentally different. Yet both ideas proved irresistible.

Once the IQ test had been developed to measure intelligence in the living, it was almost inevitable that someone should wish to test the dead. Social scientists, working under the direction of Lewis Terman, set out to ascertain the IQs of history's most famous geniuses. Terman himself, confessing his lifelong interest in "the childhood of genius," focused on Francis Galton, the author of *Hereditary Genius*, saying that "any psychologist who is familiar with the age norms of mental development" would recognize various details from Galton's biography as "convincing proof that Galton as a child had an intelligence quotient not far from 200; in other words, that his 'mental age' was about twice his actual age."[22]

Much of the excitement about IQ was linked to the growing popularity of the idea of meritocracy; instead of a hereditary aristocracy of the titled and the entitled, there would now be a new, more deserving upper class of eminent or soon to be eminent achievers. The notion that a test—any test—could be completely objective in measuring merit and intelligence faced challenges. In the second half of the twentieth century numerous attacks were made on the IQ system, which was regarded by some as inadvertently prejudicial. The anti-IQ forces were exemplified by J. L. Dillard, who criticized "an intelligence-testing procedure which is completely invalid because of its cultural and linguistic bias."[23] Yet the allure of quantifying genius remained as strong as that of genius itself.

BANKING ON GENIUS

In view of the fact that Lewis Terman's rigorous IQ testing had somehow failed to predict Nobel laureates, Pulitzer Prize winners, and Picassos, the task for a culture enraptured by the idea of genius was to find a means of identifying people of such potential and then helping them to use their gifts.

Since 1981 the John D. and Catherine T. MacArthur Foundation has given out what the media insist on labeling "genius grants" to artists, performers, architects, scientists, and scholars of all persuasions. The twenty-four recipients for 2002, for instance, include a trombonist, a physicist and Internet publisher, a computational linguist, a documentary filmmaker, a glass-bead artist, a children's book author, a paleoethnobotanist who studies fossilized plant remains, a seismologist and disaster-prevention specialist, and a roboticist. MacArthur fellows are chosen for their "individual leadership, initiative, and creativity," according to the foundation's president, Jonathan F. Fanton. The foundation, which emphasizes "the importance of the creative individual in society," scrupulously avoids the *G* word. Where genius actually enters the picture is more in the intentions and fantasies of the program's founder, J. Roderick MacArthur—the son of John D. MacArthur, a financial wizard who parlayed an insurance firm into an empire that included Florida real estate, New York office buildings, and pulp-and-paper factories.

"The idea behind this," Roderick MacArthur explained when the fellows program was begun, "is that Albert Einstein could not have written a grant application saying he was going to discover the theory of relativity. He needed to be free." Recipients have not tendered applications; nor do they submit progress reports after they receive their grants. "There was no management association looking at Michelangelo and asking him to fill out semi-yearly progress reports in triplicate," MacArthur said. "Our aim is to support individual genius and to free those people from the bureaucratic pettiness of academe."[24]

Leaving aside the patronage battles and myriad stresses and strains that did hamper Michelangelo, Einstein, and other geniuses of the past (not to mention the vexatious question of whether the obstacles they encountered perversely contributed to their achievements), what is most striking here is the persistence of the Romantic assumption that geniuses "need to be free." Or perhaps, if we hark back to the notion of genius as an attribute rather than a person, that freedom encourages people to develop their genius.

Another recent effort to foster genius is the Repository for Germinal Choice—the "genius" sperm bank founded in Escondido, California, by the eyeglass millionaire Robert Klark Graham. For twenty years the sperm bank, also described as a "genius baby farm," produced hundreds of designer babies sired by men of proven high intelligence; at least three of the initial donors were Nobel Prize winners. "There is nothing wrong with trying to improve the human race," said Graham, who died in 1997. "Think of all the gains we could have from dozens of children fathered by a Thomas Edison or Albert Einstein."[25]

OUR GENIUS COMPLEX

It is ironic that scientific objectivism about genius is mingled with a strong remnant of what looks like religious faith. The fact is that we cannot bring ourselves to renounce the dream of the superhuman, whether that superhumanity comes in an explicitly religious form or in the post-Enlightenment guise of artistic or scientific genius. Who can forget the story of Einstein's brain—weighed, preserved, for some time inexplicably lost, and finally the object of a scientific custody battle? What was the anomaly that made for his genius? Was the brain of exceptional size? Did it have other signifying traits? As the critic Roland Barthes put it, "Einstein's brain is a mythical object." Old photographs show Einstein cheerfully submitting to testing, his head wreathed with electrical wires, his brain waves mechanically recorded while he was instructed to think of relativity. "Paradoxically," Barthes wrote, "the more the genius of the man was materialized under the guise of his brain, the more the product of his inventiveness came to acquire a magical dimension, and gave a new incarnation to the old esoteric image of a science entirely contained in a few letters." For Barthes, the essence of Einstein's genius was captured in the contrast between photographs of the scientist "standing next to a blackboard covered with mathematical signs of obvious complexity" and cartoons that showed him "chalk still in hand, and having just written on an empty blackboard, as if without preparation, the magic formula of the world."[26]

Deep within us lies a certain strain of longing for genius, a genius worship, that might be described as messianic: the hope that a genius will come along to save us from our technological, philosophical, spiritual, or aesthetic impasse. Is there anything wrong with cherishing this ideal?

What all the IQ tests, brain measurements, and supposedly telltale pathologies show is that genius in a particular case can't be proved to exist, much less effectively predicted. It's not that there is no such thing as genius but, rather, that genius is an assessment or an accolade often retrospectively applied to an individual or an idea—not an identifiable essence.

The words we use shape the way we think. *Genius* has become too easy a word for us to say. The parallel here may in fact be addiction rather than religion: as a culture, we have become increasingly addicted to the idea of genius, so we are dependent on it for a certain kind of emulative high, an intoxication with the superlative. Nowadays it takes more and more genius, or more and more geniuses, to satisfy our craving. It may be time to go cold turkey for a while, to swear off the genius model to represent our highest aspirations for intellectual or artistic innovation. If we remind ourselves that what is really at stake is creativity and invention, if we can learn to separate the power of ideas from that of personality, then perhaps we will be less dazzled by the light of celebrity and less distracted by attempts to lionize the genius as a high-culture hero—as essence rather than force. It's not just another word that we need; it's another way of thinking about thinking.

CHAPTER ELEVEN

Dig It

Looking for Fame in All the Wrong Places

Despite having names of Greek shepherds (Polystyrene, Polyvinyl, Polyethylene), plastic
. . . is in essence the stuff of alchemy.
— Roland Barthes, "Plastic"

The National Book Award for Nonfiction was given in 2010 to Patti Smith for her book *Just Kids*. Since Patti Smith is a rock star as well as a poet and "punk icon," her heartfelt remarks at the awards ceremony did more for the book business than any other tribute could have done. Smith told the assembled guests that as a young woman working at the Scribner's Bookstore, shelving books emblazoned with the National Book Award logo, she had dreamed of writing such a book herself. She concluded her acceptance speech with an impassioned defense of the printed book: "Please, no matter how we advance technologically, please never abandon the book. There is nothing in our material world more beautiful than the book."[1]

Needless to say, this was gratifying. The judging panel for the nonfiction award, of which I was chair, had communicated by phone and e-mail for months, reading and discussing almost five hundred books, and one of the things we had agreed on was that we were not going to be influenced by the review attention a book had received. In his book on literary prizes, James English notes that the National Book Awards mimic the Oscars in promulgating five finalists in each award category.[2] Our five finalists were not the five most noticed books of the year but rather the five we admired the most. When we chose Patti Smith's book as the prizewinner, we felt satisfied that we had picked the best book we had read. But we could not have anticipated how effective it was to have a celebrity of this kind become a spokesperson for the importance of books.[3]

The judges were not seated together at the awards ceremony but were parceled out among the many tables reserved for authors, agents, and editors. When I returned to my seat after giving the statuette to Smith, I thought my evening was over. But to my considerable delight, the fiction prize, the last and often most anticipated award, was given to the author at whose table I was sitting. And the fiction winner, Jaimy Gordon, was a surprise, chosen over a few more famous writers. Her book, *Lord of Misrule*, was published by a tiny independent publisher based in Kingston, New York, which puts out no more than five or six books in a good year. I therefore had a front-row seat as this fine but virtually unheralded writer turned, visibly and in a matter of moments, into a literary celebrity. In the days that followed, her new book was contracted to Random House, the prizewinning book was to come out in paper with Vintage, and she was sought after for interviews and photographs, including a big piece in the *New York Times*.

It's too simple to say that Patti Smith was a celebrity who became a writer and that Jaimy Gordon was a writer who became, at least for this moment, a literary celebrity. But something like that did take place before my eyes. The star was overwhelmed with memories of her early bookshop dreams, and she spoke through her tears. The little-known author, previously appreciated by a loyal but limited readership, claimed her prize and her place in publishing history, all at once.

Writers can become celebrities, but usually not for the quality of their writing. John Grisham and Danielle Steele are celebrities; John Ashbery and John Updike are, more properly, renowned or maybe even celebrated. (I choose them because each is given an appendix in James English's book on prizes, with the long list of awards they have won.) But if Norman Mailer became a celebrity, as he did, it was not, strictly speaking, because of the books he wrote but because of his life and how he conducted it, which won him notoriety. Ditto Truman Capote, and perhaps even Susan Sontag.

In the nineteenth century, before the advent of film, radio, television, the Internet, and so on, authors could indeed be celebrities. We can all name them: figures like Byron, Alcott, Emerson, Stowe, Twain, Dickens, Wilde. But if you type "Wilde celebrity" into your browser today you get a dozen listings for the actress Olivia Wilde (who did, in fact, choose her stage name in homage to Oscar Wilde, and who is, among other things, PETA's pick for sexiest vegetarian celebrity of 2010). "Emerson celebrity" produces either Michael Emerson of the TV show *Lost* or Celebrity Nails and Spa, in Emerson, New Jersey—take your pick. Fame is fleeting.

When *Fame* is the title of a musical, *Notorious* the stage name of a rapper, and *Celebrity* the name of a cruise line (or a hair salon) we have moved into territory where these terms of approbation and rebuke have become brands. The words themselves, rather than anything or anyone they might designate, have become—to employ a recent coinage— famesque.

How lasting is this kind of celebrity?

Imagine that you are a cultural investigator of the twenty-second century and that you are doing a little fieldwork in the Los Angeles area. Your excavations turn up, in the vicinity of what your GPS map tells you is something called a "Chinese Theater," a surprising number of hand- and footprints, and indeed some hoofprints and tire tracks, each enclosed in a concrete rectangle. Looking closer, you see that each rectangle contains a name or names and a date. The earliest names you find are those of Mary Pickford, Douglas Fairbanks, and Norma Talmadge. Those dated 2010 include Jerry Bruckheimer and a mysterious individual who might be a Frenchman, since he signs his name with the single word *Cher*. Hoofprints appear next to the names of Tom Mix, Gene Autry, and Roy Rogers. (Can they have been centaurs?) Cigars mark the concrete squares of George Burns and Groucho Marx, nose prints the squares of Jimmy Durante and Bob Hope. Nothing about these names or prints strikes you as especially Chinese.

You move on to a stretch of disused roadway that seems to have been a kind of promenade or performance space. The area in question, on what your map tells you was once Hollywood Boulevard and Vine Street, is lined with coral-pink terrazzo five-pointed stars, rimmed with brass and set into a charcoal-colored terrazzo background. (Compared with the hand- and footprints, these clearly show an increase in artisan skill and wealth on the part of the indigenous society, and you as a cultural investigator of the future might well conclude that they date from a later stage of Hollywood civilization.) Your map indicates that the area was once called the Walk of Fame. Five different brass emblems differentiate what appear to be ancient entertainment categories: a classic film camera, a television set with rabbit ears, a phonograph record, a radio microphone, and a pair of comedy and tragedy masks. Some figures represented or commemorated by inlaid stars seem to belong to categories or species unfamiliar to you: Mickey Mouse, Tinker Bell, Snow White, Winnie-the-Pooh (here your taxonomy temporarily fails you: what is a "pooh"?), Lassie (perhaps a famous Scotswoman?), Rin Tin Tin (a musician?), and Kermit the Frog. There is also a single star honoring a collective set called the Munchkins, a term familiar to you from Dunkin Donuts, but since there seems to be no entertainment category for food types this may be a regional usage whose meaning is lost. A special group of images commemorates an event designated as the Apollo 11 moon landing, so that among all these images of stars you find, as well, images of four identical circular moons.

Of course, your fieldwork is not limited to Los Angeles. You also find across the United States, in a bewildering range of buildings called halls of fame, relics as various as football jerseys, torn basketball nets, and, in Tuscaloosa, Alabama, the houndstooth hat of someone or something (a totem animal?) called Bear Bryant. (Another sport seems to have had a tiger totem and been sacred to the goddess Nike, but traces of that totem disappear, abruptly, without explanation, in the early years of the twenty-first century.) "Hall of fame," it seems, is an indigenous American usage, even though the architectural iconography of these structures tends to evoke, in a generalized way, ancient Greece or (more often) ancient Rome. The original hall, the Hall of Fame for Great Americans, was founded in 1901 and by the 1970s still existed within a ruined colonnade in the Bronx, New York, but the hall itself, a vestige of its former self, lacked funds needed to commission the bronze busts of its honorands. Although in its day the Hall of Fame for Great Americans was more prestigious than the Nobel Prize, and groups like the American Bar Association and the Daughters of the American Revolution lobbied to get their candidates elected, it became a largely forgotten and neglected relic. Its place in America's heart, mind, and pocketbook was taken by dozens of other halls of fame, many commemorating sports or music heroes (baseball, football, basketball, bluegrass, rock and roll). Not to mention (but of course you will wish to in your research report) the Insurance Hall of Fame, the Burlesque Hall of Fame, the Cowboy Hall of Fame, and the Robot Hall of Fame. Clearly there was a market for them.

As you contemplate this treasure trove of archaeological information, you cannot help being struck by how much the civilization you are

investigating appears to be focused on celestial objects, gods and god-
desses, and totem signs. The discovery of a category called "American
idols" provides an especially rich area for the comparative study of religion. So-called star maps, found in excavated ancient trash barrels, seem
to have guided twentieth- and twenty-first-century pilgrims to the homes
of movie stars. It will be part of your research to discover who or what
these beings were and what was their relation to other clans, tribes, or
castes of similarly named figures, all seemingly connected to the heavens
or to mythological figures of the past: rock stars and superstars, luminaries and idols, glamazons and celebutantes. These last two, examples of
the hybrid nature of celebrity in action, appear particularly Ovidian.

You trace the dates when some of these terms became current in
twentieth-century usage. *Superstar*, an outstanding performer in theater,
music, sport, and so on, dates from as early as 1925 ("cinema superstars") and 1936 ("super-star jockey"); *supermodel* from 1977 (Margaux
Hemingway); *superhero* from 1980; *rock star*, as a general term of praise
(rock star financiers, rock star physicists), from the last quarter of the
century. *Celebutante* can be found as early as 1939 (Brenda Frazier),
though the word came into its own with Paris Hilton and Nicole Richie.

Our description of a fantasy cultural investigation of the future has
not to this point specified what kind of a researcher might pursue these
clues about celebrity. If the investigator is a sociologist or a cultural
anthropologist, he or she might be especially interested in the underlying
causes of celebrity, from an economic or a social point of view. If the
investigator is a specialist in communications, the question of technology
(print, broadcast, Internet, etc.) might be foremost in his or her mind.
In any case, these would be "material culture" investigations, looking at
the institutional substrate, the historical and political machinations, that
produced celebrity and celebrities.

But what would be a literary way of approaching this question, distinct from a sociological or economic or historical approach? I want to
suggest that such an approach would begin by taking the language of
celebrity, notoriety, and fame seriously on its own terms. By looking
at—rather than *through* or *past*—the rhetoric and imagery and metaphors that have animated this phenomenon. By contemplating a cultural
field that has stars, gods, idols, and icons and recognizing that we are
dealing with a full-blown mythographic system.

Just as titles like Duke, King, Queen, Prince, and Princess have
increasingly been applied to entertainment celebrities, becoming in the

process something less like metaphors and more like an alternative system of royalty, so the language of stars indicates an aspirational belief system, midway between religion and hero worship. But the royal and noble monikers applied to celebrities were never hierarchically precise. Would the musician known as Prince (full name Prince Rogers Nelson) outrank John Wayne (Marion Michael Morrison, known as Duke)? Is there an adequation between Aretha Franklin, the Queen of Soul, and Elvis Presley, the King of Rock 'n' Roll? How about the performer Lady Gaga and the country music group Lady Antebellum? Clearly these are moves in the direction of a cultural peerage, but they seem inchoate rather than legible, or accidental rather than essential, in the technical sense in which those terms are used in logic or textual criticism.

In contrast to this loose, nonsystematic penchant for borrowing titles and ranks, celebrity and notoriety have, in fact, evolved into a functional mythographic system, an assemblage of myths forming a complex unity. The myths are those of a particular society—call it modern, or postmodern, culture; in this case the two are the same. Like all myths, these variously explain, allegorize, narrate, and historicize. They are patterns of social credence and social desire.

For all that we hear and see about a revival of interest in traditional religion, some believers require—*instead* or *as well*—a set of myths based on local experience and sightings. Such belief structures need not conflict with or rival what we sometimes call organized religion, and they may even build on it in various ways, from adaptation (the rock opera *Jesus Christ Superstar*) to bricolage (the iconography of Madonna). Gods made flesh walk among us, and their names are symptomatic: Leonardo, Angelina. The word *celebrity* derives from a term for "thronged," not, as we might suppose, from religious "celebration," which is the result, not the cause, of the celebrious event. The presence of a throng (actual or virtual) is the only precondition: celebrity is, in a sense, a back-formation from the capacity to attract a crowd.

The hierarchy of Hollywood, old and new, depends on commonly understood rankings: superstar, star, starlet; A-list, B-list, C-list, Z-list. The Ulmer scale, founded by the film industry writer and editor James Ulmer (the author of *James Ulmer's Hot List: The Complete Guide to Star Ranking*) measures the global value of stars according to qualities like bankability, career management, professionalism, promotion, risk factors, and—last but not least—acting talent. The term *A-list*, coined to assist power brokers and financiers in the canny casting, funding, and production of motion pictures, has by now migrated across a wider field of celebrity and notoriety. *The Oxford English Dictionary* dates *A-list* in this sense to one usage in the 1930s ("an A and B list of débutantes and stag lines"), but most examples come from the 1970s and later, and those who seek a definition of *A-list* are helpfully told to compare this one with entries for *B-list*, *C-list*, *D-list*, and *Z-list* (A: "the most celebrated, sought-after, or high-ranking individuals, esp. in the entertainment industry or the media; a social, professional, or celebrity elite"; B: "moderately celebrated, sought-after," etc., "a prominent but not elite social, professional, or celebrity group"; C: "relatively unimportant members of a particular group," "minor or formerly prominent celebrities or socialites"; D: "the least celebrated or important members of a particular group, esp. in the entertainment industry or the media"; and finally Z: "the very least important individuals, esp. in the film industry; esp. used to emphasize extreme insignificance"). The dictionary's double use of the abbreviation *esp.* (for *especially*) in its definition of Z-listers seems particularly—or *especially*—pointed. Nowhere is extreme insignificance more, well, insignificant, than in the film industry. The possibility of migrating up (or cascading downward) in this alphabetical cosmology is the constant hope (or constant fear) of participants, as well as the constant entertainment and speculation of columnists, agents, and publicists. But what is more important for our present concern is that these terms have now become general. *Rock star* is a common term for a celebrity in virtually any sphere of activity. "In the world of physics," declared *Wired* magazine, "Richard Feynman was a rock star."[4]

A-list, B-list, C-list. In fact, though celebrity may look to some historically or sociologically minded observers like a business or a commodity or an ideology, in literary terms it is a mythology and a reading practice. The narratives of celebrity tell transformative stories. Like the moralized Ovid of the medieval period or the mythography of the Renaissance or the dying and reviving gods of James George Frazer's *Golden Bough*, the elaborate panoply of superstars that confronts us daily on pages of boldface names and in magazines called *Self*, *Us*, and *People* is a reminder of the quest for a new belief structure, a euhemerist vision of humans who can be transmogrified into gods.

There's perhaps no better, or more readable, short account of this process than Roland Barthes's essay "The Writer on Holiday," in his collection *Mythologies*. This brief and brilliant piece has the double advantage of being a literary analysis as well as a portrait of literary celebrity. The topic is a human interest story about a writer, shown off-duty, on vacation, wearing blue pajamas, and eating Reblochon cheese. Although the ostensible point of the article is that such a writer is human like the rest of us, "the balance of the operation," Barthes notes:

> is that the writer becomes still more charismatic, leaves this earth a little more for a celestial habitat where his pyjamas and his cheeses in no way prevent him from resuming the use of his demiurgic speech.
>
> To endow the writer publicly with a good fleshly body, to reveal that he likes dry white wine and underdone steak, is to make even more miraculous for me, and of a more divine essence, the products of his art. Far from the details of his daily life bringing nearer to me the nature of his inspiration and making it clearer, it is the whole mythical singularity of his condition which the writer emphasizes by such confidences.[5]

"Celestial habitat," "demiurgic speech," "divine essence," "mythical singularity"—these are the star qualities that are, paradoxically, ensured by the artful disclosure of human frailty. Or, as another celebrated late-century commentator on celebrity, the musical artist George Michael, remarked, "It's not that there's something extra that makes a superstar. It's that there's something missing."[6]

The gods of Olympus were powerful and flawed: jealous, ambitious, licentious, promiscuous, quick to take offense and to take revenge. Whatever they did, they were always good copy. If this reminds us of celebrity tabloids, we should not be surprised. Gods who exhibit human vulnerabilities often make for stories as compelling as those of humans who aspire to emulate the seeming perfection of the gods. The "something missing" that makes a superstar is not a negative but a positive, an opportunity for identification and connection. What such luminaries lack, what they need, what the audience—the throng—can give them, demonstrates both their godhead and their paradoxical humanity. When Patti Smith wept at the National Book Awards, accepting the prize for a book called *Just Kids*, her memories were of a teenage girl who longed to be a writer—but her tears were the tears of a star.

CHAPTER TWELVE

Anatomy of a Honey Trap

Supporters of WikiLeaks proprietor Julian Assange have protested his arrest in Sweden on sexual charges as a classic "honey trap"—a sting operation in which an attractive person is used to entrap or coerce a target. In this case the claim is that two Swedish women used sex as a way of trapping Assange. Even though the sex was reportedly consensual, the prosecutor allowed a claim of rape because it was unprotected—that is, either Assange did not use a condom (alleged by one of the women) or the condom broke (alleged by the other woman).

It won't have eluded the percipient reader that words like *consensual* and *unprotected* have some resonance in the world of international diplomacy—nor that the *leaks* in WikiLeaks are in this accusation made vividly, and disconcertingly, literal. As for *honey trap*, a phrase more familiar in Britain than the United States, its connection with *sting* seems more than coincidental. The honeybee has long been associated in literature and political philosophy with a model of human society—from Virgil's *Georgics* to Mandeville's *Fable of the Bees* to Tolstoy and Marx. Was this "honey trap" baited to protect human society from the unprotected leaking of classified documents? Was the sting set up to prevent what in apiary culture has been dubbed "colony collapse disorder"? Or were the (former) colonies in fact themselves collapsing under the weight of government dissimulation?

One of the stories that circulated widely via WikiLeaks was the saga of Bruno the bear. The two-year-old Bruno was the first wild bear seen in Germany since 1835. Initially greeted as a welcome visitor to Bavaria,

Bruno soon attracted negative attention by doing what came naturally—killing sheep, chickens, and a child's pet rabbit. The WikiLeaks cable even described him sitting on the steps of a police station, eating a guinea pig. Clearly this was, as the minister-president of Bavaria dubbed him, a Problem Bear. Calls for his assassination went out, despite the protests of schoolchildren, and after a group of Finnish bear-hunters with dogs failed to corner and capture him, Bruno was shot by "an unnamed hunter." All has not been lost however, since Bruno the Problem Bear was subsequently stuffed and put on display at the Nymphenburg Palace in Munich. The official title of the museum is the Museum of Man and Nature. In this case, as more than one commentator noticed, Man seems to have won over Nature.

Bruno's sad tale provoked a good bit of international press, as well as deep mourning within parts of Germany. In June 2006, the high point of the Bruno story, the *Guardian* published a piece on the bear's formerly "idyllic existence." What were his pastoral delights, according to this source? "Swimming in lakes, eating honey and killing the odd sheep."[1] A pattern thus begins to emerge. For Bruno, too, it now seems clear, was caught in a honey trap. Groomed as a national hero, at first expected to bring honor and glory back to Bavaria, he was shot dead within three weeks of his arrival. Was it completely an accident that calls began to be heard for the resignation of the environment minister, Werner Schnappauf? Or was Bruno a plant, and his end foreordained: suicide by honey? In some European languages, the Wikipedia article on honey notes, "even the word for 'bear' (e.g., in Russian, 'medvéd,' in Czech, 'medvěd,' in Croatian) 'medvjed' is coined from the noun that means 'honey' and the verb which means 'to eat.'" When Wiki calls to Wiki, who can fail to hear the echo?

The most famous honey-eating bear in Western literature is of course Winnie-the-Pooh, whose chronicler consistently spells the substance *hunny*. Once again, no acute reader alerted by the WikiLeaks cables can fail to spot the *hun* hidden in this apparently harmless substance. The first of the Pooh books was published in 1926, and the term *Hun* had been associated with the modern German state since 1900, when Kaiser Wilhelm II used it in an exhortation to his troops during the Boxer Rebellion in China. *Hun* was used by the Allies throughout World War I to describe the Germans and their rapacity (derived from *Attila the Hun*), and was again omnipresent in the political language of World War II. In a broadcast on the Soviet–German war in June 1941, Winston

Churchill spoke dismissively (and alliteratively) of "the dull, drilled, docile brutish masses of the Hun soldiery, plodding on like a swarm of crawling locusts." How short a line can be drawn between this Winnie and A. A. Milne's hun(ny)-eating bear? If we add to this imposing list of "coincidences" (worthy of leaking to any embassy or consulate) the fact that, according to the outlier historian David Irving, some of Winston Churchill's most famous speeches during World War II were subsequently recorded for broadcast by the English radio actor Norman Shelley—who supplied the voice for Winnie-the-Pooh on *The Children's Hour* throughout the '30s and '40s—we can begin to see the pervasiveness with which the theme of the honey trap has seeped into the political culture of the west.

And in case we are in any doubt about the interconnectedness of these themes, we have only to consult Frederick Crews's *Postmodern Pooh*, in which a discussion of the symbolism of "the amply proportioned Winnie-the-Pooh tiptoeing on a chair to reach a honey-pot in his larder" dismisses as trivial the allegorical readings of this image as Aspiration, Commodity Fetishism, or Male Rapacity. "Translation itself," we are told, "the escape from literary presence to packaged significance—is precisely the error here. What you ought to be registering is a teddy bear stretching for a honey pot. To insist on further portent is to take a step backward in sophistication."[2] The author of this timely selection signs his name Orpheus Bruno. Could there be any more convincing evidence of the honey trap/Bruno/Winnie axis we have been tracing? Indeed, it requires no translation.

In 1974 the great master of spy stories John Le Carré wrote in his novel *Tinker, Tailor, Soldier, Spy*, "I made a mistake and walked into a 'honey trap.'" But although *honey trap* was originally associated with espionage, the *Oxford English Dictionary* says that it is now a term found "especially in journalism." Since WikiLeaks itself sits at the confluence of espionage and journalism, it should perhaps come as no surprise that its founder has been stung. Yet even in this sticky situation, the documents continue to flow.

CHAPTER THIRTEEN

The Gypsy Scholar and the Scholar Gypsy

NOT AN ACADEMIC QUESTION

I begin with a pet peeve, the word *academia*, which is ubiquitous these days in the public press and seldom means anything nice. "Why is academia so scared of emotion?" asked an article in the Brown University *Daily Herald*.[1] "Politicians Resurface in Academia from Clinton Era," declared a headline in the *Boston Globe*. (What the *Globe* meant was that, having lost a national election, figures from the Clinton White House, like Donna Shalala, Richard Celeste, and Lawrence Summers had all taken jobs as college or university presidents.)[2] The now-deceased journal *Lingua Franca* was described by Kirkus Reviews as "less full of spite and despair over the current state of academia than is, say, *Newsweek* or *National Revi*ew"—and also more fun to read.[3]

It's not a surprise to find that the first citation for this term, *academia*—at least according to the indispensable *Oxford English Dictionary*—is William H. Whyte's 1956 classic work of sociology, *The Organization Man*. Here is the illustrative quotation from the *OED*: "Let's turn now from the corporation to academia. . . . If the academic scientist is seduced, it cannot be explained away as the pressures of commercialism."[4] Nineteen fifty-six has never seemed so long ago, or in such another country.

"Academia," indeed, seems to *be* another country, at least so far as some people see it: "Course management software is not universally embraced in academia," says a business writer. "Some professors have resisted posting their ideas online, considering them intellectual property that makes them unique and marketable."[5]

The *-ia* suffix in "academia" is what's doing a lot of the work here. This termination, derived from Latin and Greek, is used in English for words related to pathology (*hydrophobia, mania, hysteria*), botany (*dahlia, fuschia, lobelia*), alkaloids (*morphia, strychnia, ammonia*), and countries. (All these examples are from the *OED*.) Like Australia, Albania, Bulgaria, Nigeria, Transylvania, or C. S. Lewis's Narnia, nouns that end in *-ia* appear to be places, and—from the narrow perspective of the United States—*other* places, distant in time, space, and reality. Contrast *academia*, if you will, with the more traditional, and irenic sounding, *academe*, which dates in English as far back as Shakespeare, and which, especially in the proverbial phrase "the groves of Academe," has come to mean "the academic community, the world of university scholarship." Academe, as its poetic provenance suggests—seems both more dreamy and otherworldly, and less officious and official than *academia*. *Academe*, it is interesting to note, comes from a transferential error: in ancient Greece it denoted a garden near Athens sacred to the hero Academus; Plato's philosophical school became known as the "academy"; the Latin poet Horace wrote of the "groves of Academe"; and the phrase became common with Mary McCarthy's wicked academic novel of that title in 1951. Academus was never an academic, or a denizen of "academia."

Bearing in mind the etymology of this suffix from disease and travel ("He came down with a serious case of academia"; "I met her on the seacoast of Academia") we can see how the idea of the "academic" as the citizen of some literally "otherworldly" place has taken hold. *Academic* as a substantive noun is another such word, used only by non-academics. As I have suggested elsewhere, the term, when wielded in the media (note *-ia* suffix) seems to conflate irrelevance with arrogance.

No one has written more wittily about this than David Brooks, in his bestseller *Bobos in Paradise*. For Brooks, as for many, the land of academia is bordered by an equally fabled country, "bohemia." *Bobo* is his shorthand term for "bourgeois bohemians." When he remarks—just to give one example—that "Intellectual life is a mixture of careerism and altruism (like most other professions)" and that "today the Bobo intellectual reconciles the quest for knowledge with the quest for the summer house," Brooks's percipient observations still seem on the mark.[6] But recently members of the academic profession, and especially scholars of the humanities, have begun to be concerned, not about the new class of bourgeois bohemians (Brook's Bobos), but rather about another segment of the population: adjunct faculty trying to make it into the ranks of the fully employed. The old jokes about the "leisure of the theory class" ring a little hollow in the face of this professional and economic circumstance.

If many of today's young—or older—PhDs are packing up their lesson plans and getting into the vintage Chevy Nomad to drive down the freeway (or hopping on the A-train to go uptown or downtown in New York City) in order to teach class B at University Y, then on perhaps to teach class C at University Z, what "leisure" can they possibly have to develop a big project? When do they have time to troll in the stacks of major research libraries? And—this is the catch-22—what standing or professional cachet do they have to publish essays or articles in top-shelf journals? (Assuming that in this dire publishing climate those journals themselves continue to exist.) It's true that *PMLA*, and some other journals too, once adopted a blind-submissions policy, but of late even that practice has been augmented by the commissioning of invited essays. And the overwhelming number of journal articles printed in major humanities venues are by people with some conventional university or college ladder status (graduate student, junior faculty, senior faculty). This is what publishers call "platform"—you have to have it in order to present your work authoritatively, and you build your authority by publishing the work. It's a self-contained, circular system.

So here is the question: What can and should be done in academia about part-time and adjunct instruction, the many-tiered system of university employment that requires some journeyman instructors to commute from place to place, from school to school, in order to make a livelihood in this profession, while others move up the standard academic ladder from assistant professor to tenure?

This topic may seem dull and pragmatic, since it does not lead to a comfortable, and familiar, knock-down-drag-out, armchair-quarterback argument about content and style in the humanities—the kind of argument that has in fact animated humanists since schools, universities, and academies were founded, and that has in recent decades produced those periodic salvos loosely known as the culture wars. We know how to deal with such theoretical issues, even if we do not know how to "solve" them. Argument, in fact, is the heart of the humanities and always has been, though we sometimes tend to forget it. Not answers but questions. Not unanimity but debate.

But how can we debate the question of peoples' livelihoods, their craft and roles, the very choice to *be* a scholar, or a scholar-teacher, or a scholar-critic? These various terms for what we do—scholar, teacher, critic, theorist—are themselves nicely contestatory, and I will want to return to them. But the problem of the seasonal migration of independent scholars seeking work transcends and contain these terminological niceties, and at the same time is contained and defined by them.

My contention here will be that, although this question may look like a nuts-and-bolts issue, it is in fact profoundly theoretical and cultural, and that it also crosses into vital and discomfiting territory concerned with class and privilege—topics about which twenty-first century humanists are deeply nervous. And I will argue as well that we are in the midst of a defining transitional moment for the humanities, something akin to the recent bubble in the stock market. Some of the premises on which the current structures are based are unexamined, and others are badly in need of re-examination. One thing we need to think about, and think about soon and in depth, is whether liberal arts education will ever return to the center at colleges and universities, or whether the humanities and the arts are fated to remain, for the foreseeable future, something between a vanity item and a loss leader in the business of pre-professional, professional, and vocational instruction that now dominates so-called higher education.

The whole impetus behind the expansion of the post-war, mid-twentieth century university was the eradication of class lines. To a point, of course. It wasn't until the 1970s that some same-sex colleges went coed; affirmative action, as we've seen, still raises hackles in some quarters; and issues of affordability still create chasms of difference and privilege, with the middle class often the odd class out. Scholarships are readily available to the demonstrably poor, but students from middle-class homes find it less easy to obtain financial support. But U.S. plans from the GI bill to Pell grants, or, in Canada, social science and humanities grants, have tried to make college going, and college teaching, a more accessible goal for everyone. And this has had some unintended as well as some intended effects. It has widened the net, but it has also transformed the content of educational programs.

The problem is not—or not only—the professionalization of the academic humanities, but also the professionalization of undergraduate education. Students are steered—by their parents, by the economy, and often by schools themselves—into courses that prepare them for careers after college: pre-law, pre-med, pre-engineering, pre-architecture. The result has been a decentering or marginalization of the old "liberal arts" curriculum, and especially of the humanities. And the results have been very tangible—and discouraging—for younger (and older) humanities scholars who would like long-term or permanent jobs, but simply can't find them.

The democratization of the professoriat, however, has run up against some ingrained class prejudices from within the educated elite. People, some people at least, have a hard time sympathizing with out-of-work PhDs. (They have even less sympathy, it sometimes seems, for working PhDs.) It was easy for a *New York Times* correspondent on the Modern Language Association beat to make mock of then-president Elaine Showalter's attempt, a few years ago, to inform part-time instructors and new job candidates about opportunities beyond the academic world. That year an MLA survey had suggested that only one-third of job candidates in English found tenure-track jobs within a year of finishing their PhDs. In foreign languages the rate was slightly higher; in classics and linguistics, slightly lower. In any case, more than half the candidates looking for continuing jobs teaching humanities subjects did not find them. Showalter had arranged an opening-night forum named after David Lodge's novel *Nice Work*, at which experts spoke about work in journalism, television, movie making, speechwriting, and business. At the same time as the "Nice Work" panel, the MLA's Graduate Student Caucus met to discuss unionization. They noted that the use of part-time faculty was growing, and that 47 percent of the teaching positions in higher education were already part time.

The *Times* columnist found especially risible the dismay evinced by job candidates. A kind of inverted classism pervaded the article's tone, which made merry with the idea of a "Marxist Literary Group's cash-bar cocktail party," and asked, rhetorically, "Where could one go [at the conference] to forget the sad lives of poor migrant professors and downtrodden grad students trudging from college to college with no office and no money?"[7] The headline made the column's attitude all too clear: "Professors or Proletarians? A Test for Downtrodden Academics." Plainly, the author seemed to imply, these privileged crybabies should just stop squealing about their situation and get real about the real world. (This is what is known as the Marxist-with-the-Mercedes syndrome.) Needless to say, this is not an attitude that is especially helpful, and even the *Times* must not believe that most aspiring scholars these days are still

what used to be called, in the olden days, "dollar-a-year men," who—like
the second sons of the British aristocracy—went into the teaching profession as a kind of upscale hobby.

Columnists' witticisms aside, this remains one of the most serious
problems facing universities and colleges today: what to do about the
growing number of faculty members who teach on short contracts, often
part time, with no benefits or job security, and who wander—by necessity—from institution to institution, never attaining anything like job
security or tenure. These nomadic teachers, many but not all of them
recent PhDs, have come to be known as "gypsy scholars." The problem
is acute, but not new. The term *gypsy scholar* was in use as early as the
1980s, at the time of another supposed crisis in the humanities.

GYPSY SCHOLARS AND SCHOLAR GYPSIES

In 1982 Fred Hechinger, then education editor of the *New York Times*,
wrote a long piece for the paper's Week in Review section entitled "A
Lost Generation of Young 'Gypsy Scholars.'" Hechinger described this
"large and growing group of 'gypsy scholars'" as "recent doctoral gradu-
ates in the humanities and social sciences who wander from job to transitory job with little prospect of a stable long-term career. Some hang on
in one department, feeling exploited in low-paid, part-time positions,
but hoping for that one opening that may just lead to tenure. Others
travel from one short-term job to another. Ultimately, many drop out."[8]
By 1995 these adjunct or part-time instructors were calling *themselves*
gypsy scholars and were trying to organize, unionize, and lobby for things
like health benefits, better working conditions, and job security.[9]

"Gypsy Scholars Roam Academic Landscape," declared another article in the *New York Times* that year, noting that, according to the
National Center for Education Statistics, an estimated 15–30 percent of
all junior faculty members move from one job to another each year.
"The gypsy scholars rarely live in a place long enough to establish roots
and often feel like outsiders in their own departments," the *Times*
reported.[10] (By 1998 about 7 percent of all faculty would be full time,
non–tenure track.) It is of some interest—at least to me—that one of the
figures featured in this article, described in 1982 as "now unemployed
and disenchanted with teaching," was Russell Jacoby, now an established
historian and critic of the academy, whose publications include *The Last*

Intellectuals: American Culture in the Age of Academe (1987), *Dogmatic Education: How the Culture Wars Divert Education and Distract America* (1994), and *The End of Utopia: Politics and Culture in the Age of Apathy* (1999). Jacoby's rueful prediction back then—"We won't be hired anymore as beginners and we won't be hired as tenured professors"— happily turned out, in his case, to be untrue, and his experience clearly gave him material that fueled his polemic writing. Indeed, it's arguable that his career was shaped as much by these "lost years" of academic wandering (in the course of five years, he told the *New York Times*, he taught history at Brandeis, Boston University, UCLA, and Irvine) as by his doctoral work. By an odd quirk of coincidence—if it is that—it was Jacoby who is often credited with having coined the phrase *public intellectual*.

There is a certain irony to the occurrence and popularity of this "gypsy scholar" label, since it so directly echoes (and inverts) the title of Matthew Arnold's famous poem, "The Scholar Gipsy," a poem idealizing the life of the mind, and, in particular, the life of the Oxford scholar untrammeled by "the strange disease of modern life."

I say the poem is famous, and indeed it was so for over a hundred years. To Arnold's contemporaries, he was a poet, the author of "Dover Beach," "Stanzas on the Grande Chartreuse," and "Empedocles on Etna." To later generations he became a Victorian sage, far better known for his prose essays than for his verse, and, in the latter part of the twentieth century, a target for political and literary theorists.

The author of *Culture and Anarchy*, the passionate advocate of critical "disinterestedness" and of the value of literary "touchstones" in creating a common stock of (English) high culture, Arnold was the critic the late twentieth century loved to scorn. Held up, curiously, as the apostle of snootiness, this career schools-inspector, the author of three books on European systems of education. In *Culture and Anarchy* Arnold divided the English population into Barbarians (the aristocracy), Philistines (the middle classes) and the Populace (the working classes). What could unify, and what could improve and develop, these unhopeful-sounding groups of disparate individuals? Arnold's answer, astonishing in the light of today's general dismissal of the importance of the humanities, was *literature*.

Literature, and specifically poetry, was itself a cultural value for Matthew Arnold, one that could change the world. Arnold, professor of poetry at Oxford from 1857 to 1867, put the case for criticism, an entity that he defined, polemically, as "*a disinterested endeavour to learn and propagate the best that is known and thought in the world.*" The italics are his. He meant this to be a polemical statement, not a truism. Arnold was dismissive of much of "the current English literature of the day," preferring European criticism, "a criticism which regards Europe as being, for intellectual and spiritual purposes, one great confederation, bound to a joint action and working for a common result; and whose members have, for their proper outfit, a knowledge of Greek, Roman, and Eastern antiquity, and of one another."[11] This was one hundred fifty years ago. Criticism, says Arnold (again famously) must be "sincere, simple, flexible, ardent, ever widening its knowledge."[12] Notice *flexible*, a key term for him; it is Matthew Arnold, not Jacques Derrida, who first writes of the importance of the "free play of the mind."[13] This is the criticism that "can help us in the future." Although criticism can never approach the importance of "genuine creation" in literature—the critic should not confuse himself with Shakespeare or with Aeschylus—still "the critical power," he argued, "tends, at last, to make an intellectual situation of which the creative power can profitably avail itself," so as to make "the best ideas prevail."[14]

In an era when words like *best* are suspect intellectually—though acceptable when wielded in publications like *Zagat's* or *Consumer Reports*—Matthew Arnold has often been flattened into a caricature. But this self-confessed dandy, full of witty chat and "persiflage," was a far less stodgy figure than his opponents have wanted to assume.

"The Scholar Gipsy," Arnold's early and very successful poem, is a clear descendant of Milton, Wordsworth, Keats, and Gray. (If the poem it were a horse, we might say it was by "Lycidas" out of "The Solitary Reaper," or by "Indolence" out of "Country Churchyard.") The poet addresses a companion, conventionally described as a shepherd (literary-speak for *poet*) who is sent off to tend the flocks while the poet-speaker, lying in an English field within sight of the towers of Oxford, lies down in the shade to read a book. The companion-shepherd is sometimes identified as Arnold's friend, the Victorian poet Arthur Hugh Clough. And the format is familiar from the old medieval dream vision: the reader, drowsing, enters the world of his book, from which he will later rudely awake.

What is the speaker reading? An "oft-read tale" by the seventeenth-century Oxford student and philosopher Joseph Glanvill: the story, according to Arnold, of a poor Oxford scholar who, "tired of knocking

at preferment's door" (i.e., looking for a job), forsakes his university
friends and goes off to join the gypsies, "to learn the gipsy-lore." A few
years later the scholar encounters some college friends, and tells them
the gypsies have "arts to rule as they desired / The workings of men's
brains"—arts of insight, control, and understanding that he intends to
learn. "That said, he left them, and returned no more." But "rumours
hung about the countryside" that the scholar-gypsy has been "seen by
rare glimpses," and has then disappeared or faded away. At this point, in
chronicling the various kinds of persons who have reported scholar-gypsy
sightings, the poet-speaker changes his mode of address and begins to
speak not to his shepherd companion but directly to the scholar-gypsy:
"I myself seem half to know thy looks" (62); "For most, I know, thou
lov'st retired ground" (71); "And then they land, and thou art seen no
more!" (81) Shepherds, students, maidens, housewives, children (everyone but academics) see the gypsy—as the year turns from spring to summer to autumn to winter, and from May to June to April, the scholar-
gypsy is glimpsed in the towns and woods abutting Oxford, until finally
there takes place what seems to be a direct encounter between poet and
spectral scholar.

> And once, in winter, on the causeway chill
> Where home through flooded fields foot-travellers go
> Have I not passed thee on the wooden bridge,
> Wrapped in thy cloak and battling with the snow . . .
> (121–24)

As soon as this confrontation is suggested, however, it is withdrawn, and
the poem performs a Keatsian reversal.

> But what—I dream! Two hundred years are flown
> Since first thy story ran through Oxford halls,
> And the grave Glanville did the tale inscribe
> That thou wert wandered from the studious walls
> To learn strange arts, and join a gipsy-tribe.
> (131–34)

During this time the world has changed, and for the worse. The single-
minded seventeenth-century scholar-gypsy, who had "*one* aim, *one* business, *one* desire" (152), seems to exemplify the Unfallen Intellectual,
whose singularity of focus (here described as a quest for knowledge rather
than a search for gainful employment) puts the fallen modern world to

shame. "O life unlike to ours!" the poet exclaims. In Arnold's vision of modernity "light half-believers of our casual creeds" (172) suffer "sick fatigue" and "languid doubt" (164), and romantic suffering is its own end.

> Who most has suffered, takes dejectedly
> His seat upon the intellectual throne.
>> (183–84)

The poem's most celebrated stanza, often quoted out of context as if it embodied Arnold's own philosophy, is a ringing paean to the supposed purity of the past.

> O born in days when wits were fresh and clear,
>> And life ran gaily as the sparking Thames;
>>> Before this strange disease of modern life,
>> With its sick hurry, its divided aims,
>>> Its heads o'ertaxed, its palsied hearts, was rife—
>>>> Fly hence, our contact fear!
>> Still fly, plunge deeper in the bowering wood!
>>> (201–7)

Like Keats's nightingale, or any of a host of Victorian ghosts and specters, the scholar-gypsy, a "truant boy," eludes capture, escapes modernity and mortality, the "feverish contact," and the "infection of our mental strife." As the editor of one late-twentieth-century edition of Arnold's poems comments, "An acute sense of the special difficulties of Victorian times is needed to see the scholar-gipsy's seventeenth century as an era of 'the fond believing lyre,'"[15] but the point, of course, is that the modern world and this older, idealized figure are incompatible. The poem has elicited a variety of differing interpretations: G. Wilson Knight read the "scholar-gipsy" as a figure for the eternal Oxford undergraduate; others have seen him as an element of the English landscape, or the "tragic impasse of the Victorian age."[16]

For us, he may well be taken to represent the profession we *dreamed* of entering, the life of the mind, that drew so many of us to "academia" in the first place but that now seems so elusive and even delusory (as we wrestle with increasing amounts of committee work, letters of recommendation, papers to grade, publishing deadlines, etc.). The disappearing scholar-gipsy, like any infinite regress of wishing, is desirable in proportion to his inaccessibility. The harder he is to find, the more desirable his life seems to be.

We now need to move back two centuries, to a founding moment in the life of the mind. The story of the scholar-gypsy is taken, as Arnold notes, from Jospeh Glanvill's book *The Vanity of Dogmatizing*, published in 1661, when he was the precocious of age of twenty-five. The book was a lively, metaphorical, and enthusiastic account of intellectual life and its discontents. This is his acerbic account. We could find something similar on the op-ed pages of a newspaper today: "The disease of our intellectuals is too great, not to be its own diagnostic; and they that feel it not, are not less sick, but stupidly so. The weakness of human understanding, all will confess; yet the confidence of most in their own reasonings, practically disowns it; And 'tis easier to persuade them of it from others' lapses than their own; for that while all complain of our ignorance and error, every one exempts himself."[17]

Here is Glanvill's version of the tale of the Oxford scholar who joins the gypsies, rendered in modern spelling but retaining the episodic narrative tone of the original:

There was very lately a lad in the University of Oxford, who being of very pregnant and ready parts, and yet wanting the encouragement of preferment; was by his poverty forced to leave his studies there, and to cast himself upon the wide world for a livelihood. Now, his necessities growing daily on him, and wanting the help of friends to relieve him; he was at last forced to join himself to a company of vagabond gypsies, whom occasionally he met with, and to follow their trade for a maintenance. Among these extravagant people, by the insinuating subtlety of his carriage, he quickly got so much of their love, and esteem; as that they discovered to him their mystery; in the practice of which, by the pregnancy of his wit and parts he soon grew so good a proficient, as to be able to out-do his instructors. After he had been a pretty while well exercised in the trade there chanced to ride by a couple of scholars who had once been of his acquaintance. These scholars had quickly spied out their old friend, among the gypsies; and their amazement to see him among such society, had well-high discovered him; but by a sign he prevented their owning him before that crew; and taking one of them aside privately, desired him with his friend to go to an inn, not far distant thence, promising there to come to him. They accordingly went thither, and he follows: after their first salutations, his friends enquire how he came to lead so odd a life as that was, and to join himself with such a cheating beggarly company. The Scholar-Gypsy having given them an account of the necessity, which drove him to that kind of life; told them, that the people he went with were not such impostors as they were taken for, but that they had a traditional kind of learning among them, and could do wonders by the power of imagination, and that himself had learned much of their art, and improved it further than themselves could. And to evince the truth of what he told them, he said, he'd remove into another room, leaving them to discourse together; and upon his return tell them the sum of what they had talked of; which accordingly he performed, giving them a full account of what had passed between them in his absence. The scholars being amazed at so unexpected a discovery, earnestly desired him to unriddle the mystery. In which he gave them satisfaction, by telling them, that what he did was by the power of imagination, his fancy binding theirs; and that himself had dictated to them the discourse, they held together, while he was from them: That there were warrantable ways of heightening the imagination to that pitch, as to bind another's; and that when he had compassed the whole secret, some parts of which he said he was yet ignorant of, he intended to leave their company, and give the world an account of what he had learned.[18]

What may not be perfectly clear from this excerpt is the fact that Glanvill's entire interest was in the power of sympathetic imagination, "the motion being conveyed from the brain of one man to the fancy of another,"[19] not in the fantastic figure of the Scholar-Gypsy, which is only invoked to illustrate a general point. Once he has told the story he summarily abandons the Scholar-Gypsy to pursue the question of physiological sympathy and suggestion (laughing and yawning are contagious; the baby resembles the mother; the strings of a lute resonate together), and the subsequent chapter of his book continues this investigation into apparently impossible modes of communication (needles touched by a magnet; chiromancy, or the reading of hands and palms; the magical way Sir Kenelm Digby can cure wounds by a "sympathetic medicine").[20]

As it happens, the story of Glanvill's Scholar-Gypsy marks a turn in intellectual style. For Glanvill, also an Oxford scholar, became an admirer of many new thinkers, from Francis Bacon and Gassendi to Descartes and the Platonist Henry More. Dissatisfied with his earlier taste for "the music and curiosity of fine metaphors and dancing periods," Glanville rewrote his book in 1664 in a more sober and abstract tone, under the title *Scepsis Scientifica*, declaring his preference for a style that exhibited "manly sense, flowing in a natural and unaffected eloquence,"[21] and dedicated it to the new Royal Society—to which he was promptly elected. More than a decade later he rewrote it again, this time as an essay called "Against Confidence in Philosophy, and Matters of Speculation," in a collection called *Essays on Several important subjects in Philosophy and Religion* (1676). His career, and his writing, thus made the transition from one mode of thinking and writing to another. "Two epochs and two extremes of the human mind overlap in the three books," notes his modern editor, "roughly, the end of the scholastic era with the beginning of the scientific, and a metaphorical and figurative with an abstract and non-figurative way of describing the world."[22]

Most significantly, from our point of view, Glanville cut from the second and third versions of his book the story of the Scholar-Gypsy. In other words, the gypsy himself had escaped, a century before Arnold urged him to fly. Why did Glanvill remove the Scholar-Gypsy story? It's impossible to know. It may simply have no longer fit into the genre of his scientific narrative. Or it might be that by this time (as one scholar speculates) Glanvill had heard "the true version of the story."[23] For in fact this tale, a familiar anecdote in the period, associated by Glanvill with Oxford, and by others with Cambridge, and by still others with continental universities, is almost surely the story of Francis Mercury van Helmont, the son of Jean Baptiste (Jan Baptista) van Helmont, the "father of biochemistry," the man who bridged the world of alchemy and chemistry and invented the word *gas*. The son, Francis Mercury, was a fantastic figure, adventurer, scientist, magician, physician, philosopher, and Cabbalist who left the University (perhaps it was Leipzig) to live with the gypsies in order to learn their language and customs, not their magic arts of telepathy. Van Helmont visited England in 1670, stayed with Glanvill's friend Henry More, and inquired about another book by Glanvill (the *Lux Orientalis*), which might well mean that he had read the first. If so, the "real scholar gypsy," as Marjorie Nicolson calls him,[24] might have encountered his own shadow on the page.

In any case, Glanvill's Scholar-Gypsy performs the same kind of disappearing act (from his text) that Arnold's does from the English countryside. But where Glanville's scholar (and perhaps van Helmont's before him) joins the gypsies *to learn something* (magic, telepathy, gypsy language and lore), Arnold's scholar joins them in order *to become a kind of gypsy himself*. The whole of Glanvill's anecdote is disposed of, by Arnold, in two stanzas very close to the original (the young "Oxford scholar poor,/Of pregnant parts and quick inventive brain" was "tired of knocking at preferment's door"; the gypsies had "arts to rule as they desired/The working of men's brains,/And they can bind them to what thoughts they will"; two visiting scholars stop by and are told that the gypsies have shown him the "secret of their art"). Clearly, though, the heart of the poem is concerned not with the gypsies and their secrets but with the free-ranging of this free spirit, who becomes a kind of genius loci of the English countryside, an intellectual abiding spirit whose existence and teasing inaccessibility mark the difference between the troubled modern scholar, "divided," "palsied," "doubt[ing]," and "feverish," and the idealized scholar-gypsy, "Nursing thy project in unclouded joy,/And every doubt long blown by time away" (199–200).

Arnold had experimented with other titles for his poem, among them "the first mesmerist." Both gypsies and mesmerism were in cultural fashion in the 1830s and '40s. Indeed, a major literary prize at Oxford in 1837, the Newdigate Prize, was set for the work "The Gypsies," and the fascination of various intellectuals in the period with mesmerism was strong enough that Harriet Martineau had written on the subject. Arnold's mother herself was intrigued by mesmerism.[25] But in opting for *scholar-gypsy* over *mesmerist*, Arnold wrote himself (and his hopes and fears) into the story. "Nursing thy project in unclouded joy,/And every doubt long blown by time away." This could be the wishful mantra for every young scholar embarking on a career, or, especially, on a year of leave to write a book. But in order to enjoy a year of paid leave, it is helpful (in seeking "unclouded joy") to have a job.

THE SEACOAST OF ACADEMIA

The word *gypsy* meant originally "a member of a wandering race (by themselves called *Romany*), of Hindu origin, which first appeared in England about the beginning of the sixteenth century and was then believed to have come from Egypt."[26] (This was a population analogous to the so-called Irish Travelers who were briefly in the news recently because one member of the group, Madelyne Gorman Toogood, was caught on videotape beating her child.)[27] Gypsies made a living "by basket-making, horse-dealing, fortune-telling, etc., and [says the inevitable, and very English, *OED*] have been usually objects of suspicion from their nomadic life and habits." By the early seventeenth century the word was being used regularly in a transferential sense to mean "a cunning rogue." Interest in gypsies was apparently keen enough among nineteenth-century scholars to coin the term *gipsiologist*, and by the mid-twentieth century *gypsy* in U.S. slang meant an independent, sometimes unlicensed, vehicle and its driver (a gypsy cab, a gypsy truckdriver). It's clearly from this last sense, the American slang application of *gypsy* to mean independent operator, that the term *gypsy scholar* derives.

Meanwhile, through a series of deliberate and inadvertent slippages in geography and ethnography, the word *Bohemian* (*bohémien*) in French came to mean "gipsy." The idea was that the original gypsies had come from Bohemia (remember that in English they were thought to come from Egypt). By the late seventeenth century, *gypsy* and *Bohemian* were to a certain extent interchangeable terms. In modern French, as in modern English, *bohemian* came to mean "a gipsy of society," someone who has separated himself (or herself) from conventional society, an artist, writer, or actor who "leads a free, vagabond or irregular life, not being particular to the society he frequents, and despising conventionalities generally. (Used with considerable latitude, with or without reference to morals.)"[28]

The phrase "the seacoast of Bohemia" is usually associated with Shakespeare, and scores of commentators have taken the playwright to task for not knowing that Bohemia was landlocked. (Others have leapt to his defense, explaining either that Bohemia did once have a coast, or that Shakespeare knew it didn't, and was making a familiar joke that would have been recognized by his audience: Shakespeare never nods.) In point of fact, although an important scene in *The Winter's Tale* does clearly take place on the seashore of a country called Bohemia, the actual phrase "the seacoast of Bohemia" appears nowhere in the play, making the phrase the equivalent of its fantasmatic location: ubiquitous but undiscoverable.

In common use this phrase, "the seacoast of Bohemia," has become virtually synonymous with impossibility, and therefore with infinite possibility: if there is, or was, no such place, then the place itself may be imagined in any way one chooses. The writer Christopher Morley once declared the city of Hoboken, across the Hudson River from New York City, to be "the last seacoast of Bohemia."[29] What he meant, apparently, was that Hoboken was, in the 1920s, a "Greenwich Village West," a place of cabarets, speakeasies, nightclubs—and artists.

The German essayist Hans Magnus Enzenberger used the phrase "the seacoast of Bohemia" as the title of a playful epilogue to a book called *Europe, Europe* (1989), in which he imagined a Europe whose nation-states had been superseded by a hodgepodge of regional loyalties (Scottish, Catalan, and others). "This hodgepodge is our final shape," declares an elder statesman, "Chaos is our most important resource. We need our differences."[30] What is the relationship between Bohemia and Academia?

In one sense this conflation of gypsy and Bohemian simply does not work for the present cant sense of *gypsy*. Humanities graduate students—

and especially unemployed or underemployed, or overworked and underemployed graduate students—are arguably among the *most* conventional of persons, since they are constantly on the job market, and constantly under scrutiny. Far from rejecting society, they often long to join it at its most stable center, wishing, like so many other workers, to have a single domicile, a single job, and even a mortgage.

Of course, today there is another entire group of traveling scholars, itinerant intellectuals, whose offices are not their cars, and who sometimes fly first class. These are the so-called Public Intellectuals (a term either oxymoronic or redundant, depending upon one's point of view). But perhaps here it is more germane to mention an organization like Scholars at Risk, an international network of academic institutions organized to advocate on behalf of scholars, writers, and artists who are threatened in their home countries because of their words and ideas. Scholars at Risk arranges for temporary positions of sanctuary at universities and colleges where these scholars can continue their work. Although many scholars are able to return to their home countries after their visits, there are cases in which this is not safe or possible. Under those circumstances the organization tries to find ways for them to continue their work abroad.

That scholars, and scholarship, should be "at risk" is an all-too-familiar story in the long history of intellectual inquiry, and one with powerful resonances—and significant institutional consequences—from the recent past. Enforced academic travel, academic nomadism in flight from repressive and murderous regimes, was a founding fact of life for humanities departments in the 1930s and '40s, as it was for the sciences and social sciences. Just as Princeton's math and science faculties profited from the presence of European and later Asian and African refugees, so also did departments of art history, and literature, and philosophy. Whether or not these scholars were bohemians, with a capital or a small *B*, they brought with them an intellectual culture that made their wandering part of the panoramic vision that they offered to the world. The famous dateline to James Joyce's *Ulysses* deliberately invokes this cosmopolitan aura: Trieste–Zürich–Paris, 1914–21. (Notice that Dublin is *not* one of his cosmopolitan capitals.) Another, more extended classic example, and a particularly poignant one, is provided by the epilogue to Erich Auerbach's *Mimesis*, written between May 1942 and April 1945:

> I may also mention that the book was written during the war and at Istanbul, where the libraries are not well equipped for European studies. International

communications were impeded; I had to dispense with almost all periodicals, with almost all the more recent investigations, and in some cases with reliable critical editions of my texts.[31]

Thus his book lacks footnotes, Auerbach explains, and "it is possible and even probable" that he "overlooked things which I ought to have considered and that I occasionally assert something which modern research has disproved or modified." As for his readers, likewise dispersed by the same European disasters he is so reserved about naming:

> I hope that my study will reach its readers—both my friends of former years, if they are still alive, as well as all the others for whom it was intended. And may it contribute to bringing together again those whose love for our western history has serenely persevered.

The subtitle of *Mimesis*, readers will recall, is the equally quiet and equally telling phrase *The Representation of Reality in Western Culture*.

In her book on translation, Emily Apter challenged what she calls "Auerbach's self-portrait as a lonely European scholar," pointing out that not only had another European exile, Leo Spitzer, already established a vibrant—and global—philological school in Istanbul by the time Auerbach arrived, but that such other intellectuals as Georges Dumézil, Leon Trotsky, Fritz Neumark, and Paul Hindemith had become important presences in the 1930s. Indeed Istanbul had long been a coveted destination for exiled European scholars in a wide variety of fields, especially for Germans and Jews seeking political asylum. The question, it seemed, was not one of enforced isolation but of a preference for a "European" culture even in exile. "Spitzer allowed Turkey to shape his formation of a field of modern humanism," wrote Apter. "Auerbach resisted Turkey. Though he spent over a decade in Istanbul, he apparently never mastered the Turkish language, and there is little evidence to suggest seepage of his 'foreign' surround into *Mimesis*." The pathos of singularity that has become the mythos of Auerbach "in exile" needs correcting, she insisted: "Auerbach was in pretty good cosmopolitan company during his Istanbul sojourn."[32]

Perhaps *exile* is the wrong word; and perhaps, too, we might look for our traveling cultures closer to home. In the same period, the 1930s and '40s, a scholar writing under the very appropriate name of Max Nomad (1888–1973) lectured on politics and history at NYU and the New School for Social Research. He became the author of books like *Rebels and Renegades, Apostles of Revolution, Aspects of Revolt* and *A Skeptic's Political Dictionary and Handbook for the Disenchanted*, and was the subject of an

Edmund Wilson profile published in the *New Yorker*. The man known as Max Nomad was himself a nomad, having been born in Poland and immigrated to the United States from Austria prior to World War I. His work offered a gently skeptical account of the left from within radical politics, suggesting that what would come to be known as the "professional managerial class," once it tasted power, would itself desire to replace, rather than merely to oppose, the dictatorial rulers against which it had originally organized in protest. This might thus be said to be a story not only of gypsy scholars and scholar gypsies, but of nomad intellectuals and intellectual nomads. Or, to adapt David Brooks's phrase, of Nomads in Paradise.

In their theory of nomadology, philosophers Gilles Deleuze and Félix Guattari idealize the life of the non-sedentary scholar in an attempt to critique the search for solidity in ideas. "History is always written from the sedentary point of view and in the name of a unitary State apparatus," they write in *A Thousand Plateaus*. "What is lacking is a Nomadology, the opposite of a history." The coinage *nomadology* is a deliberate play on the philosopher Gottfried Wilhelm Leibniz's *Monadology*. Thus, while they refer to books on the Crusades, for example, as among those texts whose literal "topic is nomads," Deleuze and Guattari's "nomads" are also anagrams of *monad*, an absolute and simple unit of being "without parts, extension, or figure."[33] that possesses the power of perception: a soul; a mind; a person. (The term *monad* was used by Leibniz and adopted by him from the early modern philosopher Giordano Bruno.) In *A Thousand Plateaus* we are told "there is no visual model for points of reference that would make them interchangeable and unite them . . . they are tied to any number of observers who may be qualified as 'monads' but are instead *nomads* entertaining tactile relations amongst themselves."[34]

NOMAD INTELLECTUALS AND INTELLECTUAL NOMADS

Going to theory for a guide to praxis is exactly the kind of move often deplored by those who would condemn theory-speak to the failed recent past of "academia." But the theory of nomadology has had a quirky literalization in the proliferation of "academic nomads." In a curious way academia today is more like baseball than like Wall Street, Main Street, or bohemia: universities and colleges, like ball clubs, are located in various markets across the country, and both rookies and stars, once hired, travel to where the club is and set down roots—for a time. The farm-team system, like the junior faculty, makes it possible to move up through the ranks (to "grow one's own") but there is always the likelihood that a major player from elsewhere will be wooed and will take over a coveted position. Academia and baseball, in other words, are subject in similar ways to the power of money and celebrity. As in baseball, so also in academia, it was once the case that a new hire might well spend an entire career with the same institution, but free agency has lately become more the norm, and institutional loyalty is for many a quaint, charming, but hopelessly outmoded idea. Most young scholars, even those who get tenure as a result of their first jobs, expect to move on—perhaps from colleges to universities, or from rural campuses to cities, or to places where they and a partner can both be gainfully and happily employed. The college version of Mr. Chips is as out of fashion as the amateur faculty talent show or the cookie-baking faculty spouse.

Most U.S.-based academic novels of the 1950s and '60s situated the utopia and dystopia of campus life in literal groves of academe, leafy liberal arts colleges removed from the grit of city life and the pressure of professional schools like law and engineering. Here the college professor is still in concept a kindly, avuncular father figure. And a man. Randall Jarrell's *Pictures from an Institution* (1954) is set at Benton, described by the *New York Times Book Review* at the time as "a progressive college for women with suspicious resemblance to several real progressive colleges for women." (Other reviews characterized it as "a Bryn-Mawr-like women's college.")[35] Mary McCarthy's *The Groves of Academe* (1952) took place at Jocelyn College in Jocelyn, Pennsylvania. (McCarthy was also, of course, the author of *The Group*, her account of eight Vassar girls of the class of 1933 and their adventures in intellectual, cultural, and sexual fashion in the thirties and forties.) Edward Albee's *Who's Afraid of Virginia Woolf* (1962) featured a small New England college in the fictional town of New Carthage. The fantasy represented in these novels was of a kind of academic nuclear family, with the school itself functioning, as the saying went, in loco parentis—with a father at the head of the household.

It's not a surprise that so many of the hapless heroes of academic novels are professors of literature, since these books are largely *written* by literature professors and other humanists. (We shouldn't forget *Love Story*, the achievement of classicist Erich Segal.) But the centrality of the liberal arts, and the expectation that the students featured in these novels would be enraptured both with their professors and with the humanities, marks the genre of the academic novel as an endangered species. The coeducation of the Ivy League, some women's colleges, and the "Little Ivy" in the 1970s opened up these bastions of elite education to both sexes, and the fantasy of the small liberal arts college has receded somewhat from the cultural imagination of many of today's aspiring undergraduates. More recent "academic novels" tend to focus on university life, like David Lodge's Rummidge series, or on professional education, as in *The Paper Chase*. It may be symptomatic that professional-school memoirs, like former law student Scott Turow's *One-L*, are replacing these works of fiction as the favorite mode of academic exposé, just as the "college" experience has become for many undergraduates, at big schools and small, largely a space for professional and pre-professional training—even if the school in question has core courses or distribution requirements that keep the humanities somewhere on the table.

"What would you *do* with a degree in *X*?" is the question, whether *X* is English, French, classics, or African American Studies. *Do* means turn into a job that makes money and confers prestige. Disinterested intellectual curiosity of the kind urged by Matthew Arnold (and others) is not enough. What majors in the humanities *used* to "do" with their training in literature, art, philosophy, history and music was to use it in their own work and lives. Comparatively few became college professors or curators. But arguably some politicians wrote their own speeches, enlivened and informed by classical models and modern poetry. The spectacle of Abraham Lincoln writing the Gettysburg Address on the back of an envelope is one of the founding scenes of writing in all of American political history—maybe the greatest, certainly the most moving. And arguably others who use words, quotations, and allusions might still find pleasure and profit in thinking through and with the ideas that have been central to the disciplines of the humanities: Lawyers who write briefs, business people who make oral (not PowerPoint) presentations, friends who offer toasts on celebratory occasions, advertising copywriters who could refer glancingly to familiar phrases or images and expect their clients to respond with recognition. These days, such crossover cues tend to be musical rather than verbal; sampling has replaced quotation as what Dr. Johnson once called the *parole* of cultural life.

Our culture has changed, both globally and digitally, and no range of common references can expect to unite disparate publics or generations. Indeed it never did. But the difference between an undergraduate and a graduate education has changed as well, and "breadth" requirements are often regarded as tedious obligations rather than pleasurable or provocative opportunities. What do we want our fields to communicate to our students? For more than a hundred years—not so long, really, in the history of institutions of higher learning—academic life was imagined as largely sedentary, based in university and college towns. Institutional loyalty was an aspect of this residential rootedness, whether the institution was Oxford, Swarthmore, Berkeley, Vanderbilt, or Wisconsin-Madison. Many of the tasks, roles, and services provided by faculty members could not be quantified or assessed. The periodic crankiness of columnists (and legislators) who complain that college teachers teach only nine hours a week, with summers "off," fundamentally misunderstands the nature of a college teacher's and a scholar's work. But we are internally divided, as well, between the travelers (high and low) and the stay-at-homes. The fact is that, like law, medicine, business, or any other profession, ours has many modes, not one ideal type.

The question is: who is most likely to be free to think, the gypsy scholar wandering unwillingly from part-time job to part-time job, or the secure tenured scholar who is protected in what he (or she) says? How can freedom of thought be guaranteed? It if is truly free, it cannot. And certainly freedom of *speech* on campus has become a complicated issue again—as indeed it has always been. But perhaps it has latterly grown less easy to idealize those who remain free of institutions, those who thumb their noses at mediocrity. Bohemians, gypsies, and nonconformists of all kinds are imagined as having the capacity, and the absence of structure and routine, that will enable them to live the true life of the mind—that life that we, weighed down as we are by institutional obligations, no longer have time for. They symbolize a resistance to professionalism, to the idea of a professional scholar. This may be valid in theoretical ways, but when *The Road Less Travelled By* becomes a *New York Times* bestseller, we should wonder who it is exactly who is on the road *more* traveled by. There may, indeed, be a kind of self-deception in our supposed wanderlust that the current realities of the profession will no longer allow us. Are we ready to jettison tenure, a system initially established as a safeguard against the interference of donors with deep pockets and shallow ideas? Deinstitutionalization is a radical idea that often benefits the bottom line rather than the threshold of scholarship (or social welfare).

It would be well to remind both the insecure (who need no reminding, but may overestimate the value of the security they lack) and the secure (those who have succeeded in gaining tenure somewhere) that freedom of thought is often a fugitive virtue, if not a cloistered one. Universities have now adopted a model of "work" that resembles that of business, but the emphasis on the "bottom line" and "productivity" may itself have hastened the demise of the liberal arts and the fantasy of freedom of thought. Between the wandering many and the sedentary few, everyone should perhaps worry that it is thought itself that is at risk of dropping out.

Today's scholar gypsies and gypsy scholars are world travelers, and world citizens—some by preference, some by necessity; some in theory and some in practice; some in person and some online. I am myself, like many "academics" these days, a traveling scholar, conscious of, and grateful for, the opportunity to speak with groups large and small, in many communities across the country and the world. I am also a passionate believer in *translatio studii*, in the power of ideas and concepts to journey, with and without their intellectual begetters and guardians, from one end of the earth to the other, across spaces, times, and peoples, whether in face-to-face encounters or through the increasingly sophisticated processes of "distance learning." Evidence of this is registered every day, from the exponential growth in digital humanities research to individual exchanges between correspondents, like the email note I received from a secondary-school teacher in New Zealand, reporting that his students had seen my online lecture on *King Lear* courtesy of a free service offered by the Harvard Extension School.

We do not lack for daily reminders in the news of the world as well as the news on our campuses that the questions posed by humanists have never been more pertinent or more pressing. When we think with nostalgia about the scholar gypsies of the past, and with concern about the gypsy scholars of the present, we should also bear in mind the fact that the "humanities" have their basis in the human. As education becomes increasingly global, while remaining, at the same time, intensely local, there is probably no better investment, and no better bargain, than making the humanities the new bottom line.

CHAPTER FOURTEEN

Radical Numbers

Some people were not happy when two prominently placed pediatricians chose to speak out against the war. The message sent out to students and other concerned citizens invited them to get involved in the debates and to reflect upon the implications for themselves and for the country. Had the doctors overstepped the bounds of propriety or abused a position of cultural power? The situation seemed familiar, déjà vu all over again. In this case, though, the invitation to political activism came not from Dr. Benjamin Spock, the celebrated author of *Baby and Child Care*, the bible for a generation of anxious American parents, but from Drs. Sean and Judith Palfrey, the masters of Adams House at Harvard. The date was not 1968 but 2003. And the conflict in question was not the Vietnam War but the pending invasion of Iraq.

In January 2003 the Palfreys, both medical specialists in pediatrics, had posted an e-mail to all Adams House residents to urge them to "think about and discuss the issues [surrounding an impending war with Iraq] actively and respectfully." Citing their own work experience as child-health-care providers ("these are roles we play in our professional lives every day as we work for the health and well-being of children and families here and throughout the world"), they stressed that they were not asking recipients to agree with their position but rather to acknowledge and discuss "the high stakes inherent in our country's current rhetoric." Harvard president Lawrence Summers, who had himself been outspoken on certain moral and political issues affecting the nation and the world, was concerned about the specific question of electronic access to the house mailing list. He told the student newspaper, the *Crimson*, "It was unfortunate that the House e-mail was used to express these views." Students and other masters were asked by *The Crimson* whether they though it was appropriate for the housemasters to discuss their political views publicly. One Adams House student mentioned the possibility that those views might be taken as "the party line." But he also said he appreciated the fact that—in the paper's phrase—"the masters were taking part in the intellectual life of the house."[1]

The Palfreys' voiced expression of concern about war, written from the perspective of doctors who care for children and families, did, at least for this onlooker, call to mind the very public intervention of that other pediatrician from an earlier era of activism and engagement. On January 5, 1968, Benjamin Spock and four codefendants were charged with conspiracy "to hinder and interfere with the administration of the Universal Military and Training Act." In other words, they had advised young people to resist the draft. Arrested with Spock were Yale University chaplain William Sloane Coffin, Harvard graduate student Michael Ferber (now an English professor at the University of New Hampshire), novelist Mitchell Goodman (then married to poet Denise Levertov), and Marcus Raskin, subsequently cofounder of the Institute for Policy Studies. Although the "conspirators" had never met before, and had done only one thing in common—they appeared at a press conference to express, in separate statements, their opposition to the war and their support for draft resistance—this was enough to put them on trial. (As Noam Chomsky wrote about the incident, after the press conference "they separated, many of them never to meet again. But this is the government's concept of 'conspiracy.'")[2] All but Raskin were convicted and sentenced to two years in prison, though the conviction was reversed in the following year. This was the famous Spock trial. The defendants in the case became known as the Boston Five.

The Boston Five. The Chicago Seven. The New Haven Nine. These are my radical numbers. To at least some of today's audiences and readers, these numbers will be more mysterious than revealing. In local memory the Boston Five is a savings bank. The Jackson Five was a rock group. Spock is a pointy-eared Vulcan from *Star Trek*. Yet each of these was a group of radical intellectuals, or intellectual radicals, trying to make a difference.

It's sometimes hard to remember how ubiquitous these concerns were, or how immediate the ethical and political issues felt, no matter what side you were on. In that respect it was a very different time. When I was an undergraduate at Swarthmore my years there were framed by the civil rights movement and the Vietnam War. With a friend, Alex Capron (now a professor of legal and medical ethics), I wrote a musical comedy called "The Oddity," which was a rewriting of *The Odyssey* with a modern-day Odysseus, like his original namesake, seen as a draft resister, and moving from venue to venue in search of exemption from the war. One of the star performers, singing a torch number called "The Red Whiten Blues," was Sarah Lawrence, now Sarah Lawrence-Lightfoot, Emily Hargroves Fisher Professor of Education at the Harvard Graduate School of Education, a distinguished sociologist. Among my classmates were Michael Ferber, later to be one of the Boston Five and now an English professor; Patchen Dellinger, the son of David Dellinger, one of the Chicago Seven, now a surgeon; Nick Egleson, who upon graduation from college became the president of Students for a Democratic Society, and Cathy Wilkerson, whose father's West Eleventh Street townhouse was accidentally blown up in 1970 by a Weatherman bomb—three people died in the explosion.

My graduate-school years corresponded with the height, or the depth, of the war and the political assassinations that left the country reeling; my first year of teaching was 1969–70, the year of the Bobby Seale trial in New Haven, when Yale president Kingman Brewster opened up the residential colleges to demonstrators and provided food and space for political rhetoric. Allen Ginsberg chanted in Saybrook Courtyard while I balanced a plate of brown rice on my knees; it was May 1970, and classes had shut down for the year by common consent.

*

The Chicago Seven began as the Chicago Eight, a group of protesters at the 1968 Democratic Convention in Chicago. Across the country the Vietnam War and the civil rights movement had stirred students, professors, and other radical intellectuals to organize. In Mayor Richard Daley's Chicago that summer, Democrats were gathered to endorse the nomination of Hubert Humphrey. When riots broke out in the streets, and on television, eight protesters—all men, seven of them white—were indicted for crossing state lines with the intent to incite violence. The law they were accused of having broken was a new one: it was created by Congress in 1968 to address the felt need to control antiwar protests. The eight men—Rennie Davis, David Dellinger, John Froines, Tom Hayden,

Abbie Hofman, Jerry Rubin, Bobby Seale, and Lee Wiener—were indicted in March of 1969 and stood trial in the court of public opinion, as well as that of hard-line jurist Julius Hoffman. Seale, a member of the Black Panther Party, was bound and gagged on October 29, after shouting repeatedly at the judge, calling him a "fascist dog" and a "pig." A few days later, on November 5, he was sent to prison for five years for contempt of court, leaving the remaining defendants as the newly reduced Chicago Seven.

Of these seven, several—admittedly the least colorful—were "intellectuals" by any traditional definition. Dellinger, then chair of the National Mobilization Committee to End the War in Vietnam, or MOBE, was a Yale graduate from the class of 1937 who had refused to register for the draft in World War II. Froines, founder of the Radical Science Information Service, had a PhD in chemistry from Yale. He later joined the UCLA faculty as a professor in the School of Public Health. Davis graduated from Oberlin and earned a master's degree from the University of Illinois before joining the antiwar movement in the sixties. (He later became a venture capitalist and a lecturer on meditation and self-awareness.) Weiner was at the time of the trial a teaching assistant in sociology at Northwestern. Tom Hayden, later a state senator from California (and one-time husband of actress Jane Fonda), was the chief author of the 1962 Port Huron Statement, the statement of principles of the Students for a Democratic Society, to which several codefendants belonged. Outshone by the courtroom antics of the Yippies—Abbie Hoffman and Jerry Rubin, who had staged a Festival of Life and nominated a pig named Pigasus for president—and upstaged by Bobby Seale, these radical intellectuals were not intellectual radicals. Their ideas were familiar; it was their tactics, and their lawyer, William Kunstler, that made them memorable. But these were memorable times.

The trials, like the assassinations, kept on coming. So many in such a short period of time. The trial of the Boston Five for conspiracy to encourage draft resistance took place in 1968. Spock, Coffin, Ferber, and Goodman were convicted on June 14, a week after the assassination of Bobby Kennedy, two months after the assassination of Martin Luther King Jr., three months after the My Lai massacre. The trial of the Chicago Seven for conspiracy to cross state boundaries to provoke a riot began in September 1969 and ended with convictions and contempt citations across the board—including for the lawyers—in February 1970.

The defendants in the first trial had adopted a sober and respectful demeanor in order to make their political point; the defendants in the second trial tried a different set of tactics, calling experts from Timothy Leary to the director of the nude musical *Oh! Calcutta!* Famous writers, from Norman Mailer to William Styron, were summoned to the stand to testify. The poet Allen Ginsberg, who had chanted the Hare Krishna mantra for ten minutes in front of television cameras at a Yippie press conference, was asked by the prosecutor to recite three particularly explicitly homoerotic poems and to explain to the jury their religious significance. He was also asked to explain what a "be-in" was (and to spell it for Judge Hoffman, who found the concept elusive). The trial was itself a piece of theater, as Hoffman had intended. All the convictions in the Chicago Seven trial were reversed in November 1972 by the Seventh Circuit Court of Appeals, which cited the biases of the jury and the judge's "deprecatory and often antagonistic attitude toward the defense."

The third of these trials took place in April 1970—thus only two months after the trial of the Chicago Seven had ended. The defendants in this case were dubbed the New Haven Nine. The nine were members of the Black Panther Party, caught up in a murder-conspiracy trial that turned on the question of which member of the Panthers was a police informant; insofar as "radical intellectuals" or "intellectuals as radicals" were involved, it was the Yale campus, and the larger world of politics and culture, that provided them. But provide them it did. On May Day, May 1, 1970, as the National Guard was called out and 15,000 demonstrators converged upon New Haven, poets, playwrights, and activists mingled on the streets, in the courtyards, and on the New Haven Green. President Brewster speculated aloud about whether a Black Panther could get a fair trial in the United States of America. Henry Louis Gates Jr., then an undergraduate at Yale, helped persuade his white classmates to join the strike, convinced—like many at the time—that defendant Bobby Seale was not being tried fairly, "bound and gagged as he had been in Chicago and as we were sure he would be in New Haven."[3] By *strike* here was meant the cessation of classes, not physical violence or even picketing. The university became, for a short but significant space in time, a place of teach-ins, conferences, rallies, and constant public and private political debate. French playwright Jean Genet declared that this was "the moment of truth for Bobby Seale, for the Black Panthers, for young white Americans."[4] Decades later, conservative websites still claim that Hillary Clinton, then a law student at Yale, was one of the protest ringleaders in support of the Panthers case—a "Panther apologist," in the phrase of an anonymous and widely circulated e-mail of January 2000. (Clinton—then Hillary Rodham—had organized law students to be present at the trial to watch for civil rights abuses.)

When the poet Robert Bly accepted the National Book Award for Poetry on March 6, 1969, he invoked the moral authority of these radical intellectuals.

> We have some things to be proud of. No one needs to be ashamed of the acts of civil disobedience committed in the tradition of Thoreau. What Dr. Coffin did was magnificent; the fact that Yale University did not do it is what is sad. What Mr. Berrigan did was noble; the fact that the Catholic church did not do it is what is sad. What Mitchell Goodman did here last year was needed and in good taste. . . . In an age of gross and savage crimes by legal governments, the institutions will have to learn responsibility, learn to take their part in preserving the nation, and take their risk by committing acts of disobedience. The book companies can find ways to act like Thoreau, whom they publish. Where were the publishing houses when Dr. Spock and Mr. Goodman and Mr. Raskin—all three writers—were indicted?
>
> . . . You have given me an award for a book that has many poems in it against the war. I thank you for the award. As for the thousand-dollar check, I am turning it over to the draft-resistance movement, specifically to the organization called the Resistance. . . .

The most dated part of this speech is the amount of the check. Today's National Book Award winners each get $10,000 and a crystal sculpture.

But there is something moving, still, about this spectacle of a poet trying to change the world with "many poems against the war"—and a thousand-dollar check. Especially when we contrast it to the cancellation of the proposed White House conference on "Poetry and the American Voice," convened by First Lady Laura Bush for Lincoln's birthday, February 12, 2003. When poet and editor Sam Hamill responded to the invitation by posting an e-mail urging that invitees send him poems and statements opposing the invasion of Iraq, he received over 5,300 submissions, some from poets as well known as Adrienne Rich, Lawrence Ferlinghetti, Philip Levine, and Diane DePrima.[5] The event was "postponed" indefinitely, and the White House put out the following statement: "While Mrs. Bush understands the right of all Americans to express their political views, this event was designed to celebrate poetry." Katha Pollitt, writing in the *Nation*, observed ironically that it was "just like old times," recalling an occasion "when Robert Lowell refused to attend a poetry symposium at the Johnson White House to protest the Vietnam War."[6]

We have come, then, full circle: from e-mail to e-mail, from Adams House to the White House. Or rather, from something it was decided should not happen at Adams House to something it was decided should not happen at the White House. But these are not "old times"—they are new, and they are ours, however uncannily and disturbingly they may seem to evoke the past. E-mail itself marks the difference: instant, cheap, and global, so different from the slow-moving and amateurish mimeographed flyers of the sixties. With issues of war, justice, and race again on the horizon, we cannot postpone our own articulation of the "American voice" indefinitely. And we should allow for the possibility that expressing political views and celebrating poetry can often be one and the same act. This is the value of the humanities to our culture. (*Radicals* are roots, and *numbers* are verses.) The most radical thing the government, or the university, can do, is to encourage people to say what they think.

CHAPTER FIFTEEN

After the Humanities

Let us imagine a thought experiment. What would higher education be like without the humanities? Or, less drastically, with what we ordinarily call "the humanities" present in a very different form?

The humanities have since the sixteenth century been considered as the branch of "learning or literature concerned with human culture." From a twenty-first-century perspective, though, human culture, however defined or demarcated, would seem—to many—to be the common purview of historians, anthropologists, quantitative (as well as qualitative) social scientists, and, increasingly and preeminently, practitioners and theorists within the life sciences.

At the same time that their boundaries are being breached and expanded by adjacent disciplines, the humanities have been under persistent critique from some quarters for two mutually paradoxical reasons: first, that they are not relevant to present-day concerns and, second, that their interest in relevancy devalues traditional works and approaches. (Sometimes you can't win for losing.)

How have changes in the structure and content of higher education, and, indeed, the goals and strategies of universities and colleges, affected the standing and nature of the humanities? What is the relation of the humanities today to the sciences, the social sciences, or the creative arts? What comes after the humanities—both within university culture, and in the professional, social, and political world?

I address this big question—what comes after the humanities?—under three different but equally important headings here—headings that I might name in the following way: the humanities as cultural accessory; the humanities center as symptom; and collaborative work and the new humanities—the humanities, so to speak, after the humanities.

THE HUMANITIES AS ACCESSORY

The word *accessory* in contemporary culture has two meanings, one associated with fashion, and the other with crime. I intend both of them here. A fashion accessory contributes "in a subordinate way" to a general effect or result.[1] Gloves, handbag, shoes, umbrella, pocket square—these are fashion accessories for the human subject. For your car, you may prefer other enhancements: wheel covers, leather seats, a Bose sound system, a CD changer. Elements like four-wheel drive, safety airbags, and automatic transmission are not accessories; they are fundamental to how the machine actually works, or to its safety in operation.

The fashion accessory is the category into which the humanities have increasingly moved in cultural terms. Basic humanities courses in art, music, Shakespeare, modern architecture, the classics are still in demand as electives, and as social glue. Many successful lawyers, doctors, investment bankers, and venture capitalists return to these topics once they have made their money and established their careers; there is a booming business in upscale extension courses, lifelong learning, cultural tours, and alumni weekends. As a Shakespearean and cultural critic, I have taught or led each of these at one time or another, and enjoyed them thoroughly. It's worth noting that participants in programs like these don't generally read much contemporary literary criticism and theory or, for that matter, art-historical scholarship or music theory. They engage with the works, or in some cases with the biographies—or imagined biographies—of the artists and writers. They do often read reviews, both book reviews and reviews of stage productions, dance and musical concerts. In short, there is a real divide between the public humanities in this sense and the scholarly humanities being practiced and perpetuated in graduate school and in advanced courses in colleges and universities.

None of this will come as a surprise. But it may surprise you to learn that some of the most successful current uses of the humanities are in the realms of business, executive training, "leadership" institutes, and motivational speaking. We could call these "applied humanities." Just as a case in point, consider the remarkable number of books on Shakespeare and management (all of them have been published between 1999 and the present).

> *Shakespeare in Charge: The Bard's Guide to Leading and Succeeding on the Business Stage* (1999)
>
> *Power Plays: Shakespeare's Lessons in Leadership and Management* (2000)
>
> *Shakespeare on Management* (1999)
>
> *Inspirational Leadership: Henry V and the Muse of Fire; Timeless Insights from Shakespeare's Greatest Leader* (2001)
>
> *Say It Like Shakespeare: How to Give a Speech Like Hamlet, Persuade Like Henry V, and Other Secrets from the World's Greatest Communicator* (2001)

In one of these books, Lady Macbeth's urgent advice to her husband, "Screw your courage to the sticking point/And we'll not fail," is instanced as an example of how proper preparation can prevent professional failure. No one bothers to point out that Lady Macbeth is trying to urge her husband to kill the king.

Who teaches these sessions?

Former Reagan arms control director Kenneth Adelman is not only the coauthor of one of these books but also, with his wife Carol, the founder and salesman for a leadership training program wittily called Movers & Shakespeares. As leadership institutes become an increasingly popular option for executive training in the first decade of the twenty-first century, the Adelmans advertised on their website both their own credentials and their organization's purpose and method.[2] Let me share with you some selections from their website, since any paraphrase would not do it full justice:

> Drawing on their extensive experience in top positions in government, public corporations, and non-profit groups, Carol and Ken Ademan work closely with companies and universities to customize each program to address the key issues facing their particular organization at the time.
>
> The Adelmans select the most apt Shakespeare play to fit the program's purpose. For leadership and ethics, they draw on *Henry V*, for change management, *Taming of the Shrew*, for risk management and diversity, *Merchant of Venice*, and for crisis management, *Hamlet*.
>
> No prior knowledge of Shakespeare is required. . . .

Participants divide into small discussion groups to relate the lessons of these Shakespearean scenes to their own company practices. The groups report back to the whole seminar on whether and how the company handled the situation better (or worse) than King Henry V, Portia or Claudius.[3]

Now, I consider this pure genius. It's a fabulous gimmick. Indeed, I wish I'd thought of it. I'd be a millionaire by now. But of course, I wouldn't be—and this is the point. The Shakespeare stuff is ancillary to the organizers' expertise and résumés, "their extensive experience in top positions in government, public corporations, and non-profit groups," to quote the website once again. Just as "no prior knowledge of Shakespeare is required" of participants (and quite reasonably so), likewise the directors of "Movers & Shakespeares" are, so to speak, Movers rather than Shakespeares. They have picked up their Shakespeare along the way. Carol Adelman is the president of Movers & Shakespeares, and her résumé tells us that she has "over 25 years of theatrical experience," but her doctorate is in public health, and she has worked in government as the "top official for the first President Bush on U.S. foreign aid to Asia, the Middle East, and . . . Eastern Europe." Her husband, with "years of teaching Shakespeare" at Georgetown and George Washington Universities (I am, again, quoting his résumé) has a doctorate in political theory and a master's in foreign service studies.

In the terms in which literature departments once used to discuss the structure of a metaphor, *tenor* and *vehicle*, Shakespeare is the vehicle here, and leadership, or management, the tenor. That is to say, the real subject is leadership, and "Shakespeare" (the humanities component) is the image or comparison being used to convey the point. It is because of their credentials in government and business, not in English literature, that the Adelmans have clout in the world of the leadership institute. Contented clients like Northrop Grumman Mission Systems, the Resource Bank, General Dynamics Armament and Technical Systems, Ocean Spray products, and the Wharton School of Business have written testimonials to Movers & Shakespeares, testifying to this program as a suitable authority to advise business executives. The humanities are in this case being used to teach business. And the teachers are government and business specialists, not PhDs in the humanities.

Although humanistic scholars may well use "business" models as ways of analyzing and interpreting literature and culture (I'm thinking here, for example, of English professor Mary Poovey's work on double-entry bookkeeping and classical rhetoric in *A History of the Modern Fact*, or Marc Shell's book on *Money, Language, and Thought*), they are not regularly coappointed in business schools, much less called in to advise the U.S. Treasury or the executives of financial corporations. At least for now. (Any picture of the humanities "after the humanities" will have to take this option into account.)

The humanities today accessorize business, finance, politics, journalism, and other activities in the public sphere. Laments about the politicization of the humanities miss this point: If the humanities today are "political," or "politicized," as used to be regularly suggested, it is not because of the personal politics of the teachers in the classroom, but rather because humanities topics, authors, and works have been appropriated, and repurposed, as analogies and case studies for so-called real-life scenarios, whether in business, advertising, or any other "applied" activity. Put another way, the humanities beyond the university (and sometimes even within it) have become social sciences. In this sense we are already "after the humanities."

One of the unanticipated by-products of functional obsolescence in cultural terms (the end of "use value") is an uptick in iconic status (cultural capital; "exchange value"). Thus, as I once argued in an essay on Roman numerals, as soon as those numerals stopped being used by shopkeepers for arithmetic in the early modern period (the Roman system had no zero and thus was dysfunctional for the new math of algebra being imported from Arab countries and from India) they became iconic signs for grandiose things like the months of the French revolutionary calendar—or, in our own time, for movie sequels and the Super Bowl. So likewise, alas, with the humanities. Deemed impractical as college majors for any student wanting a future with a high-paying job, the humanities have become ornamental assets.

In a *New York Times* editorial written during the Iraq War, columnist Adam Cohen noted that the Brookings Institution, a Washington think tank, had titled a report on the Iraq war "Things Fall Apart," a famous phrase from W. B. Yeats's poem "The Second Coming"—a poem written in 1919, after the First World War. Cohen's article took note of the many out-of-context quotations often lifted from this very quotable poem ("the center cannot hold"; "mere anarchy is loosed upon the world"; "the best lack all conviction/While the worst are full of passionate intensity") while also he noted that those who cite it forget—or, more probably, never know—that Yeats's poem, and his worldview, were quite different from the sentiments these snippets seemed to suggest. "Yeats was attracted to fascism," Cohen reminded his readers, "and he rebelled as a youth against the adults' talk of progress by embracing its opposite. 'I took satisfaction in certain public disasters, felt sort of ecstasy at the contemplation of ruin,' he once wrote."[4] Cohen's article refers warmly several times to Harvard poetry critic Helen Vendler's perceptive reading of "The Second Coming" (his bio on the *New York Times* site discloses that he is, indeed, a graduate of Harvard College), pointing out in considerable detail how ironic it was to cite Yeats in the Iraq context. The *Times* headline writer picked up on the irony, entitling the piece "What W. B. Yeats's 'Second Coming' Really Says about the Iraq War." But in fact the 140-page Brookings report never mentions or cites either the poet or the poem except in that title, "Things Fall Apart," which is of course also the title of Chinua Achebe's English-language African novel of 1958 (a novel that *does* cite the Yeats poem).

It's been a long time since 1958, much less 1919, and it's not clear that the Brookings authors ever thought about Yeats at all. Their study is all politics and social science, not a literary allusion or a poetic epigraph in sight. What Adam Cohen was lamenting was the disappearance of the humanities from this kind of public discourse. (If J. M. Keynes had written the report, it might indeed be full of literary tags.) Cohen's reading of the poem was a kind of elegiac homage to an absence of poetry at the center of things. *He* knew the poem well, even if the researchers and politicians he cites did not. In this case, too, the humanities was an accessory, both before and after the fact.

One actual "accessory" that has been suggested as a must-have for instant information about the humanities in culture is *The New Dictionary of Cultural Literacy*, a 2002 offshoot of E. D. Hirsch's 1987 book *Cultural Literacy: What Every American Needs to Know*,"—a mild-mannered polemic published in the midst of what were then described as the "culture wars."

The New Dictionary of Cultural Literacy describes itself, symptomatically, in the following way: "the 6,900 entries in this major new reference work form the touchstone of what it means to be not only just a literate American but an active citizen in our multicultural democracy." All the keywords are here, from *touchstone* (made famous by Matthew Arnold in 1880, in a controversial essay entitled "The Study of Poetry") to *American, citizen, democracy* and (in a bow to the twenty-first century) *multicultural*, although significantly modified, in this instance, by *our*: "our multicultural democracy." *The New Dictionary of Cultural Literacy* is clearly conceived as a guidebook for Americans. Try to imagine, if you will, the use of this handbook as the equivalent of a Berlitz dictionary of phrases, tucked into your briefcase, handbag or backpack, ready to supply important information at a glance about Robert Burns, Joseph Conrad, "the face that launched a thousand ships," "double, double, toil and trouble," or *How the Grinch Stole Christmas*—all listings under the heading of "Literature in English."

Some of the Dictionary's entries are genuinely useful—you never know when you are going to need quick definitions of *depletion allowance, double indemnity, baud rate, chat room,*or *bioterrorism*. But if the definition of "double, double, toil and trouble" is any indicator—"lines chanted by the three witches in the play *Macbeth*, by William Shakespeare, as they mix a potion"—they may be more useful for *Jeopardy!* or Trivial Pursuits than they are for being an active citizen in our multicultural democracy. Which doesn't at all mean we can do without knowing them.

This is, in fact, the point. What used to be "polite literature" and "mental cultivation befitting a man," the very definition of the humanities as transcribed by the *Oxford English Dictionary* at the turn of the last century, is now instrumental knowledge, crossing over boundaries from literature and history to science and technology.[5] In one way, as may be obvious, this is a return to the "before the humanities" moment represented by a seventeenth-century figure like Francis Bacon, who was both scientist and humanist. It's only since the Enlightenment that "science" and "the humanities" have evolved along different paths. One way of imagining the humanities "after the humanities" is, as we will see, to repair this breach.

What about the other sense of *accessory*, the one that means accomplice in crime? This may be a little strong for what I have in mind. But I do think humanists are often complicit in the undervaluing of their disciplines, in their eagerness to claim what used to be called "relevance." Such claims amount to a doctrine of "use value" that is at once defensive and unpersuasive, but that is nonetheless (or therefore?) often heard. The chief culprit for me here—and I realize how unwelcome this observation is going to be—is the claim that the humanities "make you a better person" or "teach ethical lessons." As you can see, this is not completely different from the claim that the humanities can make you a better executive, "leader," or business manager. But what is being improved here, at least so the claim goes, is not the bottom line but the bottom of your heart. I won't go into this further now, except to say that I am myself extremely skeptical about the moral lessons literature can teach—moral conundrums, perhaps, and moral impasses, all appropriate topics for interpretation. But works of art and literature cannot be reduced (or expanded) to bromides about virtue or ethics. As is frequently noted, the plots of the Greek classics are full of parricide, fratricide, incest, and madness. The story lines of Shakespeare's tragedies are similarly aversive, and their "lessons" cannot be "don't become a Macbeth." The annals of twentieth-century history are full of tyrants who loved opera, theater, art—and, indeed, their pets. This did not make them good people.

More importantly, by the time we go down this road, translating painting or music or drama or poetry into works of moral or ethical uplift, or using the plots of novels to prove something about "human nature" rather than about writing, we have backed away from the humanities and assented to their conversion into something "useful," something connected to "progress" in social or economic or scientific terms. Literature is good to think with. It makes us better analysts, better interpreters, better readers. It doesn't supply answers. What distinguishes the humanities is their methods of analysis, interpretation, and speculation—rather than a strictly empirical investigation. (Empirical questions are asked in the context of research, of course, but the "answers" are put in the service of analysis.) This is not always acknowledged (either by those outside the humanities or within it), and it is, indeed, not always credited, or always welcome.

An article in the *New York Times* with the eye-catching headline "In Tough Times, Humanities Must Justify Their Worth,"[6] produced the usual bromides about how the humanities are "prerequisites for personal growth and participation in a free democracy, regardless of career choice." The pull quote featured below the headline evoked the most over-used, and mis-used, term of them all, what I think of as the *d*-word: it read, "Defending the virtues of the liberal arts in a money-driven world." The humanities, it seems, are always either "in crisis" or on the defense. And who were the authorities quoted on this important matter? Two former law school deans who had published books on the topic, a state commissioner of higher education, and one lone professor of literature and American studies. The education commissioner rued the fact that there was a lot of interest at what was described as the "national leadership level in higher education" on emphasizing the "practical and economic value" of a liberal education, but that "the idea [had] not yet caught on among professors and department heads." Here, I submit, we have the problem, expressed in a topsy-turvy fashion: it would be better, I think, to consult professors—humanities professors—than commissioners, law professors, or persons at "the national leadership level" about what we do, why we do it, and why it matters.

*

Let me tell you a story. When the former president of Harvard, a mathematical economist, was new to his position, he gathered groups of faculty for conversations at his home over dinner, to familiarize himself with their scholarly areas, some of which were far from his own expertise. One of the first groups he convened was a group of humanists, fifteen or so people, from a variety of departments from art history to linguistics to the language and literature programs. And he began the dinner conversation, genially, with what he assumed would be an easy question to answer, one that would situate the discipline. "Tell me," he asked, "what kinds of problems do you solve in the humanities?" A small silence greeted this invitation. Faculty members around the table glanced at each other. After a while, I plucked up my courage and spoke. "Mr. President," I said, "Humanists don't solve problems. We love our problems. We've been debating and pondering the same problems for hundreds or even thousands of years. In fact if we come close to 'solving' a problem, we try to think about it in another way, from another angle. Humanists interpret, discuss, and debate. We don't 'solve' problems so as to go beyond them toward an ideal of progress." The president smiled, and paused. Clearly he thought this was provocative, even charming, but it could not be true. Two hours later, after a vigorous but highly amiable conversation, we remained far apart on this question. The difficulty of convincing him, I see now, was symptomatic—not of anything about him, per se, but about the divide (even among academics) between the idea of education as applied to social or cultural progress, and the idea of education as about the mind. Here too we are, for better or worse, "after the humanities."

Harvard's next president, a historian, made the arts a priority in her institutional planning. But even on campuses where the humanities and arts are emphasized, I would still contend that the playing field is tilted toward the quantifiers, verifiers, statisticians, surveyors, experimentalists, and tabulators. Essential to this conversation is the matter of what constitutes evidence or proof in a given discipline, and proof in the humanities is a very different matter from scientific or social-scientific proof. One of the great challenges for humanists—whoever we are today—is to explain what evidence is for us, and how we justify it.

For many years I taught a large lecture course in Shakespeare, part of Harvard's Core curriculum, a course that enrolled as many as four to six hundred students at a time. (I gave up this course, which I loved teaching, only when I published the lectures—in revised form—in my book *Shakespeare After All.*) For some of these students, this was, perhaps, the only course in literature they would take in the four years of their college experience. One day when I was lecturing, perhaps—though I'm not sure—about *The Merchant of Venice*, I began with a presentation about how a particular issue had been interpreted. The students wrote busily in their notebooks. After about ten minutes, I said, "that was for many years the leading interpretation, but these days very few people believe it." In the lecture hall there was a pause, as students crossed out their notes. I began again with another interpretation—"instead, people began to argue that . . ." and again the students faithfully recorded this information. And again, after about another ten minutes, I stopped to say, "but this view, too, has now been set aside by most critics." Again the silence, again the vigorous crossing out. By the end of the lecture, after this process had been repeated a few more times, many students were visibly irritated (though others, I would like to think, were stimulated and engaged). I was the professor. I was the Shakespeare expert. Presumably I knew the right answer. Why didn't I just tell them? But of course what I was teaching them—or trying to teach them—was something else, and something important. That the humanities, or at least the literary humanities, are an ongoing conversation and dialogue, conducted over space and time, orally and in written form. This is not the same as saying "anything goes." There is indeed *evidence* (in the text, in history, in stage practice, and so on) about literary meanings, but those meanings are not final or finite. Works of literature, like works of art, music, and so on, are living things that grow and change over time, gathering meanings and significances through the history of their reception and performance, and in dialogue with the historical context. *The Merchant of Venice* is not the "same" play after the Holocaust as it was before, any more than Shylock, its most contested character, is the "same" as he was in Shakespeare's own time, when the part of the Jewish moneylender was played for laughs, and the actor wore a red wig and a false nose. The words of the play are the same. But the audiences are different, and the history of the play—the gradual transmutation of Shylock from comic butt, to tragic villain, to empathetic outsider, and the modern conflation of these modes—has changed what Shakespeare "means." And we could make similar claims about virtually every play, not only those in which considerations of racial, religious, or gender attitudes have changed with time.[7]

THE HUMANITIES CENTER AS SYMPTOM

As we've begun to see, there is a significant sense in which "the humanities," as we generally and loosely discuss them today—the current set of departments, courses, and approaches that cover literature, music and art, religion and philosophy—are already both "before the humanities" and "after the humanities." This is a situation in which that familiar phrase from postmodernism, *always already*, has a pertinent and accurate place. (The humanities are always already prescient and belated, both "before" and "after" their ideal and notional selves.) Let's see how this works: The medieval educational system of the trivium and the quadrivium (the trivium: grammar, logic, and rhetoric; then the quadrivium: arithmetic, geometry, music, and astronomy) was the standard mode of intellectual training for centuries. And grammar, logic—or dialectic—and rhetoric (the structure of language, the way language produces argument, and analysis, the way language can be used to persuade and instruct) are at the heart of what we now call "the humanities," although that term, and the modern educational system that employs it, was long in developing.

Renaissance humanism, a cultural and pedagogical program of recovering the Greek and Roman texts, emphasized the liberal arts—music, art, rhetoric, oratory, poetry, history, science—as a way of exploring the nature of the self, the dignity of the individual, and the heritage of the past. Here it came into conflict with a more biblically based mode of education that emphasized obedience and humility, and focused on religious rather than classical works. Scholars and writers at the forefront of this movement included Erasmus, Petrarch, Thomas More, and Pico della Mirandola. In England, schools were founded on this principle. It was, indeed, the educational system that was in practice when Shakespeare attended the Stratford grammar school, where he seems to have gotten a good classical education centering on the study of Latin texts, like Ovid's *Metamorphoses*, Virgil's *Aeneid*, and the plays of Plautus.

When the term *humanities* per se entered the European, British, and American educational systems it referred—we should note—to Greek and Latin texts of philosophy and history (not yet of literature), read in the original languages. *Lit Hum*, the Anglicized, academic version of the Latin phrase *literae humaniores* (literally, "more humanistic letters") became a degree category at Oxford around 1850—a degree also known as *Greats*, based on the primary study of Greek and Latin classics. Bear in mind that at Oxford this was initially a study of Greek and Roman *history* and *philosophy*; despite the *Lit* title, only in 1968 did it formally incorporate Roman and Greek literature. (In recent years the "Greats" degree has added art, archaeology, and modern literature and philosophy as well.)

I describe the genesis of the Oxford "Lit Hum" program because it contrasts with the American version of "Lit Hum" as it has long been taught, for example, at Columbia University. There the course, which began in 1937—in the between-the-wars period of attention to American cultural citizenship—is entirely taught in English translation. It includes many of the Greek and Roman classics, from Homer, Euripides, Herodotus, Plato, and Virgil, through more recent "classics" like Jane Austen and Virginia Woolf (supplying gender balance as well as modern perspectives), and also includes readings from the Hebrew Bible and the New Testament. Since 1947 the Columbia Core curriculum has included not only *literature* humanities but also *art* humanities and *music* Humanities, as well as the basic course "Frontiers of Science," a course in contemporary civilization (first begun in 1919 as a course on war and peace issues, it is interesting to note). Recently, courses in "Asian humanities" and "African civilizations" have been added to the Core, redressing the balance of "Western" texts.

Many, perhaps most, other U.S. universities and colleges have core curricula that resemble this to one degree or another—my own university has been engaged in a lively set of debates about what the new Harvard General Education requirement should look like—but I mention these, in particular, because they lay out the general terrain, and because they now include literature, art, and music. I want especially to underscore the fact that these are "core," "general education," or other basic requirements. They assume, usually with some accuracy, that students have not encountered most of these texts and ideas before and, indeed, that this may be their only exposure to them. In effect, even these are "after the humanities" humanities courses, because their role is to supply the substrate of basic works, themes, and ideas which are thought—or were once thought—to constitute the basic building blocks of modern (and ancient) humanistic knowledge: works, themes, and ideas with which the contemporary undergraduate is increasingly unfamiliar.

The humanities on campus have often had their fate bound up with such distribution requirements and general-education programs. Without such introductory courses, it is assumed, their enrollments would drop yet further. Thus in some places the humanities have become, in effect, a service division for universities and colleges, shoring up the "culture" side of what is, increasingly, professional education. What is the alternative to this useful but subsidiary role?

It's important to remember that the study of the literature of one's own language was not part of the university curriculum until the latter part of the nineteenth century. "The modern languages and literatures," notes Gerald Graff, "were considered mere social accomplishments," and "were looked upon as feminine preoccupations."[8] And we should also note that *English*, up until the 1860s, meant elocution and rhetoric. When Ralph Waldo Emerson was at Harvard (1817–21) he read Shakespeare, but only in extracurricular reading groups founded by enthusiastic undergraduates. Harvard's first course in English literature was taught in 1872–73, and the first Shakespeare course was offered (by Francis James Child) in 1876. At Michigan, the first English courses were combined with rhetoric, starting in the late 1850s. At the University of Virginia in 1874, out of a total of 368 undergraduates, only nine attended classes in literature. At Yale the teaching of English literature began in the 1870s, and the first Shakespeare course was offered in 1879. At Harvard, courses of instruction were not grouped by department until 1872, when English, Spanish, German, French, and Italian became departments. At Indiana University, under a visionary president, David Starr Jordan, an English major was first offered in the late 1880s. The change to a kind of professionalism in this area did not come until around 1875, when literary scholarship began to develop as a distinct field—this shift continued until around 1915. In the interim, something of the piety and religiosity of the old system—the education of a Christian gentleman, or, to cite the *Oxford English Dictionary*'s definition of humanities, the study of the "various branches of polite scholarship"—became tempered with a concern for matters like a national literary canon.

This timeline for the institutional professionalization of literary study—from the late 1870s through around 1915—dovetails in interesting ways with the emergence of social-science disciplines like anthropology, sociology, and psychology, all of which emerged as disciplines in the same time period, the last decades of the nineteenth century and the first decades of the twentieth.

Here, for comparison, is another timeline, a list not of majors but of professional organizations, humanistic and social scientific. The Modern Language Association was founded in 1883; the American Psychological Association, in 1892; the American Philosophical Association, in 1900; the American Anthropological Association, in 1902; the American Sociological Association, in 1905; and the College Art Association, in 1912.

This, in other words, was the disciplinary moment: the turn of the last century. The moment of professionalization, organization, publication, self-identification. It was, we can say, the "humanities moment," too—the first time since the Renaissance that humanists self-identified in organized ways to pursue a pedagogical program. It was a moment. It lasted about a century. And now it's over.

The organizations, of course, remain and flourish. And the scholars, the journals, the departments, the graduate programs, the bricks and mortar, the teaching staff, the clerical staff, the graduate students, the pipeline—all of these remain. But almost as soon as the humanistic disciplines began to coalesce they also began to transgress their self-constituted borders. This should not strike us as unexpected. What we need to keep in mind is that our "modernity" is a very short interval. Compared to the centuries of "humanistic practice" *before* "the humanities," which is to say, before institutional and disciplinary self-consciousness and canonicity, the time of the "English department" and the "history of art department" (previously "fine arts") and the "philosophy department" is a blip on the screen. Both the usefulness and the limitation of these categories were almost immediately felt, with some help from the government and its own instrumental goals. Thus, for example, the Cold War and the post–World War II expansion of the public universities coincided—not so coincidentally—with the growth of so-called area-studies, which brought together fields like history, geography, sociology, economics, languages, and the arts; Russian studies, Middle Eastern studies, Asian studies, African studies, American studies. Each had its itinerary, its ideology, its fit, or non-fit, with the cultural and political goals of universities, governments, and disciplines. And once this very adaptable *studies* suffix was out of the box, it could be used as a combining form for other interdisciplinary research that was not principally geographical in scope: women's studies, gender studies, African-American studies, ethnic studies, cultural studies, science studies, performance studies. These emerging and emergent paradisciplines, brought together history, the arts, politics and economics, and thus crossed over, regularly, from the division of the humanities into the social sciences, and, increasingly, into the life sciences.

Furthermore, these "studies" changed the "traditional" humanistic disciplines, like "English" or "history," both by luring away professors, scholars, and students, and also by a species of back-formation. If you look at any college or university course catalog today you will find that courses on science and technology, for example, are often taught (or cotaught) in literature departments. At the same time, law schools, medical schools, and programs in justice are increasingly teaching works of literature, visual art, and drama. One question for "the humanities" is, who is teaching these things, and what kind of training (or "credentials") do they have—or should they have—to teach them?

At the very first meeting of the Modern Language Association, over a hundred years ago, in 1883, a professor of German worried aloud that so long as "teachers of modern languages . . . do not realize, that their department is a science," people will think that "*any body* can teach French or German or what is just as dangerous, any body can teach English."[9] The speaker insisted that "our department is a science," but over a hundred years later it is perhaps less clear than ever what the scientific methods of these disciplines might be. Interpretation? Philology? Historical contextualization? In any case, the idea that "any body can teach" these subjects (Greek literature in translation, let us say, or Shakespeare, or nineteenth-century novels, all now frequently taught by law professors to enliven their courses) is alive and well. And needless to say, professors of the humanities return the compliment, teaching Blackstone's *Commentaries* and Supreme Court decisions and the history of anatomy and physiology in courses listed under "English," "Comparative Literature," and "Art History."

In one sense we have returned to the "before the humanities" moment, when "scientific" questions and questions that relate to what we now call social science were part of the purview of poets, essayists, and cultural theorists (like Bacon, like Montaigne, like Milton). But these days a new set of terms, and fields, has entered the public consciousness. Terms like *medical humanities* and *digital humanities* and *law and the humanities*. *Humanities*, in fact, is now a suffix (replacing the *studies* suffix of the 1980s and '90s). While we were busy worrying about prefixes (*post*-structuralism and *post*-modernism, *new* or *neo*-historicism) it was the suffixes that were really changing the academy. (So the "after the humanities" moment is heralded by the placement of *humanities* after the signifying adjective or noun phrase.)

The proliferation of parafields in the humanities, many of those fields adjacent to science or social science (cultural anthropology, cognitive theory, affect or the theory of the emotions) might suggest, again, that we are *already* both "post-disciplinary" or "after the humanities." But without question the strongest and most evident symptom that points in that direction is the growth of humanities centers and institutes.

This may strike you as a paradox, but in fact it is probably a historical inevitability. Humanities centers have become the places where one can do post-humanities work in the humanities. The places where disciplinary boundaries are *meant* to break down, where collaboration, cooperation, and crossfield investigations are *designed* to take place. They are, thus, institutions invented, sustained, and authorized to house the transition from "the humanities" to a future reorganization of knowledge production and practice. Humanities centers are designed to be interdisciplinary, crossdisciplinary, or transdisciplinary. They are *anaclitic*, or "propping," entities, in Freud's sense. And when they have done their work, they will disappear. As vital and vibrant as they now seem, and as they are, these institutions are a kind of scaffolding. They are places to which scholars at all career stages, and from many disciplines, can gather and work together. In other words, the growth of humanities centers, nation- and world-wide, while it looks like a progressive move toward both expanding and stabilizing the role of the humanities, may actual be a symptom of their dispersal and dissolution. They are a stage in a larger reorganization of "the humanities"—the shape of which we cannot yet entirely see. They are, in other words, transitional institutions, healthy symptoms of change.

One obvious if broad analogy here is the shift between the Ptolemaic and Copernican systems of the universe. The proliferation of epicycles necessary to chart what Ptolemy thought was the circuit of the planets around the earth altered radically—became simplified—when it was acknowledged that the earth was actually one of many planets that circled around the sun. So likewise the growth or "rise" of humanities centers, with their emphasis on crossdisciplinary, multicultural, and collaborative work, offered an alternative to the "traditional humanities," which were at once similarly de-centered and newly energized. And where twenty years ago the humanities centers might have been needed to tweak, spark, or prod reluctant departments into transgressing their own borders and boundaries, the job has by now been so successfully completed that the humanities centers now sit, comfortably (perhaps too comfortably) among the humanistic disciplines, offering funding, fellowships, platforms, and publicity for intellectual work that could—often if not always—be undertaken within the newly rethought or restructured academic departments and programs. Courses and topics once only thinkable outside departmental boundaries—and facilitated by humanities centers—have now made their way back into the departmental curriculum. Just check your own department's listings—you'll see that this is the case. Where once there was resistance, there is now cooperation.

And we should also acknowledge that there has been a generational change. Copernicus explained the illusion of the sun moving around the earth by drawing a comparison with sailors on a ship; when it is calmly floating along, the ship seems to be stationary. Humanities departments aren't stationary, either, since people retire, move, are hired, are promoted, change the direction of the department from within. "The English department" is a cultural fantasy (not everybody's, probably) as well as a budgetary line and a set of offices and classrooms. Today's English department is, most probably, staffed and run by scholars who got their start in the profession at institutions with active, innovative humanities centers. The outside has become inside. The outsiders have become insiders. Is it time for another "outside"?

In this spirit, let us consider two further kinds of innovation, one already happening, the other to my mind highly desirable, that will reposition "the humanities" after the humanities. The first is collaborative work. The second is a fundamental, top-to-bottom, reorganization of categories, departments, and programs. Both of them challenge the existing order in ways that are threatening to the existing order of things. That is one reason, but not the only reason, why they are so important.

COLLABORATIVE WORK AND THE NEW HUMANITIES

Collaborative work is an idea whose time has already come. In fact it came many centuries ago, in a variety of artistic and research areas. The workshop of Peter Paul Rubens had no difficulty in assigning various parts of a canvas to specialists: Anthony Van Dyck did the hands; Frans Snyders, the game animals. Shakespeare's plays, like those of his contemporaries, were often written with the collaborative participation of other members of the acting company. As actors improvised lines and gestures, some of them stuck; the plays changed as they were produced. Sometimes, of course, plays were actually credited to two (or more) playwrights (Beaumont and Fletcher, Webster and Dekker). But equally important, for our consideration here, are "authors" whose names didn't make it onto the title page, or into the catalogue. The innovation of copyright in the early eighteenth century seemed to resolve some questions of intellectual property, but in fact the questions remain, and have proliferated in the present day, when everything from Hollywood scripts to advertising is "pitched," and produced, in collaboration.

Scientists, of course, have long cosigned their articles; your position on the list of authors is determined either by your importance in the world or by your contribution to the specific research (sometimes both). Humanists have often worked collaboratively, in scholarship as well as in arts groups and performance (dance, orchestra, theater, film), but the problem has come with the question of evaluation.

When the authors are eminent enough, a collaboration can be taken for granted as a "good thing." Here are some quick samples of well-known collaborations among literary scholars over the last half century: René Wellek and Austin Warren wrote, in 1947, a book called *Theory of Literature*. In the preface, they describe their collaboration in some detail.

> The authors of this book, who first met at the University of Iowa in 1939, immediately felt their large agreement in literary theory and methodology.
>
> Though of differing backgrounds and training, both had followed a similar pattern of development, passing through historical research and work in the "history of ideas," to the position that literary study should be specifically literary. Both believed that "scholarship" and "criticism" were compatible; both refused to distinguish between "contemporary" and past literature.[10]

They go on to particularize which of them wrote each of the book's chapters. ("Mr. Wellek is primarily responsible for chapters . . . ; Mr. Warren for chapters . . .") "But," they insist,

> the book is a real instance of a collaboration between two writers. In terminology, tone, and emphasis there remain, doubtless, some slight inconsistences between the writers; but they venture to think that there may be compensation

for these in the sense of two different minds reaching so substantial an agreement.

Very nice. Very courtly, very forties. And only possible for established scholars. This was not a "tenure book."

The fifties brought forth a similarly influential volume, this one, a 750-page book called *Literary Criticism: A Short History*, by William K. Wimsatt Jr. and Cleanth Brooks. Again, it is worth taking note of their method of collaboration.

> The whole work has been written by a method of fairly close collaboration not only in the general plan but in the execution of each part. The authors have read and criticized each other's work closely and repeatedly at various stages. The substantial responsibility for the chapters is, however, to be divided as follows . . .[11]

and here they give a list of chapters and indicate which of them wrote which. Wimsatt and Brooks also include a long list of other scholars, editors, and students to whom they are indebted, including Wimsatt's graduate seminar. And they include an acknowledgment of their wives, in a spirit that is indicative of another kind of collaboration, often understated and underthanked:

> To Margaret and Tinkum, for labors expert, various, and unremitting, the authors join in affectionate gratitude.[12]

It's pretty clear that a good deal of "single-authored" work in the humanities has had this kind of family assistance—and perhaps the assistance of secretaries, amanuenses, research assistants, and other collaborators who make it into the acknowledgments but not onto the title page, as is the convention in humanities publishing. (And not only in the humanities—we can recall the relative invisibility of scientist Rosalind Franklin in the publication of Francis Crick and James Watson's *Double Helix*. Gender practices have changed so greatly since that time that it seems amazing to think how recently it was.)

A recent obituary for Ann DeChiara Malamud, the wife of the novelist Bernard Malamud, described her as what her daughter called "the proverbial writer's wife," typing all his manuscripts, as well as his letters of application for teaching posts. "She typed things endlessly for him," said the daughter, Janna Malamud Smith, "not always 100 percent happily. She could be a very, very direct person. . . . If she didn't like something she would tell him. . . . He was a guy who didn't like to be criticized. And she was a person who could become very quickly very critical." After her husband's death, Mrs. Malamud went through all his papers and manuscripts, and placed them in libraries for posterity. "It was a continuation of what she did in life for him," her daughter said. "Her work was the work of his career, basically."[13] This too is collaboration, of a kind that went unheralded and uncompensated in the sweepstakes of fame. The obituary headline said it all in a nutshell: "wife nurtured novelist's career."

For a change of gender politics, let's look at one last famous scholarly collaboration, Sandra Gilbert and Susan Gubar's 1979 book, *The Madwoman in the Attic.* Their introduction gives the intellectual background ("This book began with a course in literature by women that we taught together at Indiana University in the fall of 1974") and goes on to record the "exhilaration of writing [that] has come from working together." Gilbert and Gubar, too, divided up the chapters in ways that they detail, but, they add,

> We have continually exchanged and discussed our drafts, however, so that we feel our book represents not just a dialogue but a consensus. Redefining what has so far been male-defined literary history in the same way that women writers have revised "patriarchal poetics," we have found that the process of collaboration has given us the essential support to complete such an ambitious project.[14]

Thus for Gilbert and Gubar the collaborative project is not only collegial and intellectually stimulating, but also thematized and political. They too thank their spouses ("the revisionary advice and consent of our husbands, Elliot Gilbert and Edward Gubar") and also their children, as well as several pages of colleagues, students, and friends.

Now, two is not the magic or inevitable number for collaboration. For every dyad like Marx and Engels, there is a creative collaborative team like the Marx Brothers. Nor is it most likely, these days, that collaborations will be between individuals with very similar trainings, as is the case in all of these earlier examples. More often, a collaborative project will bring together, say, an art historian, a historian of science, and a scientist, or a literary scholar, a philosopher, and a political theorist. And in these cases, the reviews of their work, both in the public sphere and within the confines of the university, are going to cross departmental, field, and subject lines. Evaluating participation in such projects will become all the more difficult—and proper protocols for evaluation, more and more urgent. But collaboration should not be a privilege reserved, in the humanities, for the already tenured. And what about dance companies and theatre companies? Actors, directors, dramaturges, techies. Not to mention the entire field of the digital humanities, which heralds an era of what might be called Big Humanities, modeled after the Big Science of the mid to late twentieth century—teams of experts working together, with the aid of technology, to make texts, images, and other materials available for analysis. The humanities have, for a very long time, been identified with the "solitary genius" model—even though in fact most of the people labeled geniuses in the twentieth century (unlike those past) have been scientists.[15] We need to take another look at how our research and creative thinking is actually being done. How can we figure out a way to give credit to truly collaborative projects put together by study groups, performance troupes, conference planners, and so on? Again, I should emphasize that an enormous amount of such work is already taking place in what I am tempted to call—echoing a term in literary theory—the humanities under erasure, or—following a tip from popular culture—the division formerly known as the humanities (although Prince seems to have reclaimed his name, or title, and perhaps we will need to do that, too). Indeed, this is the very kind of work most often sponsored by humanities centers, even if they have residential fellows.

Setting up standards for the evaluation of collaborative work is an issue for departments, university administrators, and professional organizations like the MLA and the American Historical Association. There's nothing that generates credibility quicker than the prestige conferred by competitive awards of this kind, especially when they are peer reviewed. And I regard this as a matter of intellectual ethics as well as of institutional change. Here it may be useful to remember Mrs. Malamud, perpetually typing in another room, doubtless soundproofed away from the cogitations of genius at work. But this is not about credit so much as it is about methodology and opportunity. To repeat: from the seminar to the study group to the conference to the performance, much work in the humanities today (and yesterday) has been conceived and carried out collaboratively, even before the advent of the digital humanities. Any vision of the humanities "after the humanities" should not only restore that invisible work to visibility, but also rethink what it means to have an idea, to articulate it, to share it and to see it develop, grow, and change.

I come now to my own pet project, the one I dream of doing, even beyond getting collaborative work recognized, funded, and tenured. I'm afraid it's a scheme that sounds all too much like Mr. Causabon's "Key to All Mythologies" in *Middlemarch*—a hopelessly ambitious project, incredibly time consuming, and well beyond the capacities of the person who dreams of doing it.

It's my contention that there is, hidden beneath the "large, loose, baggy monster" of every university's list of course offerings in the humanities (the phrase is, of course, Henry James's description of the novel) a hidden order, if we could only winkle it out. I am guessing that if we were to try to find affinities between and across departments and programs, course by course, we would find them: approaches, authors, genres, styles, applications, histories; technology, science, art, the public, the private, the urban, landscape, animals, vegetables, minerals—you see, perhaps, what I mean. If we were to index all courses under keywords, and then look at how they were grouped, and if we were to do this not only university by university or college by college but, in a next stage, in groups of similar institutions across the country, I think we might be able to deduce some patterns that would tell us something about how the humanities are actually being taught. Which is to say, how they are being understood, theorized, and practiced.

I want to put some emphasis on this word *practice*. We hear a lot these days about "knowledge production," a phrase I'm not crazy about, because I never like nouns used as adjectives. But in any case the ways knowledge is produced, or recognized, may account for some disciplinary differences, but not for all of them. For me the question of a practice is central: what do you *do*? Interpret? Experiment? Theorize? Hypothesize? Close read? Contextualize? Historicize? Compare? Contrast? Debunk? Put in question? And, to recur to a question I raised early on, what kinds of *evidence* or *proof* are persuasive in your practice? Put slightly differently: what is the value of counterintuitive thinking, as well as of "rational" thought, in the intellectual, cultural, and political work you do? Practices always develop in advance of institutions.

It is indeed in consideration of the realm of *practice* that I would, for example, link the arts with the experimental sciences, rather than with the humanities. Art making, like certain kinds of science and engineering, involves space, materials, experiment, repetition, failure, expensive and precise machinery. It's often done by groups of individuals rather than singly—major artists today, if they deal in sculpture, installations, or earthworks of unwieldy size, may have fabricators to assist them in actually producing the work. Film, theater, and dance are clearly collaborative enterprises, each linked increasingly with technology, anatomy, kinesiology—and practice, in both senses of the word: repetition and craft. The humanities disciplines that deal with art, music, and literature are interpretative and textual or material but they are often also historical. If we called artists' studios *laboratories* (as, in fact, once was the case) we would see the structural similarities even more clearly. A laboratory, after all, is a place where work—labor—takes place. And every artist I know talks of his or her practice not so much as "painting" or "sculpture" but as "making work."

So the questions I would ask of every scholar, every theorist, every scientist and artist connected with higher education would be: What is your practice? What is the object of your research? What kinds of institutional spaces make your work possible (archives, libraries, theaters and concert halls, studios, laboratories, playing fields, forests, deserts). I think that if we are willing to take the risks—intellectual, institutional, individual and collective—of a major reorganization of educational categories, these are the kinds of issues we will need to address. We need to locate affinities between and among scholarly practices—practices of research, interpretation, argument, proof, and "making"—that will come closer to matching up what we teach, and how we teach it, with the rubrics, categories, and disciplinary "homes" that hire, promote, and sustain contemporary education. I have imagined this project as one of cutting and pasting, to begin with, removing every course from its "home" and rethinking its place and its intellectual affinities. But this is only a first step, a heuristic. With this raw information in hand, we need to think big about changes.

This will make many people unhappy, I suspect, at least in the short run. It will involve—if we have the courage to do it—a major rethinking, and, far more discomforting, a major reallocation of resources. It's very unlikely that most institutions, committed as they are to functioning degree programs, existing buildings, and a cast of characters including not only tenured professors but also myriad in-place deans and administrators, will really want to reorganize that complicated and ill-defined area I have called the humanities under erasure. But, as I say, humanities centers are symptoms—palpable, effective, healthy symptoms—of the problem we have been facing (or refusing to face) for some time. The opportunity for rethinking is an opportunity for thinking. We should not pass it by.

One other thing we will need to realize, and to work on, is the fact that "the humanities" today is a topic for lifelong learning, and not just for the traditional college years. We can start earlier, with secondary school students, to develop a critical appreciation of humanities fields. But what we should certainly do is prepare to focus on post-graduate and post-college study, whether in continuing-education programs, in alumni colleges, or, indeed, in leadership institutes and ideas festivals. It is both a truism and a truth that the value of studying literature, art, philosophy, language, and culture is often something that is understood belatedly, after graduation from college rather than before—especially in the present economic climate. Faculty and graduate students in the humanities should welcome the opportunity to teach in such venues— and should develop strategies for doing so.

I began my own scholarly and theoretical work on Shakespeare with a book on dreams and then a book on ghosts. And the logic behind both of these books was the logic of the "after/before," the untimely appearance, or reappearance, of something that never seems to be fully present, but always returns. The humanities is such a dream, and such a ghost.

Let me move toward an end, then, by circling back to where I began. With the idea that "the humanities" (themselves, or itself, an "idea") had a cultural moment when it looked as though they were one thing, or a recognizable set of things. But that both before that moment and now after it—in my polemical terms, "before the humanities" and "after the humanities"—the opportunities for collaboration, crossfertilization, and a commonality of interests across boundaries and borderlines are there for us to take. We should resist the idea that the humanities are merely an aspect of "general education" at the same time that we embrace the chance to teach so many students so early in their academic careers. We should get used to the idea of talking as generalists as well as specialists—something we are actually better at than we get credit for being. Young humanities scholars, in particular, can start adding this to their arsenals, talking with alumni, parents, freshmen, and nonspecialists (in their own departments and across the university) about what excites them in their work. It's only a matter of emphasis, I believe, of bringing the "what is at stake" question to the forefront. At the same time, we should be ready to rethink the entire disciplinary apparatus—moving our offices, our classrooms, and our places of publication as well as our questions—across the broader university. But we should also hold fast to the idea that it is possible and meaningful to specialize in the humanities, especially now. And this means understanding the use, or useful uselessness, of the humanities for students who are not intending to become college professors. Otherwise we wind up inadvertently outsourcing our enterprise to the law school, the medical school, and the schools of government and diplomacy. Perhaps coappointments with those schools lie in the future, for those of us trained as humanists. Or for our students.

"After the humanities" does not mean that something is finished, but rather than something is starting. What comes after the humanities—for humanists and for scholarship in general—will be unexpected, unforeseen, transformative. If we could predict it with certainty, we would not be looking far enough ahead.

Notes

INTRODUCTION: LOADED QUESTIONS

1. This passage was used in Britain by Lord Atkin in his dissenting judgment in the seminal case *Liversidge v. Anderson* (1942), where he protested about the distortion of a statute by the majority of the House of Lords. It also became a popular citation in U.S. legal opinions, appearing in 250 judicial decisions in the Westlaw database as of April 19, 2008, including two Supreme Court cases (*TVA v. Hill* and *Zschernig v. Miller*).

2. Andrew Motion, "An Introduction to the Poetry of John Keats," *Guardian*, January 23, 2010.

3. "A modern work it is said must have a purpose," the longer passage reads. "*An artist* must serve Mammon—he must have 'self concentration' selfishness perhaps. You I am sure will forgive me for sincerely remarking that you might curb your magnanimity and be more of an artist, and 'load every rift' of your subject with ore." John Keats to Percy Bysshe Shelley, 16 August 1820.

4. Guyon in fact rejects the blandishments of the "Money God," as he calls Mammon (2.7.39:1). The advice being tendered is tender but also tough. The loading of the verse, and of the poem's subject, both enriches and threatens "heauy ruine" (2.7.28:6).

5. Raymond Williams, *Keywords: A Vocabulary of Culture and Society* (New York: Oxford University Press, 1983).

6. Sigmund Freud, "The Antithetical Meaning of Primal Words" (1910), in *The Standard Edition of the Complete Psychological Works of Sigmund Freud*, ed. and trans. James Strachey (London: Hogarth Press and the Institute of Psycho-Analysis, 1957), 11:155.

7. Roland Barthes, *Mythologies*, trans. Annette Lavers (New York: Hill and Wang, 1972), 12.

1. LOADED WORDS

1. Lawrence Summers, "Remarks at NBER Conference on Diversifying the Science and Engineering Workforce," Harvard University, accessed January 14, 2005, www.president.harvard.edu/speeches/2005/nber.html.

2. See Kenneth Chang and Dennis Overbye, "Planet or Not, Pluto Now Has Far-Out Rival," *New York Times*, July 30, 2005.

3. Dennis Overbye, "9 Planets? 12? What's a Planet, Anway?," *New York Times*, October 4, 2005.

4. Alexander Pope, "An Essay on Criticism," *The Poems of Alexander Pope*, ed. John Butt (New Haven, Conn.: 1963), 151, lines 215–16.

5. Oxford English Dictionary, 3rd ed., s.v. "data."

6. John Adams, entry for 30 Nov. 1778, *Diary and Autobiography of John Adams*, ed. L. H. Butterfield, Leonard C. Faber, and Wendell D. Garrett, 4 vols. (Cambridge, Mass., 1961), 2:324.

7. Richard Dawkins, interview in John Brockman, *The Third Culture* (New York: Simon and Schuster, 1995), 23.

8. Evelyn M. Witkin, letter to the editor, *New York Times*, September 28, 2005. Witkin is professor emerita of genetics at Rutgers University and a 2002 National Medal of Science recipient.

9. Joseph Priestley, "Experiments and Observations relating to Air and Water," *Philosophical Transactions* 75 (1785): 280. Lavoisier published an attack on the phlogiston theory in 1786, and his work on oxygen and combustion, replacing the theory of phlogiston, was presented to the Academy of Scientists in a memoir in 1779 (published 1781). See Antoine-Laurent Lavoisier, *Traité élémentaire de chime* (Paris: E. Arnold and Company, 1789).

10. See J. H. White, The History of the Phlogiston Theory (London: 1932).

11. "Si vera nostra sunt, aut false, erunt talia, licet nostra per vitam defendimus. Post fata nostra, pueri, qui nunc ludent, nostril iudices erunt." (Linnaeus, quoted in J. R. Partington and Douglas McKie, *Historical Studies on the Phlogiston Theory* [New York: Arno Press, 1981], 149.)

12. Raymond Williams, *Keywords: A Vocabulary of Culture and Society* (New York: Oxford University Press, 1983), 115.

13. Oxford English Dictionary, 3rd ed., s.v. "empirical."

14. Ibid.

15. Williams, *Keywords*, 117.

16. Clark Kerr, *The Uses of the University*, (Cambridge, Mass.: Harvard University Press, 1963), 87.

17. See Michael Frayn, *Copenhagen* (New York: Anchor, 2000), 99–100.

18. David Auburn, *Proof* (New York: Faber and Faber, 2001), 47.

19. John Patrick Shanley, *Doubt: A Parable* (New York: Dramatis Play Service, 2005), vii, ix–x.

20. ALIA Institute, "Authentic Leadership in Action," www.shambhalainstitute.org/core_prog.html

21. ALIA Institute, "Fieldnotes," www.shambhalainstitute.org/Fieldnotes/Issue9/index.html. In spring 2006 the third largest course in Harvard College was

"The Psychology of Leadership." (See Johannah S. Cornblatt, "Psych Courses Draw Full Houses," *Harvard Crimson*, February 14, 2006.) The course description reads as follows: "How can leaders—in the business sector, politics, or education—create an environment that facilitates growth? Topics include transformational leadership, personal identity, change, ethics, experience and peak performance, motivation, and systems thinking."

22. Paulo Freire, *Pedagogy of the Oppressed*, trans. Myra Bergman Ramos (1968; New York: Continuum, 1987), 58.

2. MAD LIBS

1. Sigmund Freud, *The Interpretation of Dreams* (1900), in *The Standard Edition of the Complete Psychological Works of Sigmund Freud*, ed. and trans. James Strachey (London: Hogarth Press and the Institute of Psycho-Analysis, 1953), 4:318, quoted in "The Antithetical Meaning of Primal Words," *Standard Edition* (1957), 11:155.

2. Freud, "Antithetical Meaning," 161.

3. Jacques Lacan, "The Agency of the Letter in the Unconscious or Reason since Freud," in Écrits, trans. Alan Sheridan (New York: W. W Norton, 1977), 146.

4. Lacan, "Agency," 162.

5. Lacan, "Agency," 174.

6. Michel Foucault, *History of Madness*, "Reply to Derrida," in *History of Madness*, trans. Jonathan Murphy and Jean Khalfa (New York: Routledge, 2006), 589. First published in French as *Folie et déraison: Histoire de la folie à l'âge classique* (Paris: Librarie Plon, 1961). The Routledge edition is a translation of *Histoire de la folie à l'âge classique* (Paris: Galimard, 1972).

7. Freud, "Extracts from the Fliess Papers," Draft J—Frau P. J." *Standard Edition* 1:216.

8. William Shakespeare, *All's Well That Ends Well*, 5.3.263

9. John Dryden, preface to *Cleomenes* (London: Jacob Tonson, 1717).

10. Jane Austen, *Mansfield Park* (London: T. Egerton, 1814), 3.12.228.

11. D. H. Lawrence, *Sons and Lovers* (New York: Penguin, 1977), 4:79.

12. *Daily Mail*, November 7, 1966. The prior five citations are all from the *OED*.

13. Robert Abele, "At the Movies: Alan Arkin, Totally in Control," *Los Angeles Times*, June 19, 2008.

14. Theodore Roosevelt, *History as Literature* (New York: Scribners, 1913), 305.

15. The changes from *DSM-III* (1974) through *DSM-IV* (1994) and the current *DSM-IV TR* (text revision, 2000) involved, among other things, reclassifying sexual orientation so that homosexuality was no longer listed, as it had been in *DSM-III*, as a category of disorder. The *DSM* categorizes and classifies things from clinical disorders to underlying personality conditions. But none, of course, are called madness.

16. E.g., Ros Davidson, "How Mad was Ted Kaczynski?," *Salon*, November 14, 1997; and "The Mad Bomber: FBI Holds Suspect in Unabomber Case," *Current Events*, April 29, 1996.

17. Noah Feldman, "Becoming bin Laden," review of *Messages to the World: The Statements of Osama bin Laden*, ed. Bruce Lawrence, *New York Times*, February 12, 2006, Sunday Book Review.

18. Leonard Stern, "A Happy History of Mad Libs," in Roger Price and Leonard Stern, *Best of Mad Libs* (New York: Price, Stern, Sloan, 2008).

19. Sally Lodge, "At 50, Mad Libs Continues to (verb)," *Publishers Weekly*, March 31, 2008.

20. Tony Hiss and Jeff Lewis, "The 'Mad' Generation," *New York Times,* July 31, 1977.

21. See Colonel Alan J. Parrington, USAF, "Mutually Assured Destruction Revisited: Strategic Doctrine in Question," *Airpower Journal* (Winter 1997).

22. Milton S. Katz, *Ban the Bomb: A History of SANE, 1957–1985* (New York: Greenwood, 1986).

23. Keir A. Lieber and Daryl G. Press, "The End of MAD? The Nuclear Dimension of U.S. Primacy" *International Security* 30, no. 4 (Spring 2006): 7–44.

24. *Hamlet* 2.2.205–6; 3.4.189–90.

25. Sidney Gottlieb, ed., *Hitchcock on Hitchcock: Selected Writings and Interviews* (Berkeley: University of California Press, 1997), 160. Donald Spoto notes that on April 11, 1946, *The Daily Film Renter* announced that Hitchcock would direct for Transatlantic Pictures "a modern version of *Hamlet*—a project that must certainly have caused consternation among those who thought that serious dramatic art was inconsistent with Hitchcock's presumably pedestrian and commercial concerns." Spoto, *The Dark Side of Genius: The Life of Alfred Hitchcock* (1983; New York: Da Capo Press, 1999), 295.

26. *Hamlet* 2.2.374.

27. *Hamlet* 3.2.4–5, 8–11.

28. *Salon*, November 15, 2007. In this article Hamm is chosen "Sexiest Man Living 2007."

29. Ernest Lehman, *North by Northwest* (London: Faber and Faber, 1999), 3.

30. *Hamlet* 3.1.32; 2.1.63.

31. Lehman, *North by Northwest*, 6.

32. Richard Hofstadter, *The Paranoid Style in American Politics and Other Essays* (Cambridge: Harvard University Press, 1964), 25–26.

33. Daniel Patrick Moynihan, *Washington Post*, December 29, 1991.

34. Hofstadter, *Paranoid Style*, 3–4.

35. Ibid., 4.

36. Phyllis Schlafly, *A Choice Not an Echo* (Alton, Ill.: Pere Marquette Press, 1964), 25–26.

37. Vance Packard, *The Hidden Persuaders* (New York: D. McKay, 1957).

38. Packard, "Politics and the Image Builders," chap. 17 in *The Hidden Persuaders*.

39. Mark Evanier, *Mad Art* (New York: Watson-Guptill, 2002), 294–98.

40. Richard H. Rovere, *Affairs of State: The Eisenhower Years*, quoted in Packard, *Hidden Persuaders*, 302.

41. John A. Stormer, *None Dare Call It Treason* (Florissant, Mo.: Liberty Bell Press, 1964), 158.

42. G. Brock Chisholm, in *Psychiatry*, February 1946, quoted in Stormer, *None Dare*, 158.

43. Sir John Harington, *Epigrams*, book 5, epistle 5.

44. Robert H. Welch Jr., *The Politician* (Belmont, Mass.: privately printed, 1963), 223, quoted in Hofstadter, *Paranoid Style*, 28.

45. Scott Shane, "China Inspired Interrogations at Guantánamo," *New York Times*, July 2, 2008.

46. Alfred D. Biderman, "Communist Attempts to Elicit False Confessions from Air Force Prisoners of War," *Bulletin of the New York Academy of Medicine* 33, no. 9 (1957): 616–25. Biderman was a sociologist working for the Air Force.

47. Maureen Dowd, "The Wrong Stuff," *New York Times*, July 2, 2008.

48. *Oxford English Dictionary*, 3rd ed., s.v. "brainwashing."

49. Stuart Rogers, "How a Publicity Blitz Created the Myth of Subliminal Advertising," *Public Relations Quarterly* (Winter 1993): 12–17. See also Wilson B. Key, *Subliminal Seduction* (New York: Signet, 1973).

50. Richard Gafford, "The Operational Potential of Subliminal Perception," Central Intelligence Agency, CIA Historical Review Program, September 18, 1998.

51. Amy M. Spindler, "How Much Glamour Can a Man Take?," *New York Times*, June 30, 2004.

52. Maria Menounos, quoted in the *Boston Globe*, July 8, 2008. The interview aired on *NBC Nightly News* and on *Access Hollywood*.

53. Foucault, *History of Madness*, 547. See the longer quotation in the epigraph to section 1, "Counterintelligence."

54. The *OED* dates this meaning of *pitch* from 1943. The first citation for *brainwashing* in the *OED* is dated 1950. See also Tim Weiner, "Remembering Brainwashing," *New York Times*, July 6, 2008.

55. George W. Bush, interview by Tim Russert, *Meet the Press, with Tim Russert*, NBC, February 8, 2004.

3. A TALE OF THREE *HAMLETS*; OR, REPETITION AND REVENGE

1. The Tragedie of Hamlet, Prince of Denmarke: William Shakespeare, ed. J. Dover Wilson (Weimar: Cranach Press, 1930).

2. Originally published in *Shakespeare's Ghost Writers: Literature as Uncanny Causality* (New York: Routledge, 1987), 124–76; reprinted in Marjorie Garber, *Profiling Shakespeare* (New York: Routledge, 2008), 29–75.

3. The term was popularized by Jung in 1907; Freud used it in phrases like "the Oedipus complex," "the castration complex," and "the father complex"; all of these, in his theory, were linked to Shakespeare's play. "The word 'complex,'" Freud wrote in 1914, "has become naturalized, so to speak, in psycho-analytic language; it is a convenient and often indispensable term for summing up a psychological state descriptively. None of the other terms coined by psycho-analysis for its own needs has achieved such widespread popularity or been so misapplied to the detriment of the construction of clearer concepts." "On the History of the Psycho-Analytic Movement" (1914), in *The Standard Edition of the Complete Psychological*

Works of Sigmund Freud, ed. and trans. James Strachey (London: Hogarth Press and the Institute of Psycho-Analysis, 1957), 14:7–66, esp. 29–30.

4. In a poem called "When I Read Shakespeare," D. H. Lawrence wrote, "And Hamlet, how boring, how boring to live with,/so mean and self-conscious blowing and snoring/his wonderful speeches, full of other folks' whoring!" *Pansies: Poems* (London, Martin Secker, 1929).

5. Unused blocks include a court scene (page 12), actors (62), Hamlet greeting the actors (63), King Claudius (114), a draped figure, and an image of the sea in flames. For further information, see "Craig, Edward Gordon, 1872–1966. Proofs for the Cranach Press edition of Shakespeare's *Hamlet*: Guide," Houghton Library, Harvard College Library, Harvard University., accessed November 1, 2009, http://oasis.lib.harvard,edu/oasis/deliver/~hou01927.

6. "An Expostulation with Inigo Jones," in *Ben Jonson, The Complete Poems*, ed. George Parfitt (New Haven: Yale University Press, 1982), 346, lines 49–50.

7. *The Collected Poems of W. B. Yeats* (New York: Macmillan, 1964), 336.

8. Letter to Martin Shaw, cited in Michael Holroyd, A Strange Eventful History: The Dramatic Lives of Ellen Terry, Henry Irving, and Their Remarkable Families (New York: Farrar, Straus, and Giroux, 2008), 390.

9. Nina Auerbach, *Ellen Terry, Player in Her Time* (New York: W. W. Norton, 1987), 177, 175.

10. Ellen Terry, *Ellen Terry's Memoirs* (New York: Benjamin Blom, 1969), 123–24, quoted in Auerbach, *Ellen Terry*, 179.

11. J. L. Styan, *Modern Drama in Theory and Practice*, 3 vols. (Cambridge University Press, 1981), 2:17.

12. Christopher D. Innes, *Edward Gordon Craig* (Cambridge: Cambridge University Press, 1983), 15.

13. Quotations from the play are from the Arden2 *Hamlet*, ed. Harold Jenkins (London: Routledge, 1993), cited parenthetically within the text.

14. Edward Gordon Craig, *Henry Irving* (New York: Longmans, Green, 1930), 32.

15. Edward Gordon Craig, "The Actor and the Über-Marionette," in *On the Art of the Theatre* (New York: Theatre Arts Books, 1956), 54–94, esp. 81.

16. Ibid., 75.

17. Ibid., 79.

18. Ibid., 81.

19. Ibid., 78.

20. Ibid., 56.

21. Ibid., 81.

22. Edward Gordon Craig, "The Art of the Theatre: The First Dialogue," in *On the Art of the Theatre*, 137–81, esp. 143–44. A "piece for the theatre," by contrast, would be "incomplete when printed in a book or recited," in fact, "incomplete anywhere except on the boards of a theatre" (144). For Craig, the masques and pageants of the Renaissance stage were such theater pieces—a very different kind of art form from *Hamlet*.

23. T. S. Eliot, "The Love Song of J. Alfred Prufrock," in *The Complete Poems and Plays 1909–1950* (New York: Harcourt, Brace, 1959), 7; and T. S. Eliot, "Hamlet

and His Problems," in *Selected Essays, 1917–1932* (New York: Harcourt, Brace, 1950), 121–26.

24. Edward Gordon Craig, "Shakespeare's Plays," in *On the Art of the Theatre*, 281–85, esp. 281–82. Craig is here voicing a common misconception about the plays, which were often cut for performance from the earliest years of their stage history. A 1676 quarto of *Hamlet*, adapted by William Davenant, included the following note "To the Reader": "This Play being too long to be conveniently Acted, such places as might be least prejudicial to the Plot or Sense, are left out upon the Stage." See *The Tragedy of Hamlet Prince of Denmark* (London, 1676), sig. A2r; Wing S2950. I am grateful to Peter Stallybrass for this reference.

25. Craig, "Shakespeare's Plays," 284–85.

26. Quoted in Laurence Senelick, "The Craig–Stanislavski 'Hamlet' at the Moscow Art Theatre," *Theatre Quarterly* 6 (1976): 70.

27. Craig, "The Actor and the Über-Marionette," 85, 94.

28. Konstantin Stanislavski, *My Life in Art*, trans. Jean Benedetti (London: Routledge, 2008), 294.

29. "When we used conventional means Craig's version looked like piece of theatrical trickery and reminded us for the hundredth time of the uselessness and crudeness of our methods of staging. . . . We were obliged to abandon Craig's plan for staging 'To be or not to be'" (Stanislavski, *My Life in Art*, 294).

30. Quoted in Senelick, "Craig–Stanislavski 'Hamlet,'" 73.

31. Senelick, "Craig–Stanislavski 'Hamlet,'" 63, 82. The "Volapuk of Russian and German" phrase is from a letter written by Kachalov, the actor cast as Hamlet in the Moscow production. Volapuk was a constructed language, a forerunner to Esperanto.

32. Innes, *Edward Gordon Craig*, 170; Stanislavski, *My Life in Art*, 295; and Senelick, "Craig–Stanislavski 'Hamlet,'" 107.

33. Craig, "Shakespeare's Plays," 285, note added in 1912.

34. Innes, *Edward Gordon Craig*, 210, 212.

35. As a result of studies of *Hamlet*, "black figures" also came to refer to Craig's method of inking one side of a piece of wood and producing a print that resembled a church brass rubbing. See Holroyd, *Strange Eventful History*, 467–68.

36. Laird McLeod Easton, *The Red Count: The Life and Times of Hary Kessler* (Berkeley: University of California Press, 2002), 139.

37. Innes, *Edward Gordon Craig*, 155.

38. Ibid., 174.

39. Stephen Orgel, "The Desire and Pursuit of the Whole," *Shakespeare Quarterly* 58 (2007): 290–310, esp. 308, 310.

40. Harry Kessler to Edward Gordon Craig, 4 June 1929, in *The Correspondence of Edward Gordon Craig and Count Harry Kessler, 1903–1937*, ed. L. M. Newman (London: W. S. Maney and Son, 1995), 242. A similar phrase appears in a letter of 15 May 1929 (241). A German edition in 1928, with a translation of the second quarto text by Gerhart Hauptmann, preceded this English edition. See *Die tragische Geschichte von Hamlet, Prinzen von Dänemark* (Weimar: Cranach Press, 1929). The source texts from Saxo Grammaticus and François de Belleforest are included in the

German *Hamlet*; Dover Wilson's editorial commentary was added for the English version.

41. Alexander Pope, "The Preface of the Editor," in *The Works of Shakespear: In Six Volumes; Collated and Corrected by the Former Editions, by Mr. Pope* (London, 1725), vol. 1, section 34: "I have discharg'd the dull duty of an Editor to my best judgment, with more labour than I expect thanks, with a religious abhorrence of all Innovation, and without any indulgence to my private sense or conjecture."

42. J. Dover Wilson, *What Happens in "Hamlet,"* 3rd ed. (1951; repr., Cambridge: Cambridge University Press, 2003), 12; see also 7.

43. John Dover Wilson, *Milestones on the Dover Road* (London: Faber and Faber, 1969), 179.

44. Terence Hawkes, *That Shakespeherian Rag: Essays on a Critical Process* (London: Methuen, 1986), 110.

45. "The Road to Elsinore; Being an Epistle Dedicatory to Walter Wilson Greg," in J. Dover Wilson, *What Happens in "Hamlet,"* 2–23.

46. W. W. Greg, "Hamlet's Hallucination," *Modern Language Review* 12 (1917): 393–412.

47. Letter from Kachalov, the actor playing Hamlet, quoted in Senelick, "Craig–Stanisklavski 'Hamlet,'" 97).

48. Dover Wilson, *What Happens in "Hamlet,"* 7.

49. Ibid., 7.

50. Ibid., 14.

51. Ibid., 13.

52. Ibid., 21. So here he has the analogy consciously in mind. He does not regard Granville-Barker, a dramatist and man of the theater, as a foe or a rival. "The bout was played to the sound not of drums and trumpets but of laughter, and though the swords were unbated and quarter was neither asked nor given, there was nothing 'incensed', still less 'venomed', about our 'points'" (21). This again is donnish wit, academic raillery. He's quoting, and he knows he's quoting.

53. *Shakespeare Restored: Or, a Specimen of the Many Errors, as Well Committed, as Unamended, by Mr. Pope in His Late Edition of this Poet. Designed Not Only to Correct the Said Edition, but to Restore the True Reading of Shakespeare in All the Editions Ever Yet Publish'd. By Mr. Theobald* (London: Samuel Aris, 1726).

54. *The Dunciad Variorum*, in *The Poems of Alexander Pope*, ed. John Butt (New Haven: Yale University Press, 1966), 317–459.

55. See F. P. Wilson, "Sir Walter Wilson Greg, 1875–1959," *Proceedings of the British Academy* 45 (1959): 307–54, esp. 310, 320.

56. Dover Wilson, *What Happens in "Hamlet,"* 11.

57. Ibid., 23.

58. Hawkes, *That Shakespeherian Rag*, 103–11. Dover Wilson himself had been stationed in Russia and wrote about it with caution and concern. Hawkes's very pointed political critique, written in the 1980s in Thatcherite England, claims that "these crucial events of 1917 helped to shape the way in which influential critics read the plays of Shakespeare." His argument is that the field of English studies arose in part as "a bulwark against the spread of revolution" (120).

59. Dover Wilson, *What Happens in "Hamlet,"* 14.

60. G. Thomas Tanselle, "The Life and Work of Fredson Bowers," *Studies in Bibliography* 46 (1993): 1–154, esp. 32, discussed by Jeffrey Masten, "Pressing Subjects; or, the Secret Lives of Shakespeare's Compositors," in *Language Machines: Technologies of Literary and Cultural Production*, ed. Jeffrey Masten, Peter Stallybrass, and Nancy J. Vickers (New York: Routledge, 1997), 75–107; see 88.

61. Tanselle, 32; cf. Masten, 88.

62. Ibid.

63. George Fabyan, *Hints to the Decipherer of the Greatest Work of Sir Francis Bacon, Baron of Verulam, Viscount St. Alban* (Geneva, Ill.: Riverbank Laboratories, 1916); and William F. Friedman and Elizabeth S. Friedman, *The Shakespearean Ciphers Examined: An Analysis of Cryptographic Systems Used as Evidence That Some Author Other Than William Shakespeare Wrote the Plays Commonly Attributed to Him* (Cambridge: Cambridge University Press, 1957).

64. Masterman, *Double-Cross System*, 118–20.

65. [Thomas Lodge,] *VVits Miserie, and the VVorlds Madnesse Discouering the Deuils Incarnat of this Age* (London: Adam Islip, 1596), 56: "ye ghost which cried so miscrally at ye Theator, like an oister wife, *Hamlet, reuenge*."

66. Michael Innes, *Hamlet, Revenge!* (London: Victor Gollancz, 1937; London: Penguin, 1961), 283.

67. See Ernest Jones, "The Oedipus Complex as an Explanation of Hamlet's Mystery: A Study in Motive," *American Journal of Psychology* 21 (1910): 72–113; "A Psychoanalytic Study of Hamlet," in *Essays in Applied Psycho-Analysis* (London: International Psycho-Analytical Press, 1923), 1–98; and *Hamlet and Oedipus* (New York: W. W. Norton, 1949).

68. J. I. M. Stewart, *Myself and Michael Innes: A Memoir* (London: Victor Gollancz, 1987), 133.

69. Michael Innes, introduction to "The Hawk and the Handsaw," in Rayner Heppenstall and Michael Innes, *Three Tales of Hamlet* (London: Victor Gollancz, 1950), 14.

70. Stewart, *Myself and Michael Innes*, 135; see Ernest Jones, "The Death of Hamlet's Father," *International Journal of Psycho-Analysis* 29 (1948): 174–76.

71. Dover Wilson, "Preface to the Third Edition," *What Happens in "Hamlet,"* vii–viii, esp. vii.

72. Ibid., ix–xv, esp. ix–x. Dover Wilson commented, "Granville-Barker was one of the greatest producers alive, while I am only an academic scribe on the wrong side of the curtain" (x).

73. In another intricate twist to this tale, the Westminster Theatre was bought in the late 1940s by the international religious movement Moral Re-Armament (MRA), whose famous "Four Absolutes" (absolute honesty, absolute purity, absolute unselfishness, and absolute love) were derived from the Oxford group headed by its founder, the Reverend Frank N. D. Buchman. Buchman served as the head of MRA from 1939 until his death in 1961.

74. Dover Wilson, *What Happens in "Hamlet,"* xi, note 1.

75. Stewart, *Myself and Michael Innes*, 119; and F. P. Wilson, quotation from "Sir Walter Wilson Greg," 331.

76. Innes, introduction to "The Hawk and the Handsaw," 13–15, esp. 14.
77. Dover Wilson, textual notes to the Cranach Press *Hamlet*, 184.
78. Stanislavski, *My Life in Art*, 294, 296.
79. Dover Wilson, *Milestones*, 178–79.
80. Ibid., 178.
81. Masterman, *Double-Cross System*, 177–78.

4. SHAKESPEARE IN SLOW MOTION

1. A. C. Bradley, *Shakespearean Tragedy* (London: Macmillian, 1924), 6.
2. Reuben A. Brower, "Reading in Slow Motion," in *In Defense of Reading*, ed. Reuben A. Brower and Richard Poirier (New York: E. P. Dutton, 1962), 3–21. Originally published in *Reading for Life*, ed. Jacob M. Price (Ann Arbor: University of Michigan Press, 1959).
3. Paul de Man, "The Return to Philology," in *The Resistance to Theory* (Minneapolis: University of Minnesota Press, 1986), 23. Originally published in the *Times Literary Supplement*, December 10, 1982.
4. Ibid., 24.
5. Ibid., 23.
6. Brower, "Reading in Slow Motion," 4.
7. Ibid., 5.
8. Ibid.
9. Ibid., 9.
10. Ibid., 3n1.
11. *Oxford English Dictionary*, 2nd ed., s.v. "slow."
12. An artist, not a scientist, Muybridge did not hesitate to manipulate his materials to produce the visual effect of an unbroken photographic sequence. "When a phase of the movement was missing—perhaps a camera failed or a negative broke or was fogged—Muybridge assembled the negatives that remained, gave them internal consistency, and renumbered them to appear consecutively in the print. At times he even went so far as to compile a sequence whose individual elements came from separate picture-taking sessions." In this practice he differed from his French counterpoint, Marey, whose work would come to influence cardiology, aviation, and anatomy, as well as early cinema. Marta Braun, *Picturing Time: The Work of Etienne-Jules Marey, 1830–1904* (Chicago: University of Chicago Press, 1992), 238. Marey's animal studies were produced with a chronophotographic gun that allowed him to show several phases of movement in the same photograph. His own celebrated experiment, demonstrating that a cat always lands on its feet, offered visual evidence to disprove Newton's law that once an object is in motion only an external force can change the direction of that motion. (Marey's longtime collaborator, Georges Demeny, split off from him in the 1890s to pursue a wider application of the technology; in 1892, Demeny invented a simple projector called a phonoscope and began to produce short films. Both Marey and Muybridge died in 1904, the year that Musger patented his design for a slow-motion device.)

13. Sigmund Freud, *The Psychopathology of Everyday Life* (1901), in *The Standard Edition of the Complete Psychological Works of Sigmund Freud*, ed. and trans. James Strachey (London: Hogarth Press and the Institute of Psycho-Analysis, 1960), 6:1–279.

14. Ibid., 97–98.

15. Walter Benjamin, "The Work of Art in the Age of Mechanical Reproduction," in *Illuminations*, ed. Hannah Arendt, trans. Harry Zohn (1936; New York: Schocken Books, 968), 235.

16. Ibid.. The internal quotation here is from Rudolf Arnheim's *Film als Kunst* (Berlin: Ernst Rowohlt, 1932), 138; see Benjamin, "Work of Art," 236. In the English translation of Arnheim, the phrase reads as follows: "Slow motion has hardly been applied at all yet to artistic purposes, although it should be very useful. It might, for instance, serve to slow down natural movements grotesquely; but it can also create new movements, which do not appear as the retarding of natural movements but have a curious gliding, floating character of their own. Slow motion should be a wonderful medium for showing visions and ghosts." Rudolf Arnheim, *Film as Art* (Berkeley: University of California Press, 1957), 110–11. This dreamlike capacity of slow motion in cinema was utilized, to strong effect, by filmmakers like Sergei Eisenstein and Dziga Vertov.

17. Arnheim, *Film as Art*, 111.

18. Benjamin, "Work of Art," 237.

19. Maya Deren, *An Anagram of Ideas on Art, Form and Film* (Yonkers, N.Y.: Alicat Book Shop Press, 1946), 47.

20. Deren, *Anagram*, 48.

21. Ibid.

22. *OED* cites as early instances "what Hollywood has perfected as the 'double take'" (1941) and "a double take worthy of Oliver Hardy" (1957), while "take" as a term from cinematography ("a continuous section of film photographed at one time; an instance of such filming") dates from 1922. *Oxford English Dictionary*, 2nd ed., s.v. "double take."

23. Judith Butler, "Endangered/Endangering: Schematic Racism and White Paranoia," in *Reading Rodney King / Reading Urban Uprising*, ed. Robert Gooding-Williams (New York: Routledge, 1993).

24. Ibid., 15–16.

25. Ibid., 16.

26. Ibid., 20.

27. Ibid., 16.

28. Ibid., 21.

29. Ibid., 20–21.

30. Although this piece is sometimes associated with the events of September 11, 2001, both the object of the actors' gaze and the emotions they display are fictional, which does not at all mean that they are not real.

31. Walsh notes that slow motion is also a key device for some of Viola's contemporaries, like the Scottish artist Douglas Gordon and the Dutch artist Aernout Mik. John Walsh, "Emotions in Extreme Time: Bill Viola's Passions Project," in

Bill Viola: The Passions, ed. John Walsh (Los Angeles, Calif.: Getty Museum, 2003), 60–61.

32. "I'm an artist, not a philosopher. I don't make meanings. I make art. The responsibility of an artist is not to say what something means, but to ask 'What does it mean?' The only reason to do a play is because you don't understand it. The moment you think you understand a work of art, it's dead for you. The last moment in any play must be a question. What happened? What was said? What is this? A play doesn't conclude. It should stay open ended. The last word must be a beginning, a door opening, not closing. A play is not a lecture in a classroom. I don't dictate meaning to the viewer. Theatre that imposes an interpretation is aesthetic fascism. By emptying out the meaning of a sentence, the text becomes full of meaning—or meanings. Actors, however, are trained to interpret; they feel it's their responsibility to color the text and the situation for the audience. So they reduce the possibilities of meaning. But in my theatre, the audience puts it all together, and each person puts it together differently. And each night the play is different. The audience makes the meaning. I once told an actor to read the text as if he didn't understand language. There's so much going on in a line of Shakespeare, that if the actor colors the voice too much, the audience loses too many other colors." Robert Wilson, quoted in Arthur Holmberg, *The Theatre of Robert Wilson* (Cambridge: Cambridge University Press, 1996), 61–62.

33. Mel Gussow, "At Home With: Robert Wilson," *New York Times*, January 6, 1994.

34. The Goold production opened at the Chichester Festival Theatre in the summer of 2007, then moved to sold-out engagements in London and New York.

5. THE SHAKESPEARE BRAND

1. Thomas Garbett, *How to Build a Corporation's Identity and Project Its Image* (Lexington, Mass.: Lexington Books, 1982), 151, 127.

2. Lynn Woolley, "Busting the Republican Brand," *Human Events*, May 22, 2008.

3. Thomas Davis III (R-Va.), quoted in Jonathan Weisman, "Republicans See Storm Clouds Gathering," *Washington Post*, March 16, 2008.

4. Tim Russert, *Hardball with Chris Matthews*, MSNBC, April 11, 2008; John Harwood, *Hardball with Chris Matthews* MSNBC, April 16 and 30, 2008.

5. *Oxford English Dictionary*, 3rd ed., s.v. "maverick."

6. Brock Vergakis, "Utah Faces Boycott After Push by Mormons vs. Gay Marriage," *Boston Globe*, November 9, 2008.

7. Glenn Collins, "A Critic, Insatiable and Dismissed," *New York Times*, November 26, 2008.

8. Danny Hakim and Raymond Hernandez, "Kennedy Brand Leaves a Rival Feeling Stymied," *New York Times*, December 20, 2008.

9. By the Statute of Vagabonds enacted under Edward VI (1547), vagabonds, gypsies, and brawlers were ordered to be branded, the vagabonds and gypsies with

a *V* on the breast, the brawlers with an *F* for "fraymaker." The law was not repealed until 1636.

10. We might compare the stigmatizing "noting" of Hero by Claudio in *Much Ado About Nothing*, or Antony's cynical concurrence in *Julius Caesar*, to the executions of those whose names are "pricked" in a political purge: "Look, with a spot I damn him" (4.1.6).

11. On *figura*, see Erich Auerbach, *Mimesis: The Representationn of Reality in Western Literature*, trans. Willard Trask (Garden City, N.J.: Doubleday, 1953), 64.

12. First used by Alexis de Tocqueville in 1831, *American Exceptionalism* has come to cover both a sense of manifest destiny and also a sense of national entitlement—the idea that the United States, because of its history, its political institutions, its ideals, the beliefs of its Founding Fathers, its ethnic diversity and its position in the world, is—or was—unique among nations.

For examples, see Ronald W. Dworkin, *The Rise of the Imperial Self* (Lanham, Md.: Rowman and Littlefield, 1996); Deborah L. Madsen, *American Exceptionalism* (Jackson: University Press of Mississippi, 1998); Jonathan A. Glickstein, *American Exceptionalism, American Anxiety: Wages, Competition, and Degraded Labor in the Antebellum United States* (Charlottesville: University of Virginia Press, 2002); Michael Ignatieff, ed. *American Exceptionalism and Human Rights* (Princeton, N.J.: Princeton University Press, 2005); and Seymour Martin Lipset, *American Exceptionalism: A Double-Edged Sword* (New York: W. W. Norton, 1997).

13. For examples, see Edwin Durning-Lewis, *The Shakespeare Myth* (London: Gay and Hancock, 1912); and Walter Ellis, *The Shakespeare Myth* (London: Bacon Society, 1946).

14. Graham Holderness, "Bardolatry," in *The Shakespeare Myth*, ed. Graham Holderness (Manchester: Manchester University Press, 1988), 10–13.

15. Roland Barthes, *Mythologies*, trans. Annette Lavers (New York: Hill and Wang, 1972), 110, 142, 129.

16. Ibid., 129–30.

17. Marjorie Garber, *Shakespeare and Modern Culture* (New York: Pantheon, 2008), xxi–xxii.

18. Q Scores, last modified 2011, http://www.qscores.com.

19. Matt Warburton, "Treehouse of Horror XIX," *The Simpsons*, dir. Matt Groening, aired November 2, 2008.

20. Immanuel Kant, *Critique of Aesthetic Judgment*, trans, J. C. Meredith (1790; Oxford: Clarendon Press, 1911), section 46.

6. TRANSLATING F. O. MATTHIESSEN

1. Letter to Russell Cheney, September 23, 1924, in *Rat and the Devil: Journal Letters of F. O. Matthiessen and Russell Cheney*, ed. Louis Hyde (Boston: Alyson, 1978), 29.

2. Letter to Cheney, April 30, 1925, in Hyde, *Rat and Devil*, 138.

3. Harry Levin, *The Power of Blackness: Hawthorne, Poe, Melville* (Athens: Ohio University Press, 1958), vii.

4. Ibid.

5. Giles Gunn reports that "Matthiessen's original intention had been to write a dissertation on the poetry of Walt Whitman, but the proposal was summarily rejected on the ground that Whitman had been by this time pretty well exhausted as a subject of literary study." Gunn, *F. O. Matthiessen: The Critical Achievement* (Seattle: University of Washington Press, 1975), 32.

6. F. O. Mattheissen, "New Standards in American Criticism," *Yale Review* 18, no. 3 (March, 1929).

7. Letter to Cheney, October 17, 1929, in Hyde, *Rat and Devil*, 163.

8. Letter to Cheney, November 30, 1929, in Hyde, *Rat and Devil*, 174.

9. Letter to Cheney, December 12, 1929, in Hyde, *Rat and Devil*, 177.

10. F. O. Matthiessen, *American Renaissance: Art and Expression in the Age of Emerson and Whitman* (London: Oxford University Press, 1941), xviii.

11. Ibid., 415.

12. Jonathan Arac, "F. O. Matthiessen: Authorizing an American Renaissance," in *The American Renaissance Reconsidered*, Selected Papers from the English Institute 1982–1983, ed. Walter Benn Michaels and Donald E. Pease (Baltimore: Johns Hopkins University Press, 1985), 95.

13. Matthiessen, *American Renaissance*, 203.

14. Ibid., 352.

15. Ibid., 219.

16. Ibid., 346.

17. Ibid., 351.

18. Ibid., 559.

19. Ibid., 558.

20. Ibid., 571n13.

21. Ibid., xiii.

22. Ibid., 189.

23. Ibid.

24. Ibid., 407n4.

25. Ibid., 413n3.

26. Ibid., 423.

27. Ibid., 424.

28. Ibid., 425.

29. Ibid., 432.

30. Ibid., 634, emphasis added.

31. David Caute, *The Fellow-Travellers: Intellectual Friends of Communism*, rev. ed. (1973; New Haven, Conn.: Yale University Press, 1988), 80n.

32. William L. O'Neill, *A Better World: The Great Schism; Stalinism and the American Intellectuals* (New York: Simon and Schuster, 1982), 174.

33. David K. Johnson, *The Lavender Scare: The Cold War Persecution of Gays and Lesbians in the Federal Government* (Chicago: University of Chicago Press, 2004).

34. Herman Melville, "Hawthorne and His Mosses," *The Literary World*, August 17 and 24, 1850. I am grateful to Lawrence Buell for drawing my attention to the relevance of this essay.

35. Matthiessen, *American Renaissance*, 189.

36. Ibid., 190.

37. Ibid., 57.

38. Ibid., 519.

39. Letter to Cheney, January 30, 1930, in Hyde, *Rat and Devil*, p. 200.

40. George Steiner, "Thomas Mann's *Felix Krull*," in *Language and Silence: Essays on Language, Literature, and the Inhuman* (New Haven, Conn.: Yale University Press, 1998), 271.

41. *Oxford English Dictionary*, 3rd ed., s.v. "traduce."

42. F. O. Matthiessen, *Translation: An Elizabethan Art* (1931; New York: Octagon Books, 1965), 3.

43. William E. Cain *F. O. Matthiessen and the Politics of Criticism* (Madison: University of Wisconsin Press, 1988), 52. See also Gunn, *F. O. Matthiessen*, 32–37.

44. Cain, *F. O. Matthiessen*, 231.

7. GOOD TO THINK WITH

1. Maurice Maeterlinck, *The Blue Bird: A Fair Play in Six Acts*, trans. Alexander Teixeira de Mattos (New York: Dodd, 1911; Project Guttenberg, 2005), http://www.gutenberg.org/ebooks/8606.

2. Claude Lévi-Strauss, *Totemism*, trans. Rodeny Needham (Boston: Beacon, 1963), 89.

3. Ibid. The original French text reads: "Les animaux du totémisme cessent d'être, seulement ou surtout, des créatures redoutées, admirées, ou convoitées: leur réalité sensible laisse transparaître des notions et des relations, conçues par la pensée speculative á partir des donées de l'observation. On comprend enfin que les espéces naturelles ne sont pas choisies parce que 'bonnes à manger' mais parce que 'bonnes à penser.'" Claude Lévi-Strauss, *Le totémisme aujourd'hui* (Paris: PUF, 1962), 128.

4. Francis Bacon, "Of Studies," *The Essays*, trans. Judith Boss (Renascence Editions, 1601; Eugene: University of Oregon, 1998), http://hdl.handle.net/1794/679.

5. Ibid.

6. Ben Jonson, "Inviting a Friend to Supper," *The Oxford Book of Seventeenth-Century Verse*, ed. H. J. C. Grierson and G. Bullough (1612; Luminarium, 2006), http://luminarium.org/sevenlit/jonson/supper.htm.

7. Thomas Browne, "Notes on the Natural History of Norfolk," in *Miscellaneous Writings*, ed. Geoffrey Keynes (London: Faber, 1931), 382.

8. "Movers & Shakespeares," last accessed June 14, 2008, http://www.moversandshakespeares.com.

9. "National Initiatives: The Big Read," National Endowment for the Arts, last accessed June 14, 2009, http://www.neabigread.org.

10. Wallace Stevens, "Notes toward a Supreme Fiction," in *Collected Poetry and Prose* (New York: Library of America, 1997), 348.

8. THE MARVEL OF PERU

1. Catalina de Erauso, *Lieutenant Nun: Memoir of a Basque Transvestite in the New World*, ed. and trans. Michele Stepto and Gabriel Stepto (Boston: Beacon, 1996), 4, 5, 7.

2. Pierre de Brantome, *La vie des dames galantes* (Paris: Garnier-Frères, 1841).

3. R. C. Dallas, *Correspondence of Lord Byron with a Friend* (Paris: Galignani, 1825), 41–42.

4. See Ursula K Heise, "Transvestism and the Stage Controversy in Spain and England, 1580–1680," *Theatre Journal* 44, no. 3 (October 1992): 357; and Stephen Orgel, "Nobody's Perfect: Or Why Did the English Stage Take Boys for Women?" in "Displacing Homophobia," ed. Ronald R Butters, John M. Clum, and Michael Moon, special issue, *South Atlantic Quarterly* 88, no. 1 (Winter 1989), 28.

5. Pedro Calderón de la Barca, *Life is a Dream*, trans. Roy Campbell, in *Six Spanish Plays*, ed. Eric Bentley (New York: Doubleday Anchor, 1959), 3.2.490–94.

6. Erauso, *Lieutenant Nun*, 37.

7. William Prynne, *Histriomastix*, 2nd ed. (London: 1633).

8. Marjorie Garber, *Vested Interests: Cross-Dressing and Cultural Anxiety* (San Francisco: HarperCollins, 1993).

9. Michele Stepto, "Introduction," *Lieutenant Nun*, xxix–xxx.

10. Rudolf M. Dekker and Lotte C. van der Pol, *The Tradition of Female Transvestism in Early Modern Europe* (New York: St. Martin's Press, 1989), 95–96.

11. Jonathan Goldberg, *Sodometries: Renaissance Texts, Modern Sexualities* (Stanford, Calif.: Stanford University Press, 1992), 184.

12. Julie Wheelwright, *Amazons and Military Maids: Women Who Dressed as Men in Pursuit of Life, Liberty and Happiness* (London: Pandora, 1989).

13. Nadezhda Durova, *The Cavalry Maiden*, trans. Mary Fleming Zurin (Bloomington: Indiana University Press, 1988), 78.

14. Michele Stepto and Gabriel Stepto, translators' introduction to *Lieutenant Nun: Memoir of a Basque Transvestite in the New World*, by Catalina de Erauso (Boston: Beacon, 1996), xlvii–xlviii.

15. Louis Sullivan, *From Female to Male: The Life of Jack Bee Garland* (Boston: Alyson, 1990), 9.

16. Ibid., 17.

17. Ibid., 3.

18. Erauso, *Lieutenant Nun*, 30, 39, 252–53.

9. THIRD-PERSON INTERRUPTION

1. Samuel Coleridge, *The Poems of Samuel Taylor Coleridge*, ed. Ernest Hartley Coleridge (1912; London: Oxford University Press, 1961), 296.

2. Stevie Smith, "Thoughts about the Person from Porlock," in *New Selected Poems of Stevie Smith* (New York: New Directions, 1988), 87.

3. "Porlock Wins Best Village," Porlock Tourist Association, http://www.porlock.co.uk/about/bestvillage.php.

4. Top Dating, http://www.topdating.com.

5. *Oxford English Dictionary*, 3rd ed., s.v. "person."

6. Fanny Burney, *Cecilia; Or, Memoirs of an Heiress*, vol. 4 (London: T. Peyne and Son, 1782), 222.

7. Sigmund Freud, *Beyond the Pleasure Principle* (1920), in *The Standard Edition of the Complete Psychological Works of Sigmund Freud,* ed. and trans. James Strachey (London: Hogarth Press and the Institute of Psycho-Analysis, 1955), 18:40.

8. Samuel Coleridge, preface to "Kubla Khan," in *The Poems of Samuel Taylor Coleridge*, ed. Ernest Hartley (1912; London: Oxford University Press, 1961), 296.

9. Samuel Johnson, "Lives of the Poets" (London: Dent, 1968), 1:108.

10. Jacques Derrida, *Adieu Emmanuel Levinas* (Palo Alto, Calif: Stanford University Press, 1999), 9.

11. Plato, *The Dialogues of Plato*, vol. 1 (Oxford: Clarendon, 1871), 506.

12. Freud, *Beyond the Pleasure Principle*, 57–58.

13. Ibid.

14. Ibid., 58.

10. OUR GENIUS PROBLEM

1. Gordon Edes, "Patriot's Coach has Well-Earned Reputation," *Boston Globe* February 2, 2002.

2. Mike Freeman, "Defensive Genius," *New York Times*, February 4, 2002.

3. Ian McEwan, *Amsterdam* (New York: Anchor Books, 1998), 143.

4. Ibid., 174, 190, 191, 176.

5. Todd Silver, *Think Like a Genius* (New York: Bantam, 1999), 5.

6. Immanuel Kant, *Critique of Judgment*, trans. J. H. Bernard (London: Collier Macmillan, 1951), 150.

7. Henry Fielding, *The History of Tom Jones, a Foundling* (New York: Washington Square, 1963), 604.

8. William Hazlitt, "On Shakespeare and Milton," in *Lectures on the English Poets*, ed. Alfred Rayney Waller and Ernest Rhys (1819; Project Gutenberg, 2005), http://www.gutenberg.org/files/16209/16209.txt.

9. Samuel Taylor Coleridge, "Shakespeare's Judgment Equal to His Genius," in *Critical Theory since Plato*, ed. Hazard Adams (New York: Harcourt Brace Jovanovich, 971), 470–71.

10. Richard Ellman, *Oscar Wilde* (New York: Vintage, 1988), 160.

11. Gertrude Stein, *The Autobiography of Alice. B. Toklas* (1933; New York: Vintage, 1990), 87, 114.

12. Robert McAlmon, *Being Geniuses Together,* rev. Kay Boyle (Baltimore: Johns Hopkins University Press,1997), 228.

13. James Gleick, *Genius: The Life and Science of Richard Feynman* (New York: Vintage, 1992), 378.

14. Sylvia Nasar, *A Beautiful Mind* (New York: Touchstone, 1998), 94, 95, 136, 144, 146, 199, 208, 219, 228.

15. Rex Stout, *The League of Frightened Men* (New York: Farrar and Rinehart, 1935), chap. 1.

16. Gleick, *Genius*, 159.

17. Sir Francis Galton, *Hereditary Genius* (London: Macmillan, 1869).

18. Havelock Ellis, *A Study of British Genius* (London: Hurst and Blackett, 1904), 191.

19. W. R. Bett, *The Infirmities of Genius* (London: Christopher Johnson, 1952).

20. Richard C. Paddock, "The Secret IQ Diaries," *Los Angeles Times Magazine*, July 30, 1995.

21. E.g., Jeffrey A. Frank, "What Sununu Knew as He Flew," *Washington Post*, April 28, 1991.

22. Catherine Morris Cox, *The Early Traits of Three Hundred Geniuses*, with the assistance of Lela O. Gillan, Ruth Haines Livesay, Lewis M. Terman (Stanford, Calif.: Stanford University Press, 1926), v.

23. J. L. Dillard, *Black English* (New York: Random House, 1972), 29.

24. Diane K. Shah, "A Fund for Geniuses," with Richard Manning, *Newsweek*, August 13, 1979.

25. Katherine Lowry, "The Designer Babies Are Growing Up," *Los Angeles Times Magazine*, November 1, 1987; "The Man Who Plays God," *Advertiser*, January 6, 1996; and Robert Lee Holtz, "Robert Graham, Founder of Exclusive Sperm Bank, Dies," *Los Angeles Times*, February 18, 1997.

26. Roland Barthes, "The Brain of Einstein," in *Mythologies*, trans. Annette Lavers (New York: Hill and Wang, 1986), 68–71.

11. DIG IT: LOOKING FOR FAME IN ALL THE WRONG PLACES

1. "National Book Awards—2010." *National Book Foundation*, n.d. Web, August 5, 2011.

2. James F. English, *The Economy of Prestige: Prizes, Awards, and the Circulation of Cultural Value* (Cambridge: Harvard University Press, 2005), 35.

3. Newspapers and other media outlets across the country highlighted Smith's remarks about the fate of the book, mentioning her experience as a salesperson at Scribner and her eloquent defense of printed books as "beautiful" and crucially important. See, e.g., Jem Asward, "Patti Smith Wins National Book Award," CNN, last modified November 22, 2010, http://www.cnn.com/2010/showbiz/celebrity .news.gossip/11/22/patti.smith.national.book.award.roll/index.htm; Julie Bosman, "National Book Award for Patti Smith," *New York Times*, November 17, 2010; Dan Deluca, "Patti Smith, National Book Award Winner," *Philadelphia Inquirer*, November 18, 2010; Macy Halford, "Patti Smith's Levels of Reality," *New Yorker*, last modified November 18, 2010, http://www.newyorker.com/online/blogs/books/ 2010/11/patti-smiths-levels-of-reality.htm; Hillel Italie, "Patti Smith's *Just Kids* Wins National Book Award for Nonfiction," *Washington Post*, November 18, 2010; Carolyn Kellogg, "Rocker Patti Smith Takes Nonfiction Prize at National Book Awards," *Los Angeles Times*, November 18, 2010; Bob Minzesheimer, "Patti Smith's Memoir *Just Kids* Wins National Book Award," *USA Today*, November 17, 2010; and Megan O'Grady, "Rock Star Memoir: Patti Smith Wins a National Book

Award," *Vogue*, last modified November 18, 2010, http://www.vogue.com/culture/article/rock-star-memoir-patti-smith-wins-a-national-book-award.

4. *Oxford English Dictionary*, 3rd ed., s.v. "rock star."

5. Roland Barthes, *Mythologies*, trans. Annette Lavers (New York: Hill, 1972), 21.

6. George Michael, *Money, Music, Love, Faith*, electronic press kit, 1988. I am indebted to Nancy Vickers for this reference.

12. ANATOMY OF A HONEY TRAP

1. Luke Hardin, "Bruno the Bear Shot Dead," *Guardian*, June 26, 2006.

2. Frederick C. Crews, *Postmodern Pooh* (New York: North Point, 2001), 69.

13. THE GYPSY SCHOLAR AND THE SCHOLAR GYPSY

1. Kerala Goodkin, "Emotion Has Its Place Within the Classroom," *Brown Daily Herald*, April 22, 2002.

2. Chryss Cada, "Politicians Resurface in Academia from Clinton Era, A Wave of Top Executives," *Boston Globe* June 18, 2002.

3. Review of *Quick Studies: The Best of Lingua Franca*, ed. Alexander Star, *Kirkus Reviews*, August 1, 2002.

4. W. H. Whyte, *The Organization Man* (New York: Simon and Schuster, 1956), 217.

5. Helena Payne, "Course Management Software Transforms Higher Education," *Associated Press Business News*, August 11, 2002.

6. David Brooks, *Bobos in Paradise: The New Upper Class and How They Got There* (New York: Simon & Schuster, 2000), 152–53.

7. Sarah Boxer, "Professors or Proletarians? A Test for Downtrodden Academics," *New York Times*, January 16, 1999.

8. Fred M. Hechinger, "A Lost Generation of Young 'Gypsy Scholars,'" *New York Times*, May 2, 1982.

9. Abby Goodnough, "On Campus: Army of Adjuncts Seeks to Organize on State College Campuses," *New York Times*, April 30, 1995.

10. Andrew Yarrow, "'Gypsy Scholars' Roam Academic Landscape," *New York Times*, January 10, 1982.

11. Matthew Arnold, "The Function of Criticism at the Present Time," in *The Norton Anthology of Theory and Criticism*, ed. Vincent Leitch et al. (New York: Norton, 2001), 824.

12. Ibid, 825.

13. Ibid., 813.

14. Matthew Arnold, "The Function of Criticism at the Present Time," in *The Norton Anthology of Theory and Criticism*, ed. Vincent B. Leitch et al., 2nd ed., (New York: Norton, 2010), 712, 713.

15. Kenneth Allott, ed., *The Poems of Matthew Arnold* (New York: Barnes & Noble, 1965), 342n. He quotes Keats's "Ode to Psyche," line 37.

16. A. E. Dyson, "The Last Enchantments," *Review of English Studies*, n.s., 8 (1957): 265.

17. Joseph Glanvill, *The Vanity of Dogmatizing: The Three Versions*, ed. Stephen Medcalf (Sussex: Harvester Press, 1970), 62–63.

18. Ibid., 196–98.

19. Ibid., 201.

20. Ibid., 207.

21. Ibid., cited in Stephen Medcalf, introduction to *The Vanity of Dogmatizing: The Three Versions* (Sussex: Harvester Press, 1970), xxi.

22. Medcalf, introduction, xiii. As he is quick to add, "The two pairs do not necessarily coincide, although there are reasons . . . for seeing an affinity between them."

23. Ibid., xiv. See also M. Nicolson, "The Real Scholar Gypsy," *Yale Review*, n.s., 18 (1928): 347–63.

24. Marjorie Nicolson, "The Real Scholar Gipsy," *Yale Review*, n.s., 18 (1928): 347–63.

25. J. P. Curgenven, "*The Scholar Gipsy*: A Study of the Growth, Meaning and Integration of a Poem," *Litera* 2 (1995): 45.

26. *Oxford English Dictionary*, 3rd ed., s.v. "gypsy."

27. The Irish Travelers are descendants of a group of nomadic Irish traders and tinsmiths know as the Tinkers, who immigrated to the United States in the 1840s to flee the potato famine in Ireland. They are often called gypsies because of their nomadic lifestyle. Toogood's public declaration of her ethnic identity dismayed some of the Travelers, who have preferred to live in a closed society, resisting outsiders, whom they call "country people." Many travelers make their living as itinerant home-improvement workers; some have been implicated in "scams" that have attracted the attention of the Better Business Bureau. See Lynne Duke, "Unwelcome Stares at Quiet Clan," *Washington Post*, October 20, 2002; and Larry Copeland, "Travelers Roam the Nation for Jobs, and, Sometimes, Home-Repair Scams," *USA Today*, September 24, 2002.

28. *Oxford English Dictionary*, 3rd ed., s.v. "Bohemian."

29. Christopher Morley, *Seacoast of Bohemia* (Hoboken, N.J.: Doubleday, 1929), 57.

30. Hans Magnus Enzenberger, *Europe, Europe: Forays into a Continent* (New York: Pantheon, 1989), 283, 309.

31. Erich Auerbach, *Mimesis: The Repesentation of Reality in Western Culture*, trans. Willard R. Trask (Princeton, N.J.: Princeton University Press, 1953), p. 557.

32. Emily Apter, *The Translation Zone: A New Comparative Literature* (Princeton: Princeton University Press, 2006), 50, 53, 59.

33. *Oxford English Dictionary*, 3rd ed., s.v. "monad."

34. Gilles Deleuze and Félix Guattari, *A Thousand Plateaus: Capitalism and Schizophrenia*, trans. Brian Massumi (Minneapolis: University of Minnesota Press, 1987), 493.

35. Orville Prescott, "Books of the Times," *New York Times Book Review*, May 5, 1954.

14. RADICAL EDUCATION

1. Elisabeth S. Theodore, "Summers Questions Masters' Use of House List," *Harvard Crimson*, January 30, 2003; and Sean Palfrey, e-mail, "The Specter of War," January 2003.

2. See Noam Chomsky, *Radical Priorities* (Montreal: Black Rose Books, 1981), 193.

3. Henry Louis Gates Jr., interview by June Cross, "The Two Nations of Black America: Are We Better Off?" *Frontline*, PBS, February 10, 1998.

4. Jean Genet, "Here and Now for Bobby Seale," trans. Judy Oringer, *Ramparts* 8, no. 12 (1970): 30–31.

5. On a new website, http://www.poetsagainstthewar.org.

6. Katha Pollitt, "Poetry Makes Nothing Happen? Ask Laura Bush," *The Nation*, February 24, 2003.

15. AFTER THE HUMANITIES

1. *Oxford English Dictionary*, 3rd ed., s.v. "accessory."

2. "Movers & Shakespeares," last accessed November 23, 2006, http://www.moversandshakespeares.com.

3. Ibid.

4. Adam Cohen, "What W. B. Yeats's 'Second Coming' Really Says About the Iraq War." *New York Times*, February 12, 2007.

5. The original edition of *Cultural Literacy*, then subtitled *What Every American Needs to Know*, included an appendix, a list compiled by professors of English, history, and physics, that ran alphabetically from *abbreviation, abolitionism, abominable snowman*, and *abortion* to *Zapata, Zeitgeist, zero-sum, Zeus*, and *Zionism*. The updated *Dictionary* of 2002 makes it even clearer that "culture" now includes the sciences, business, medicine and technology.

6. Patricia Cohen, "In Tough Times, Humanities Must Justify Their Worth," *New York Times*, February 25, 2009.

7. I told this story in *The Use and Abuse of Literature* (New York: Pantheon, 2011). I include it here, in the context of expectations about humanistic instruction, because it so vividly illustrates the problem of what, and how, the humanities teach.

8. Gerald Graff, *Professing Literature* (Chicago: University of Chicago Press, 2007), 37.

9. Cited in Graff, *Professing Literature*, 68.

10. René Wellek and Austin Warren, *Theory of Literature* (New York: Harcourt Brace, 1947), vi.

11. William K. Wimsatt Jr. and Cleanth Brooks, *Literary Criticism: A Short History* (New York: Knopf, 1957), xi.

12. Ibid., xii.

13. "Ann DeChiara Malamud; Wife Nurtured Novelist's Career," *Boston Globe*, March 25, 2007.

14. Sandra M. Gilbert and Susan Gubar, *The Madwoman in the Attic* (New Haven, Conn.: Yale University Press, 1979), xiii.

15. See "Our Genius Problem," page 124 in this volume.

Index